MASTERING

COMPUTERS

30/3/87

MACMILLAN MASTER SERIES

Banking
Basic English Law
Basic Management
Biology
British Politics
Business Communication
Chemistry
COBOL Programming
Commerce
Computer Programming
Computers
Data Processing
Economics
Electrical Engineering
Electronics
English Grammar
English Language
English Literature
French
French 2

German
Hairdressing
Italian
Keyboarding
Marketing
Mathematics
Modern British History
Modern World History
Nutrition
Office Practice
Pascal Programming
Physics
Principles of Accounts
Social Welfare
Sociology
Spanish
Statistics
Study Skills
Typewriting Skills
Word Processing

MASTERING
COMPUTERS

SECOND EDITION

G. G. L. WRIGHT

MACMILLAN

First edition 1982
Reprinted 1982 (3 times), 1983 (twice)
Second edition 1984
Reprinted 1985

Published by
MACMILLAN EDUCATION LTD
Houndmills, Basingstoke, Hampshire RG21 2XS
and London
Companies and representatives
throughout the world

Printed in Hong Kong

ISBN 0-333-31293-7 (hardcover)
ISBN 0-333-37596-3 (paperback – home edition)
ISBN 0-333-38714-7 (paperback – export edition)

CONTENTS

CONTENTS

FIGURES

FIGURES

ACKNOWLEDGEMENTS

My thanks are due to the following companies for approval to use diagrams, which are individually acknowledged in the text:

Hewlett-Packard Computers Ltd
The Open University
Digital Equipment Corporation Ltd
The Automobile Association
The National Computing Centre
Computing Publications Ltd
Acornsoft Ltd
ACT (UK) Ltd
Epson (UK) Ltd
Welsh Joint Education Committee

I also wish to thank Barbara Miles for typing from the manuscript written in my own fair handwriting, and Eric Huggins for permission to call upon his helpful explanation of the binary system, from his book *Microprocessors and Microcomputers*, published by Macmillan.

Finally, I wish to dedicate this book to my wife Jane in gratitude for her help in reading the draft copy and correcting obscurities and omissions, and for her continued support at a very busy time.

INTRODUCTION

The ascent of man into twentieth-century civilisation has been intricately bound up with the development of machines, from the five basic devices of the ancient Greeks — the lever, wheel, pulley, wedge and screw — to today's highly complex and interlinked technology. This development has not always occurred at a steady pace or with acceptable social consequences — the first Industrial Revolution, for instance, in the space of fifty years transformed Great Britain from an agricultural and village-based economy into an industrial town-based economy. And almost exactly a hundred years ago a spate of inventions occurred of particular significance to our subject — the first telephone in 1876, the first typewriter in 1879, the first commercial electricity service in 1882. We are now in the prelude of the second Industrial Revolution, one which is likely to have the same large-scale and not always desirable consequences as the first. At the heart of this revolution is a spate of invention and innovation associated with the computer, or the electronic digital computer to give it its formal title.

And yet, when the first computers were developed forty years ago, there were influential and informed opinions (including, it is alleged, that of the founder of IBM, now the world's largest computer manufacturer by a very wide margin) that no more than a handful of these machines would ever be needed.

So what is it about the computer that makes it so different and so powerful? What makes it so versatile that it can become an integral part of the work of scientists, engineers, accountants and many other professional people and yet at the same time can enrich the leisure time of adults and children at home? Why is it that the computer, which has helped to take man to the Moon, is now being blamed as a threat to millions of jobs? This book sets out to answer such global questions. At the end of most chapters in the book the reader will also find a list of specimen questions which indicate the type of detailed questions asked of students in first-level public examinations in Computer Studies – O level, A level, CSE and National Diploma. This book is therefore intended to provide the answers both to questions of fact and interpretation that will enable the interested reader to start mastering the computer.

CHAPTER 1

INTRODUCING

THE COMPUTER

1.1 WHAT IS A COMPUTER?

Mastering computers calls for an understanding of computers as machines in the service of man, and how they have come to be the characteristic machines of our age to such an extent that this part of the twentieth century is often called 'The Computer Age'. The popular image of a computer as an electronic brain, or the professional jargon which attributes 'intelligence' and 'memory' to computers, serves only to confuse a proper understanding of computers as machines designed and built by people, for use by people. Although it is not easy to describe a computer in a few words, in principle the computer is a simple machine, or rather a group or system of simple machines, co-ordinated by a novel form of automatic control. Its full name is the electronic digital computer:

- *electronic* because it consists of electronic components: transistors, capacitors, resistors and now of course the ubiquitous integrated circuit or microchip. These components are activated by electrical impulses;
- *digital* because these electronic components are designed to represent and perform operations on digital as opposed to analog signals. The best way to explain the difference between the words *analog* and *digital* is to consider the two types of clocks and watches now currently available. They both measure time, but the digital watch divides time up into a series of separate or 'discrete' packets: seconds or some fraction of a second. The analog watch, on the other hand, exactly copies the 'flow' of time (like an 'ever-rolling stream') by the continuous movement of hands over a dial;
- *computer* because originally (but not necessarily now) these operations were concerned with numerical computation.

1.2 THE COMPUTER AS AN INFORMATION PROCESSOR

These digital values, coded into an appropriate electrical form, can be made to represent information of any and every sort, and a computer can therefore best be described as an *information-processing machine*. Information is provided to the computer from the real world — people or other machines — in the form of messages, signals, numbers, instrument readings, letters, business transactions, enquiries, etc. It has to be encoded in such a manner that the computer can understand and respond correctly to it. As an electronic device a computer can only comprehend electronic signals — electrical impulses — and so, if the information has been originally encoded on paper tape, magnetic discs or any other medium, the codes retained on these have to be converted by an appropriate device into the electrical impulses which the computer can understand.

Once processing of information has taken place the electrical signals which constitute the output from the computer have to be converted by the electronics attached to a screen or a printer, or even a voice 'output unit', into a form understandable by human beings. This means that the computer is *interfaced* with the outside world by devices which convert data understandable to humans into data comprehensible to the computer, and vice versa. If required, the output signals from the computer can be fed directly to machines in order to control their operation. This constitutes automatic control or *automation*.

Fig 1.1   *the computer as an information processing system*

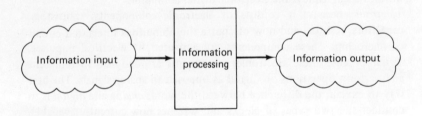

We talk of these stages as *input*, *processing* and *output* (see Fig. 1.1), and the equipment which feeds information to the processing unit and relays the results of processing from it as *input/output* (I/O) *devices* or *peripherals*. Computer *terminals*, or just terminals, are a particularly important class of I/O device because they are designed for use by people at their normal place of work, like any other piece of domestic or office equipment (see Chapter 4). Our ability to connect a computer to so many different types of I/O device is part of the general-purpose power of a computer. I/O devices are described in more detail later. There is another class of computer equipment which, although not connected directly to the machine, is essential to its working. These are data preparation devices and are the devices which perform the task of encoding data on to paper tape, punched cards or the now popular 'floppy' disc. The functional components of a computer are shown in Fig. 1.2.

Fig 1.2 *the five functional components of a computer*

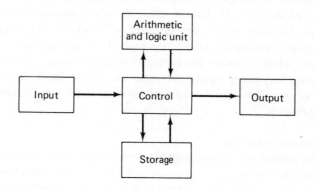

(a) The processor

The heart of the computer is called the central processing unit (CPU), or *processor*. All computers contain a CPU but some larger machines can contain several of these, hence the term *multiprocessor*. The actual definition of what is contained in a CPU is not entirely consistent. Certainly they all contain what is termed an arithmetic and logic unit (ALU) and a control unit. Opinion is divided as to whether the CPU contains the internal storage of the computer. Whether it does or does not need not really concern the reader at this time since the term *internal storage* or *main memory* will always be used in an unambiguous way. The function of the CPU is to perform a series of clearly defined operations consisting of the following:

  (i) arithmetic operations (for example, ADD, SUBTRACT);

 (ii) logical operations (logical choices resulting from a comparison of two pieces of data);

(iii) I/O operations (from READ, WRITE to various parts of the computer system);

(iv) internal data movements (moving data between parts of storage);

 (v) data manipulations (changing the structure of pieces of data);

(vi) jump instructions (for example, JUMP, GOTO instructions whose particular and unique contribution will be discussed later in this chapter).

The actual list of instructions which any computer can execute is known as its *basic instruction set*.

Data is stored and manipulated inside the processor in the form that is most efficient for the electronic implementation of these operations — the *binary* form (see Section 3.1). Binary means taking only one of two possible values at a time — on/off, up/down, 1/0 — and the basic unit of binary information is called the *bit* or *binary digit*.

It is beyond the scope of this book to enter into a deep discussion of the electronic workings of a computer; suffice it to say that by the conversion of all data into bit format, even, say, the continuous temperature readings of a thermometer, the computer can process it using very simple techniques of arithmetic and Boolean logic (Boolean logic deals only with true/false values — another good reason for using a binary system.) There are in fact very many simple electronic kits which demonstrate the elements of computer logic for those who wish to investigate this fascinating subject further.

(b) A computer program

It is the *control unit* which gives the computer its ability to decode and then execute a stored program. It acts rather like a very complex switching centre sending instructions to various parts of the computer and causing the millions of electronic switches or *gates* to be opened and closed. A computer operates under the control of instructions selected from its basic instruction set in order to perform a specific task. This list of instructions is known as a computer *program*. A program is fed, via the CPU and its control unit, into its internal storage. The program is started off, usually (but not always) by a human operator, and it continues automatically, instruction by instruction, until it finishes. At that point the program can either be executed again using perhaps a different set of data, or can be replaced by another program and the sequence repeated. For this purpose the control unit contains:

- a program counter, to initiate and control the performance, or 'execution', of the instructions in a program in the required sequence, one at a time (or 'serially');
- a register to hold the instruction currently being executed and the data currently being operated on (or 'operands');
- a decoder to activate the action required by an instruction, either through the ALU, if it is an arithmetic or logical operation, or by causing transfers of data within the processor or between the processor and I/O devices;
- a clock to control the timing of operations; and
- registers to hold the current result of processing (the 'accumulator') and other intermediate data.

(c) Internal storage (or 'main memory')

This is required to support the processor for two reasons; firstly to hold the stored program(s) currently being executed, and secondly to hold the data which is being processed by these programs, in one of three states: 'raw' data transferred in from an input device, partly processed data, and fully processed data ready for transfer to an output device. This second purpose is vital because a processor works at much higher speeds than input/output devices, and therefore it needs to work from data that has already been made ready and waiting for it. This use of internal storage is known as 'buffer' storage. The control unit and internal storage are linked by what is called a data *bus* or data *highway* and it is along this, which is merely a set of wires rather like an electricity ring main, that data flows both to and from internal storage.

The fundamental unit of storage within a computer is the bit (*binary digit*) as has already been described. However, a single bit is not a conveniently sized unit of data. For most purposes, the smallest unit in which useful data can be stored is the *byte*, which consists of 8 bits. Larger units of data storage are called *words* which in general consist of 2 or more bytes, although some very large machines use a word consisting of 60 bits. It is by the size of its internal storage that the size of a computer is often judged. Storage sizes are usually quoted in multiples of 1024 (2^{10}) bytes. 1024 bytes is known as 1 K. (K is used as a close approximation of 1024 although the K prefix usually means 1000.) A computer which is said to be a 32 K machine has an internal storage of $32 \times 1024 = 32\,768$ bytes. Similarly, larger computers often have internal storage in the megabyte range. One megabyte (1 M) is $2^{20} = 1024 \times 1024 = 1\,048\,576$ bytes, or approximately 1 million.

Fig. 1.3 shows the way in which the various units of the processor work together, in a functional rather than operational form. Chapter 3 will describe the way in which a computer works in more detail.

(d) The self-modifying program

The concept of a program, as a list of instructions for performing a task, will be a familiar one: a recipe is a program for preparing food and a crochet pattern is a program for producing an item of clothing (see Fig. 1.4). Even a gramophone record is a form of program where the instructions, in analog form for the conventional vinyl disc, control the movement of the air carrying the music to your ears. A computer is as useless without a computer program as a record player without records. Operating under the control of an appropriate stored program, the computer can perform any of a wide range of tasks, to be investigated more fully in the next chapter, without human intervention and therefore at full electronic speeds, measured now in fractions of a second and ultimately limited only by the speed of light. Early computers took their program instructions from an external source which could have been punched paper tape,

Fig 1.3 *the working organisation of a computer*

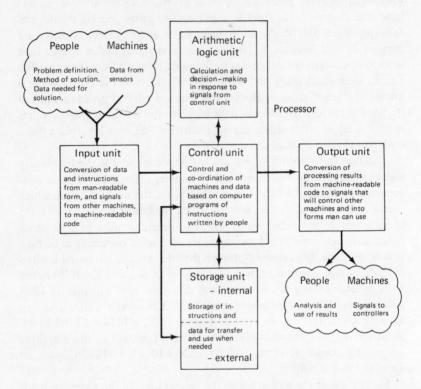

punched cards or even plug boards which actually connected certain memory locations together with wires. The big advance in computing technology was made when computers were built which could 'remember' a set of instructions and execute them whenever required.

Not every stored-program machine, however, qualifies as a computer; other machines can be equipped with automatic control to enable them to perform a sequence of operations automatically, such as an automatic washing machine. The significant difference is that, in addition to those classes of instructions already described, a computer program can also include instructions that can cause a variation in the sequence in which other instructions are executed. Instead of instructions being performed in a fixed sequence, one by one from beginning to end of a program, the sequence can be varied, with *conditional* and *unconditional jump* instructions. A computer can be programmed to make logical decisions so that it appears to have a glimmer of 'intelligence'. But because all its decisions are based on a set of simple arithmetical or logical comparisons no element of judgement is introduced. In other words the computer can decide the

Fig 1.4 *examples of 'programs': a computer program, a recipe and a crochet pattern*

```
>LIST
    10 REM THIS PROGRAM CALCULATES THE DAY OF THE WEEK
    20 REM ON WHICH ANY DATE FALLS
    30 REM BETWEEN 1ST MARCH 1900 AND 28TH FEBRUARY 2100
    40 DIM DAY$(7)
    50 DATA "SUNDAY","MONDAY","TUESDAY","WEDNESDAY"
    60 DATA "THURSDAY","FRIDAY","SATURDAY"
    70 FOR X=1 TO 7: READ DAY$(X): NEXT X
    80 PRINT "ENTER DATE AS DAY,MONTH,YEAR IN NUMERICAL FORM"
    90 INPUT DAY,MONTH,YEAR
   100 IF MONTH>2 THEN N1=INT(365.25*(YEAR))
   110            ELSE N1=INT(365.25*(YEAR-1))
   120 IF MONTH>2 THEN N2=INT(30.6*(MONTH+1))
   130            ELSE N2=INT(30.6*(MONTH+13))
   140 N3=N1+N2+DAY-621049
   150 DAYN=(N3 MOD 7)+1
   160 PRINT DAY;"/";MONTH;"/";YEAR;" FALLS ON ";DAY$(DAYN)
   170 END
>
>
>RUN
ENTER DATE AS DAY,MONTH,YEAR IN NUMERICAL FORM
?17,10,1983
          17/10/1983 FALLS ON MONDAY
>
```

HOT CHICKEN SALAD

2 cupfuls cooked chicken; ½ head celery; 1 small green pepper; 1 medium onion; ½ can concentrated chicken soup; 2 tablespoons mayonnaise; juice of ½ lemon; 1 teaspoon salt; For the topping: 50 g grated Cheddar cheese; 1 cupful chrushed potato crisps.

The amounts of the ingredients are 'more or less'. Cut the chicken into neat pieces. Chop the celery and pepper coarsely and the onion finely. Combine the chicken, vegetables, soup, mayonnaise, lemon juice and salt in a large bowl and stir well. Put the mixture into a gratin dish and smooth over. Make the topping by combining the cheese and crisps and scatter over the dish to cover completely. Bake in a preheated oven at regulo 5, 190 °C (375 °F) for about 20 minutes. Serve hot.   [*Serves 4 to 6*]

MOTIF (Make 64)

With L., work 5 ch.; join into ring with sl.st.

1st round—With L., 3 ch., 2 tr. into ring (1 ch., 3 tr. into ring) 3 times, 1 ch.. join to 3rd of 3 ch. with sl.st. Break off L.

2nd round—With M., join yarn in last 1 ch. sp. of previous round, 3 ch., 2 tr. in same sp., (1 ch., 3 tr., 2 ch., 3 tr. in next sp.) 3 times, 1 ch., 3 tr. in next sp. 2 ch., join to 3rd of 3 ch. with sl.st. Break off M.

3rd round—With D., join yarn in last 2 ch. sp. of previous round, 3 ch., 2 tr. in same sp., (1 ch., 3 tr. in next sp., 1 ch., 3 tr., 2 ch., 3 tr. in next sp.) 3 times, 1 ch., 3 tr. in next sp., 1 ch., 3 tr. in next sp., 2 ch., join to 3rd of 3 ch. with sl.st. Break off D.

Using D. join 48 motifs into strip 4 × 12, and rem. 16 into square 4 × 4. Join one edge of square to top edge of 1st. 4 motifs along strip, then opposite edge of square to top edge of last 4 motifs of strip.

amount of someone's pay rise according to the amount of pay already earned, but it cannot decide if the person is worthy of a pay rise.

A conditional jump can be used to cause one of two alternative subsequences (or 'paths') to be followed, depending on the result of a calculation or test ('IF . . . THEN . . . ELSE . . .'), or to repeat a sequence of instructions a fixed number of times or until a certain point has been reached ('DO . . . UNTIL . . .'). An unconditional jump takes the flow of control away from the next instruction to another instruction elsewhere in the program ('GOTO . . .'). Chapter 6 deals with the construction of a program using these and the other classes of instructions in various forms known as 'programming languages'.

The self-modifying program, as this attribute is known, is the final distinguishing mark of a true computer, and makes it a general-purpose and flexible information-processing machine, because it can perform information-processing tasks as they really are (to be described in the next Chapter). Most tasks are not a single unvarying list of actions, but involve alternatives, such as income tax deductions at varying rates of tax depending on income and allowances, or mathematical work involving iterative calculations. It is also this feature of a computer which leads to descriptions of computers taking decisions, or solving problems – both peculiarly human attributes. In truth, the computer is merely obeying the rules and instructions programmed into it by a human programmer; it is the program which incorporates selection or decision-making, and the computer is a machine which executes such a computer program.

(e) Data storage and communication

The various types of computer programs that are needed for computers to handle a variety of tasks with efficiency and ease are known collectively as 'software', to distinguish them from the bare machine, known as 'hardware'. Most computers now need so much software (which will be discussed more fully in Chapter 7) that it cannot all be held in internal storage, and one of the two main functions of *external* or *backing storage*, or mass memory, is to store that part of a machine's software that is not currently required inside the processor for processing. The other, and usually predominant, use of external storage is as a repository for information of all types which is required permanently for processing, such as mathematical and business tables, library indexes, and all the 'files' of information that every business needs on employees, customers, products, shareholders, accounts, stocks, machines, etc. Information processing has come to rely heavily on large volumes of stored information which can be retrieved ('accessed') speedily, brought into the processor, and then either returned to external storage if it has been changed ('updated') during processing, or merely transmitted to an output device.

Most forms of external storage hold data in binary form on some form of magnetic medium, either tape or disc. Disc storage has the advantage of providing access directly to any part of the stored data, and is known as a *direct access storage device* or DASD. This works rather like a gramophone record: just as you can place the stylus at any position you wish on the record, the magnetic read/write head can be positioned easily over any part of the disc. If tape is used as a storage medium it is essential that any search begins at the start of the tape. This is called a *serial* search and is exactly the method which has to be used for finding a piece of music stored on a recording tape. A DASD can be functionally regarded as an extension of internal storage, as shown in Fig. 1.3, but usually operates as a fast I/O device.

The final element of a computer system is the link between its various components. These linkages can be very short, or 'local', that is, all the components are in one room or equally near.

Local communication links are sometimes known as 'buses' or 'channels', and it is usual for a computer to have at least an external storage device and one I/O device (for operator use, known as a 'console') connected locally by an I/O bus. Other I/O devices, however, can be connected 'remotely', such remoteness even extending to other continents. Remote connections can use most appropriate forms of telecommunication – cables, microwave radio links, satellite radio links. The combination of computers and telecommunications is generally thought to be the single most significant development in computing, and it enormously improves the power (and, for some people, increases the threat) of the computer to be able to process data physically input hundreds or thousands of miles away, or merely to output data at locations remote from a central storage unit.

1.3 COMPUTERS TODAY

At this point we can describe computers as machines, or systems of machines to denote their multi-machine organisation, with the following characteristics:
- an organised aggregate of mainly electronic units – processors, I/O devices, local storage, external storage devices – and communication links to make it operate as a single system;
- able to work on digital information coded in a binary format for processing at electronic speeds;
- under central processor control in the form of stored computer programs, composed of basic machine instructions including self-modifying features;
- and thus able to perform a wide variety of information-processing tasks in such diverse fields as business, engineering, education and finance.

(a) Computer performance

In Chapter 3 we shall be looking in more detail at computer hardware and how it works, but the main concern of this book is with what computers can be used for, and how they can be put to use. The first true electronic computer was invented around 1945 and, after four decades of rapid development, it has encompassed a wide range of performance, capability and cost. In fact, the range between the smallest computer and the largest is probably greater, proportionally, than any other class of machines in existence – certainly greater than the difference between the smallest and largest road or air transport vehicles, and perhaps on a par with electrical power generators. The tiny electronic computer installed as a controller in automatic washing machines and the largest supercomputers working in weather forecasting all share the same characteristics, but with vastly different performance capabilities.

The two dimensions of performance in computers are *speed* and *capacity*. The fractions of speed are very small, the complement of capacity very large, and the scale of measurement will be familiar only to those who have mastered SI units (see Table 1.1).

Table 1.1

Prefix	Description	Abbreviation	Application
Milli	1 thousandth	m ⎫	
Micro	1 millionth	μ ⎪	
Nano	1 billionth (American) i.e. 10^{-9}	n ⎬	seconds
Pico	1 billionth (British) i.e. 10^{-12}	p ⎭	
Kilo	1 thousand or 1024*	K ⎫	
Mega	1 million or 1024^2 *	M ⎪	bytes, words,
Giga	1 billion (American) or 1024^3 *	G ⎬	hertz, bauds
Tera	1 billion (British) or 1024^4 *	T ⎭	

*The reason for this alternative value will be given in Chapter 3.

The principal features of a computer in which speed and capacity vary, and which are therefore commonly used in describing a particular computer and its component units, are given in Table 1.2.

(b) Important types of computer

Within this wide range are some major types of computer (see Fig. 1.5) which either represent different starting or stage points in the evolution of computers, or form distinctive products for different markets – principally

Table 1.2

Component	Feature	Units of measurement
Processor	Instruction speed (time taken to execute one instruction — ADD, SUBTRACT, STORE, etc.); Sometimes quoted as the number of instructions carried out per second	Nanoseconds or micro-seconds Millions of instructions per second (MIPS)
Internal storage	Total storage capacity Access time*⎫ Cycle time* ⎭	⎰Kilobytes or megabytes ⎱Kilowords or megawords Nanoseconds
External storage	Capacity Transfer rate (to/from processor) Access time (DASDs only) Density of storage	Megabytes or gigabytes Megabytes/second Milliseconds Bits/inch (b.p.i.)
I/O devices	Speeds (of input/ output) Capacity of I/O media (e.g. screen, card, paper)	Cards, lines or characters, etc., per second Characters
Communication links	Speeds — remote lines — data and I/O buses	Bits/second (≈ bauds) ⎰Bytes/second ⎱Words/second

*These two terms refer to the speed with which data is transferred between internal storage and the processor and will be defined in Chapter 3.

mainframe computers, minicomputers, microcomputers, small business computers, word processors, personal computers, supercomputers. They are the equivalents of the different types of road transport vehicles — saloons, sports cars, HGVs, etc. An appropriate starting point for a knowledge of how to use a computer is to select the appropriate class of machine in the first place.

12

Fig 1.5 *cost and performance of different types of computer*

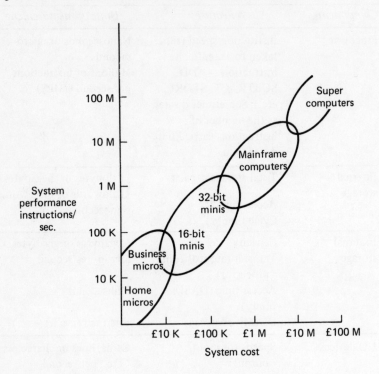

(i) Mainframe computers

Mainframes are the current descendants of the orginal computers, still
built on the same structure (which we call the Von Neumann machine in
honour of one of the significant contributors) but with vastly different
technology. These significant shifts in technology we used to call 'generations' and we had reached the third generation by the late 1960s. Because
of the rapid and continuous developments of the 1970s, this term has
ceased to have any real meaning except as a sales blurb, but we are sup-
posed (in 1984) to be using and selling fourth generation equipment now.
Mainframes are still large and expensive, costing from £250 000 upwards
to about £10 000 000; their use is synonymous with single-processor,
centralised computing, in which significant economies of scale are thought
to exist (typified in Grosch's law: the power ratio of two computers varies
as the square of the ratio of their costs; that is, if you buy a computer
twice as expensive you should get four times the power). This indicates
that along with their high costs they are used mostly by large companies

for gainful reasons (cost-reduction or profit-improvement).

Other characteristics of mainframes are that they:

- are mainly American manufactured; ICL is the sole significant non-American manufacturer outside the protected Japanese market;
- require a large volume of software, partly because of multi-user requirements, and also because they need to run several programs simultaneously ('multi-programming') to keep a large processor busy, so they also require a large internal storage capacity;
- need environmental support in sealed rooms; this is because many of the moving parts on such devices as disc drives are affected by excess dust or wide variations of temperature or humidity;
- generally demand quite a large number of professional staff to run them;
- are available in a variety of versions of processor and storage capacity, but often with a limited range of I/O device types; this enables them to be tailored, or 'configured', to satisfy both storage-dominated and processor-dominated applications, and to meet a company's specific requirements.

Fig. 1.6 shows a typical mainframe computer system, with still relatively large separate units, connected by cables hidden in false floors.

Fig 1.6 *a typical mainframe computer system*

A - Central processing unit and internal storage
B - High-speed printer
C - Operator console
D - Card reader
E - Magnetic disc drives
F - Magnetic tape drives

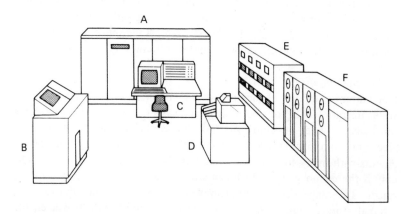

(ii) Minicomputers

Minicomputers ('minis') began to emerge in the 1960s, still recognisably based on the original computers but primarily designed for different uses. They were able to exploit some of the first moves towards miniaturisation in electronics, or integrated circuits, so that they gained in compactness and cheapness. They were designed primarily for various types of engineering and control work (particularly characterised now by industrial robots in the automotive industry), which led to some important demands and characteristics:

- high reliability;
- ease of use;
- limited number of uses, often dedicated to single use;
- relatively simple software;
- ease of device attachment;
- robustness for use in uncontrolled environment, and packaged in rack-mounted units (see Fig. 1.7).

This resulted in a significantly different internal organisation of hardware and software (or 'architecture'). Typical configurations (much less variety) cost from £15 000 to £500 000. Minis are manufactured by a different sector of manufacturers, still US-dominated but with some significant indigenous manufacturers. Their software and the ready availability of simple terminals made them a great step forward in approachability and usability, and their benefits have, in the process of time, moved them away from their original markets.

Minis are now often found in supporting roles to mainframes (for example, as 'front end processors' where the preparation and checking of data are performed by a separate minicomputer before the data is handed over to the mainframe for processing) and, as rivals to smaller mainframes, they have been promoting a trend away from centralised computing (known as 'distributed computing'). The latest 32-bit 'superminis' are among the most sophisticated and effective computers systems on the market.

(iii) Microcomputers

One current end-point of the process of miniaturisation, through the large-scale integration (LSI) of electronic circuits, is a range of products available on a silicon wafer or 'chip'. An LSI chip contains at least 500 separate electronic components. Next comes the VLSI (very large-scale integration) circuits with many thousands of components. A good example of a VLSI chip is the memory chip which can store 64 000 bits on a single wafer of silicon. This range includes semi-complete processors (the microprocessor), internal storage chips and various interface modules which will enable devices such as magnetic discs, printers, graph plotters and video displays to be connected to the computer. Contrary to public belief, we do not

Fig 1.7 *a typical rack-mounted minicomputer and a small business system of about the same power*

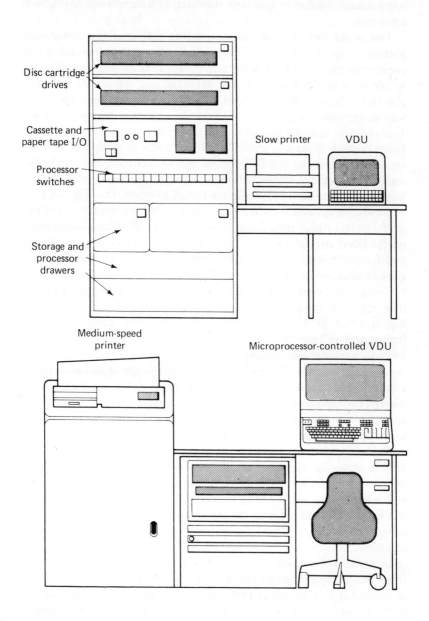

Disc cartridge drives

Cassette and paper tape I/O

Processor switches

Storage and processor drawers

Slow printer   VDU

Medium-speed printer

Microprocessor-controlled VDU

have a computer on a chip, but components of a computer. A complete computer on a chip, to be called a transputer, is likely to form the basis, when linked together in very large numbers, of a completely new type of computer.

One of the uses of these components is to build small low-cost general-purpose computers known as microcomputers or microsystems, along with commensurately scaled down I/O and storage devices, and with relatively simple software. Microcomputers, with limited user options, are now available from about £100 upwards to £20 000. Smaller systems are mostly sold as *personal computers*, for individual and general non-specialist use. The cheapest systems are often provided with 'domestic' I/O devices, audio cassette drives and small TV sets and come in partly assembled or even kit form for the real DIY enthusiast. Personal computers are in fact reaching a 'hobby' market of unexpected proportions, with sales of hundreds of thousands per year in the United Kingdom. (See Fig. 1.8.)

The larger systems are often packaged as *small business computers* (see next section) where they compete with small minis. Microsystems based on the latest class of microprocessors are now beginning to rival medium mainframes in their processor performance, though still limited in their I/O and mass storage capacity.

Components containing integrated circuits of various types are finding their way into computers of all sizes, even the largest mainframes. The biggest effect to the public of microelectronics technology will be the replacement of mechanical components such as timers and controllers in washing machines and cookers. We have already seen the effect on the Swiss watch industry of the electronic watch, and the replacement of the slide rule and hand-cranked calculator by the electronic calculator. Computerised car instrumentation and continuous monitoring of car performance by microprocessor are not uncommon now. The toy market has been joined by video games and microprocessor-controlled toys.

Much computing equipment now uses microprocessors within I/O devices and communications links. We are seeing more and more 'intelligent' terminals which are capable of a certain amount of simple processing before handing the data over to the main computer. One good example of this is the VDU which allows the characters displayed on its screen to be edited before the information held on the screen is dispatched to the computer.

In none of these uses are they programmable by their end users; they come mostly with programs already fixed, or 'blasted', into special types of internal storage known as ROM (read-only memory). However some of the larger video games do enable ambitious users to write small programs as an intermediate form leading up towards a personal computer for home use.

Fig 1.8 *typical microcomputers for (a) business and (b) personal use*

(courtesy of ACT (UK) Ltd)

(a)

VIDEO MONITOR

MICROCOMPUTER

DISK UNIT

(b)

DISKS

PRINTER

(courtesy of Acornsoft Ltd)

(iv) Small business computers

Very small mainframes, minicomputers and larger microcomputers are now, to the user, virtually indistinguishable particularly when built up with extra software and more sophisticated attachments for the business market. Companies who operate in this way generally buy the basic computer from the original manufacturer (who is known as the 'original equipment manufacturer' or OEM in this context) and produce their own 'product' with their own packaging and brand name. Such companies are sometimes known as 'systems houses'.

Small business computers often represent well-designed and fashionably packaged systems for specific uses. A good example is the class of small computers known as word processors. These emanated from the intelligent typewriters, or memory keyboards, developed by typewriter manufacturers to provide typists with extra speed. They are now sold in a variety of forms, ranging from standalone machines dedicated solely to this task, to fully multipurpose microcomputers, fitted with special software and high-performance terminals with the objective of performing a variety of functions associated with the production and storage of office documents. Word processors are also, when linked to other similar machines and to other normally independent machines such as photocopiers or dictation machines, the basis of electronic office systems, which currently represent a major area of development and innovation in computer system design and usage.

The marketing success of word processors can be attributed to two features apart from their purposeful hardware and software and overall packaging: firstly a playing down of their computer applications, and secondly a close attention to making them as unobtrusive and sympathetic in an office environment as possible (see Fig. 1.9). In the business field small systems of this type are taking a lot of the mystery and mystique out of computers (an unfortunate legacy from the days of mainframe domination) just as personal computers are doing in our homes.

(v) Supercomputers

The largest conventional mainframe computers in use today can execute about 10 million typical instructions per second. However astounding that speed may appear, it is still too slow to permit the solution by the comter of certain problems in science, such as instant weather forecasting, aircraft design simulations and flood or earthquake predictions. Such tasks, whose solution could make great contributions to personal safety and energy usage, can take days to run on conventional machines or are too big to work at all. So, while the growth elsewhere has been in very much smaller machines, scientists have required the development of *supercomputers*, some built on completely different designs from conventional

Fig 1.9 *a small business computer in an office environment*

(courtesy of Hewlett-Packard Ltd)

computers in that they allow the execution of multiple instructions in parallel (rather than the serial processing of single instructions), through one of several alternative mechanisms.

Current supercomputers, which have been ordered in surprisingly large numbers, can perform up to about 100 million instructions per second, properly programmed for the appropriate tasks. Already, however, NASA (the US National Aeronautics and Space Administration) has called for designs for a supercomputer ten times faster than the current models, with a performance of about 1000 million instructions per second, for wind tunnel simulation. It seems that there will always be a place for bigger and faster computers — users will be continually finding bigger and bigger problems to tackle with them.

(*vi*) *Portable computers*

At the same time our computers have been contracting in the reverse direction. For several years it has been possible to buy a true stored-program computer of the size of a pocket calculator, and many of the smallest home computers would fit into a shopping bag, but their lack of an external storage facility limits their usefulness. Now we have a truly portable computer, with a fuller keyboard, narrow-width printer and the new 3-inch floppy disc drive in one ruggedised package with carrying handle. The development of a high-power long-life electric battery will finally free us from the restrictions of the power point, (though some models can be powered from a conventional car battery), so that a computer may go wherever man may go.

SPECIMEN QUESTIONS

In this list of specimen examination questions, and in all the lists at the end of later chapters, those marked '*' have been based on or derived from questions set in the A level, O level or CSE examinations in Computer Studies of the Welsh Joint Education Committee in the years 1981-3.

1. Define a computer and describe its essential characteristics.

2. Describe the development of computers since the 1940s by referring to
   (i) the three generations of computers;
   (ii) minicomputers and microcomputers.
   In each case name one distinctive feature and name one typical application for each type of computer.   *

3. Differentiate between a microprocessor and a microcomputer.

4. Outline the changes that have taken place in computing over the last thirty years, explaining how the reliability, power, and speed of hardware and software have developed. What effects do you think these changes have had on the use of computers?   *

5. Explain how the recent rapid developments in computer technology have led to a situation in which a huge variety of different types and commercial sources are available on the market.   *

6. Explain briefly the following terms and abbreviations:
   (a) bit, (b) byte, (c) k, (d) Mb, (e) ms, (f) CPU, (g) ALU.

7. Outline the distinguishing characteristics of micro, mini and mainframe computers in terms of costs, hardware and software capacities and types of application.

CHAPTER 2

THE WHO, WHAT AND WHY OF COMPUTERS

Although reliable official statistics are not available, the best estimate is that computer hardware accounts for 15 per cent of the UK's annual investment in plant and equipment and that in the UK one home in five now contains a personal computer. More important, in the face of world-wide stagnancy and even decay in trade and production, expenditure by business and domestic users on computers is likely to grow at a rate of about 15 per cent per annum until the end of the decade.

The figures do not show, however, the wide ranges of uses which computers have found, nor do they reveal how deeply they have become embedded in some aspects of our life. Like many other features of modern life, we only realise their impact when they become unavailable for one reason or another, as for instance when computer operators come out on strike and make their machines inoperative. Such action brings most of the routine work of their companies to a halt, and trade unions have come to realise the strategic position which computers and their staff now occupy. In their forty years of use and development, computers have moved into many and different applications, any classification of which is merely arbitrary, but it is most meaningful to identify their uses in the following areas:
- numerical computation;
- data processing;
- automatic control;
- personal computing;
- information processing.

2.1 COMPUTERS IN NUMERICAL COMPUTATION

As their name suggests, computers were originally invented as computing machines (compute: 'determine by calculation' — *Shorter Oxford English Dictionary*). They succeeded and replaced mechanical calculating machines or engines (a term which, incidentally, has returned to use for a type of microcomputer) which dated back 100 years and which can now be seen in museums such as the Science Museum in London. Much scientific work has always demanded numerical computation that was beyond human capabilities in terms of:

- volume (number of operations), and therefore speed of completion;
- accuracy (freedom from induced errors);
- precision (level of detail).

The calculation of paths of stars and comets in astronomy, and of tide tables in meteorology, are two long-standing examples and, more recently, military and space programmes have added a greater urgency to this demand.

The particular features of computers which made possible a transfer of this work were firstly their ability to perform arithmetical operations very fast, and secondly the use of a stored program to enable sequences and combinations of simple arithmetic to be performed automatically and repeated as required. These are common features of all true computers, with the result that numerical work features prominently in the use of most computers, from the highest flights of scientific experimentation (where there remain some problem areas unsolvable without a further step ahead in computer power), down to the domestic computer which can be programmed to keep a family's budget, or merely to perform some difficult or tedious piece of arithmetic. At this level, its use is not too far removed from that of an electronic calculator; the dividing line between programmable calculators and very small computers is a fine one, but significant differences include:

- calculators handle only numerical values;
- programmable calculators are still very difficult to program;
- programmable calculators have very limited storage.

This should do no more than emphasise that nowadays people use computers for different reasons — what is essential to a scientist is a convenience to a home computer fanatic. The middle ground is occupied by what most people experience from computers — the performance of simple but repetitive tasks such as calculating pay and printing a payslip or providing electricity or gas bills. This is the work generally classified as data processing. Such work is not impossible without computers, but vastly more superior results in terms of speed and accuracy accrue from the use of computers, and for a public gas supplier it is the speed with which a bill can be produced after a meter is read that makes all the difference. Fig. 2.1 shows a simplified procedure for calculating a gas bill as a sequence of arithmetical operations, in the form of a *flowchart*, which is widely used in computing and which will be examined in Chapters 5 and 6.

Fig 2.1 *arithmetical procedure for gas bill calculation*

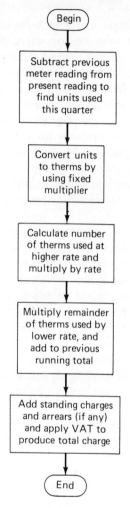

For highly demanding computational work (popularly known as 'number-crunching') the following features of a computer are of particular importance:

- the way that numbers are represented and held in the computer;
- the way that arithmetical operations are performed;
- the way that a computer can be programmed to perform mathematical functions other than add, subtract, multiply or divide, such as square roots, by a process known as 'numerical analysis';
- the sets of rules (or algorithm) through which a solution will be found for a mathematical problem if followed long enough.

2.2 COMPUTERS IN DATA PROCESSING

Despite their name and origin, and despite the prominence (but not pre-dominance) of numerical work on computers of all types, it would be wrong to think of computers just as giant calculating machines. The large majority of non-domestic computers today are used in the context of *business data processing*. Data processing (DP) was a term that pre-dated computers by about a generation (in human, not computer, terms!), and was used to describe a part of company work that dealt with the routine computational work that any company has to arrange, such as calculation of pay, production of accounts and keeping of ledgers) and the mainten-ance of its information ('data') on employees, customers, suppliers, products, etc., kept in collections known as 'files'.

Our inheritance from pre-computer data processing is widespread and includes:
- business machines now connected to a computer on-line, so that a direct connection is made between user and computer via a specific piece of peripheral equipment. The opposite of 'on-line' is 'off-line' where data is prepared on a device which is not connected to the computer. The out-put from an off-line device could be punched cards or punched paper tape, for example, and this is then loaded into a computer peripheral device so that the data stored on the tape or cards can be transferred to the computer's storage for processing;
- media such as cards, tape, listing paper and forms;
- techniques and methods of handling input and files.

The first of these factors is particularly important because it changes the shape of computers.

The use of a computer as the heart of a data processing activity, now described as electronic data processing (EDP) or automatic data processing (ADP), turns what was originally a single machine into a multi-machine system. In such a computer system the value and importance of peripherals typically far exceed that of the processor itself. Fig. 1.6 shows a typical computer configuration from a mainframe data processing department, and identifies the principal peripherals surrounding the processor, and in most senses overshadowing it. Fig. 1.6 does not show the off-line equipment supporting the computer system: pre-processing equipment such as data preparation devices and post-processing equipment such as bursters, collators, and envelope fillers. Fig. 2.2 shows a typical complete machine system in EDP, and an extension of the flowchart of the gas billing calculation of Fig. 2.1, illustrating the changed balance of comput-ing in data processing.

Business systems are also procedural systems of great width and depth;

Fig 2.2 *data processing and the computer*

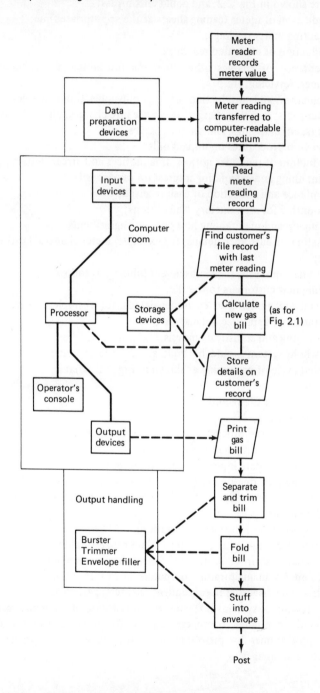

a typical gas billing system contains many other functions beyond the procedure shown in Fig. 2.2, and could encompass:
- production of meter reading sheets at the appropriate time;
- accepting meter readings;
- production of estimated readings;
- acceptance of charges other than gas for billing, for example, coke, fittings, servicing, etc.;
- calculation and production of gas bills plus other charges including meter rents, standing charges, appliance hire charges, hire purchase repayments, coke, fittings, and service charges;
- follow-up procedures on unpaid bills;
- production of reminder notices, final notices and arrears letters;
- maintaining and calculating interest on gas deposits;
- acceptance and allocation of cash received;
- accounting for all monetary transactions;
- setting-up and maintaining hire purchase agreements;
- updating of customer details, for example, meter changes, tariff changes, etc.;
- customer removals, their subsequent billing and follow-up;
- adding new customers to the file;
- general amendments to customer details, for example, change of name, alteration of appliance details, etc.;
- accounting and statistical analysis.

The whole system would be built around the customer master file, in a repeated cycle of processing as shown in Fig. 2.2. That is:
- read input data
- update master file record
- produce output.

The role of the processor in data processing is thus a reduced but still central one, primarily devoted to:
- the control of data input, storage and output devices;
- the running of one or more computer programs, mostly of limited computational content and rather more heavily concerned with the handling of data in files;
- the supervision of the entire operation.

In this way the use of a computer in data processing is more akin to its use in automatic control (see next section). It has led to a number of technical developments in mainframe computers of immense significance, some of which will be discussed in subsequent chapters, particularly:
- the creation of systems software, which is a suite of programs designed to allow the computer to process its data efficiently and to act as an aid to the programmer by providing him with ready-made routines such as 'sorts' and 'merges';

- easier programming methods for business computing;
- computers capable of running many programs concurrently (multi-programming).

It exposed the computer to a vastly wider market, which in turn created economies of scale in manufacturing and led ultimately to the much cheaper machines of today. It finally created both the computer industry and the computing profession as we know them today, and particularly the key role of systems analysis in business computing.

Equally the computer in business has significantly affected business organisations themselves. There are very few organisations with more than, say, 100 employees who do not find it advantageous to use computers in one or other aspect of their data processing, and many large companies are very heavily dependent on them.

What such organisations find in computer-based systems are the basic advantages of mechanisation over manual work − speed, accuracy, reliability and lower costs − plus some added and less quantifiable benefits such as better customer service through real-time systems, integration of company activities through the use of data communications, and the ability to survive in an environment in which ever more information is required of them and in which ever more information is available to them (and to their competitors).

In turn this has affected us, the public, who are mostly employees of, and certainly customers of, computer-using organisations. As customers, we receive numerous bills, letters and other computer-produced documents through the post; as both employees and customers, records about us are held on the computer files of those organisations: banks, building societies, police, county and district councils, Post Office, gas, electricity and water boards, government departments, trade unions . . . the list for a typical citizen is very long. Some of the potential consequences of this are discussed in Chapter 10.

2.3 COMPUTERS IN CONTROL

Automatic control of machines (or automation) is a long-established feature of industrial manufacture. We are also familiar with domestic controls such as temperature thermostats in electric irons and in our central heating systems, and the timer controls in an automatic washing machine. These examples represent two classes of control. In the first case, there is a feedback from the thermostats to the heater or fan which comes on intermittently to maintain the desired temperature, known as *closed-loop control*. In the second case, there is no feedback but simply a sequence of instructions followed automatically, known as *automatic sequence control* (ASC) or *open-loop control* (see Fig. 2.3).

Fig 2.3 *automatic control and the computer*

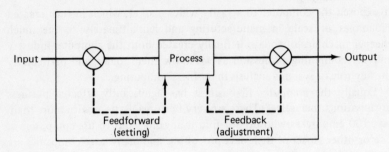

(a) *closed loop control*

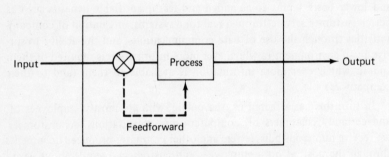

(b) *open loop control*

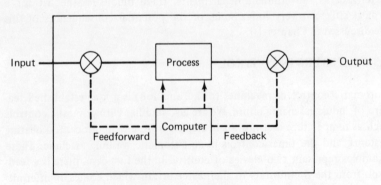

(c) *the computer as a controller*

Engineers have long been using these forms of control in manufacturing processes, and have used computers as the controlling device linked by suitable 'interfaces' (devices which enable one piece of equipment to communicate with another) to instruments ('sensors') which record production variables such as temperature, speed, weight, and to controllers ('activators') which can change some aspect of the operation of the process or machine. The most important function of these interfaces is to convert non-digital signals ('analog') into digital form, as analog-to-digital converters.

In *process control* the computer is used to supervise the operation of conventional controlling devices in large-scale continuous or semi-continuous production such as oil, chemical, paper or metal processing, or ultimately to replace them in the form of direct digital control. To do so, a computer program needs to input an instrument reading, compare it to a stored or computed value, and return a value or a correction factor to the activator in keeping with the pace of the process which it is controlling, or 'in real time'. This term is also now widely used in business computing, where it refers to computer programs which process individual transactions or enquiries on demand (while people wait), and is also known there as 'demand' or 'transaction' processing. Examples of real-time applications are in airline booking systems and any system which requires fast updating of files of information. In conventional data processing, as mentioned earlier on p. 24 for example, where bills and invoices are produced, the data is collected together in batches and processed at regular intervals throughout the work period. Such a system is called 'batch' processing.

Numerical control refers to the use of a computer to generate a sequence of activator movements for machine tools such as drills, lathes and presses, and is a type of control that was boosted by the availability of the smaller and cheaper *minicomputers* which were primarily designed for this and other smaller-scale control applications. A particularly important application of this type is in the control of traffic flow using computer-controlled traffic lights. In the transmission of electricity via the National Grid, the supply of power is controlled by demand and the use of computers is essential to the efficient utilisation of the electricity supply.

The minicomputer also became useful to engineers in the design of machine and components; under program control, a computer could store and display a representation or drawing on a graphics terminal (see Fig. 4.16) where it could be modified, tested under a variety of simulated conditions and ultimately refined before a prototype need be built. Computer-aided design (CAD) is now an important tool for design engineers, architects and planners, and is often linked with computer-controlled production and manufacture.

Progress with minicomputers in automation was steady but unspectacular and largely unknown to the general public, until the well-publicised advent of the microprocessor — the current end-point of the on-going process of miniaturisation and large-scale integration (LSI) of electronic circuits. Microprocessors are finding widespread engineering and control applications as low-cost controllers in small domestic machines such as cars, washing machines and cameras, and finally as the control units in industrial robots and in assembly-line automation.

There is little doubt that the use of these computers in controlling other machines will be greatly extended as engineers learn to use them as one of their basic building blocks. For machines currently controlled by other types of device, the microprocessor is cheaper, more reliable, more flexible and has a faster response; for machines not yet taken over by the long advance of automation, microprocessors will provide all the advantages of automatic control — better quality of output and higher performance, at a lower overall cost. It is also an inevitable and long-standing conse-quence of automation that manual labour is dispossessed — but more about this in Chapter 10.

2.4 PERSONAL COMPUTING

The common theme running through all the different uses of computers described so far is that they are employed by public and private organ-isations because they can perform various tasks more effectively and therefore more economically than other machines or people; in other words they cut costs and/or improve profits. Until about five years ago the sheer basic cost of a computer ruled it out as a medium of individual, educational, cultural, recreational or social enrichment. Up to that time the only opportunities for that form of non-profit-making computing was provided by multi-access computers, in which the hardware and software are designed to support a large number of simultaneously active terminals, usually by giving each terminal a short share ('time-slice') of computer time in sequence. This mechanism gives the appearance and much of the reality of continuous computer availability to terminal users. Special software also assists in making the use of multi-access terminals as simple as possible, by providing a process of question/command and answer/response between the computer user at a terminal and the computer system, a form known as interactive or conversational computing (see Chapter 7). Multi-access computer systems are highly sophisticated machines, and introduced com-puting to a decade of students, schoolchildren and other non-professional users. One noteworthy group of people who were able to exploit this limited and costly opportunity were a section of modern artists, who could use a computer's power to generate complex geometric patterns and create fine line-drawings, in an activity that is known as Computer Art.

However, the personal computer did not become a reality until progress in microelectronics produced the microcomputer, based on microprocessor and storage chips and interfaces to cheap and small-scale terminals. At the cheapest level there are now many models costing less than £100, using mostly TV sets or video monitors and cassette recorders as terminals. Personal computing is now a major and unique sector of the computer industry, supported by computer shops, an enormous number of magazines, cottage-style software suppliers and computer clubs. Personal computers have also made possible the growth of computing in schools, which has itself fostered a home computing mania among schoolchildren of somewhat alarming proportions.

The foundation of home computing is undoubtedly the video game, employing sophisticated computer graphic displays in full colour. The common feature of a computer game is that the computer has been programmed to respond to your inputs and then display the consequences and either continue playing or even, as in Computer Chess and Draughts, make a similar move of its own. We have enjoyed computer games of a less addictive kind for many years, mostly as a diversion for bored computer programmers awaiting their next assignment, and more importantly as a means of introducing people painlessly to a computer. The computer-games manufacturers are now inventing new games of great ingenuity and technical sophistication; Space Invaders and Pacman are yesterday's favourites. The dividing line between a purely video game machine and a true home computer is a marginal one, but nearly all now allow full programming facilities. Even at this level the personal computer permits the same type of facilities as do other and larger computers – computation, control and data handling – but obviously to a degree limited by the size and environment of personal computing. The more expensive and robust machines are therefore useful to small businesses, self-employed professional people, teachers, managers in large businesses. For this purpose they are usually sold with floppy or small hard disk devices and better-quality displays, along with pre-written programs for standard and predictable business functions.

Given the low and decreasing cost of useful personal computers and their ready availability in chain stores and even supermarkets, the supply and distribution of good-quality software remains an unsolved problem. One solution on the horizon is electronic distribution of proven software from a single and central storage point – a concept known as 'Telesoftware'. Such a service will operate over a public Videotex facility (see next section) or via an intermediate link, requiring only an additional interface unit which will in effect put the personal computer user in touch with a library of programs from which he or she may select for temporary usage at little or no cost.

Personal computing, whether for gain, leisure or pleasure, is one of the most welcome developments in modern computing, first because it offers a completely new form of leisure pursuit to help fill the increasing amount of leisure time that modern technology (computers included) will be giving us when the 35- or 30-hour working week arrives; and second because it humanises and democratises the computer as no other experience or media presentation can. When we all have a computer in the home, we will better appreciate what large computers can do for and to us, in our place of work and in the other large organisations which shape our lives.

2.5 INFORMATION PROCESSING AND INFORMATION TECHNOLOGY

The extension of the boundaries of computing which started with the use of computers in data processing, has also been assisted by the developments in micro-electronics, two forms of which, the microprocessor and the microcomputer, have been mentioned in the earlier section of this chapter. The relative costs of this movement are interesting in that while the cost of processors has, in one estimate, been dropping at the rate of 20 per cent per year, the cost of storage has been falling at the higher rates of 30 per cent (internal storage) and 40 per cent (backing storage). The economics of computer hardware have been leading users further into pure information processing (= information storage, retrieval and dissemination), with little or no computational content at all, into what has been (re)defined as *informatics* (after the French term *l'informatique*). This inelegant term is an attempt to redress the balance of meaning that is still inherent in the term 'computing'. Perhaps it should be mentioned at this point that in some contexts there is a difference between the words 'data' and 'information': data can be considered the raw material of information.

One example of information processing is what constitutes one of the most common business uses of a computer; the keeping of names and addresses for circulation control. We are all on the receiving end of *name-and-address systems*: directly, with computer-printed stick-on labels, envelopes, magazine wrappers and the like, and indirectly in the form of computer-printed bills with a name and address appearing through window envelopes. The sole function of this (part of a) computer application is to set up, maintain, store and print out a (potential) customer's name and address, (along with some other information relating to credit or registration status); a simplified example will be used throughout this book to illustrate some points about computer systems and programming and their impact.

Videotex is another example of an information system, whose main function in its various forms is to distribute stored information (including computer programs, as we have seen above) from a central computer to primarily domestic TV receivers via a special interface/decoder unit. Public videotext systems may be classified into Teletext and Viewdata systems; Teletext (for example Ceefax) uses spare capacity in normal TV broadcasts on microwave channels to transmit a few lines of data per cycle to build up screen displays in a fixed sequence, any one of which may be requested by a viewer, but does not permit data to be returned by the viewer (at the moment – this may change when domestic cable channels are used to carry TV transmissions). Viewdata systems use telephone lines to transmit entire screens of data ('pages') of information requested by individual viewers, and also allows a customer to respond to displayed information (for example, to reserve a room at a hotel from a list on the screen) via a Videotex keypad (see Fig. 4.9).

This combination of computer technology and data communications is the essence of what has become politically known as 'Information Technology'. This term, unfortunately abbreviated to IT, is semi-officially defined as 'the acquisition, processing, storage, dissemination and use of vocal, pictorial, textual and numerical information by a microelectronics-based combination of computing and telecommunications'. Jargon-ridden as this definition may be, Information Technology does convey a change of emphasis away from conventional static computing into an acceptance that the communication of stored information is a fundamental objective of computing. Thus for a user of Ceefax or Prestel the location of the computer which holds the stored information and may accept a response is immaterial; it is the immediate availability of stored information in the home that is the essence of the service. A similar shift of emphasis is evident within Word Processing, where communication between word processors both within and between companies is seen as one of their main objectives, one of the forms of 'electronic mail' which could take us into the automated, paperless office. Domestic electronic mail is also available, in somewhat embryonic forms at the present, in most public viewdata systems.

Finally, computers and telecommunications have also contributed to the objectives of *collecting and disseminating knowledge*. It is often said that automation is changing our way of life from a labour-based society to a knowledge-based society, and therefore the organisation of knowledge bases must make a significant contribution to this process. Traditionally, our formal knowledge has been written in books, stored in book libraries, with a passive information service. Increasingly, references to, and abstracts of, knowledge are stored in very large bibliographic or statistical databases, and are available for searching and retrieval via a terminal. There are both disciplinary and inter-disciplinary banks of data (databases) available, covering most branches of science, technology and business, while details of most books published in the United Kingdom since 1950 and in the United States since 1968 are available through the British Museum's BLAISE system.

The extension of on-line databases to text storage and display, either on microfilm or on Prestel terminals, has led to predictions about the eventual disappearance of printed books and newspapers altogether. Without agreeing with such a far-fetched prediction, the fact that computers are bound to have some impact on our organisation, and therefore perspective, of knowledge shows how far we have come in forty years from the days of the automatic calculator. How one machine can extend its functions so far is one of the main themes to be explored in succeeding chapters.

SPECIMEN QUESTIONS

1. Explain the difference between data and information. What attributes must information possess to be of value?

2. What is meant by a real-time system and how does it differ from a conventional computer system? Give one example of a real-time system, clearly stating its hardware configuration and software requirements.   *

3. What are the major characteristics of a microprocessor? Why are these characteristics of particular value in the field of control applications?   *

4. Give a detailed definition of data processing. What additional features are implied by the newer term 'information processing'?

5. Write an account of a computer installation or application that you have studied. Include in your answer: (i) the hardware used, (ii) how and why the computer is used, (iii) two advantages that using the computer has brought for the user, (iv) any disadvantages of the application.   *

6. What is 'word processing'? Account for the origin and growth of WP as an area of computer usage.

7. Define 'information technology', and give four examples of it in action.

CHAPTER 3

HOW THE COMPUTER
WORKS

The survey of computer usage in the previous chapter has emphasised the diversity of computer applications and the versatility of the computer. Three factors make this possible and this chapter deals with two of them. The first is the way that data of many different types, arising from different sources, is represented and handled within the computer; the second is the way that program instructions in a computer program are able to perform the processing of that data.

3.1 DATA REPRESENTATION

(a) The binary system

The fundamental form in which *all* information — numbers, characters, and program instructions — is handled in the computer is the binary number form.

In everyday life quantities are normally represented in multiples of ten — 'decimal' counting or counting to 'base' ten. This system goes back into prehistory and comes naturally to a human being who has a total of ten fingers and thumbs on his two hands. It is not the only system in general use, however, and until recently the English-speaking world used the Imperial system of measures, which has a bewildering assortment of bases:

    2 pints to a quart;
    3 feet to a yard;
  14 pounds to the stone;
  16 ounces to the pound, etc.

In the binary system, the base is 2, and it therefore has only two figures, 0 and 1. In the decimal system, there are no figures higher than 9, so whenever 1 is added to a 9 in any order (or column), the 9 is changed to 0 and 1 is added to the next higher order. In binary, where there is no figure greater than 1, this change has to happen more frequently. In decimal the orders are often called

... thousands, hundreds, tens, units

which can be represented as powers of ten

... $10^3, 10^2, 10^1, 10^0$

In binary the orders can be called

... eights, fours, twos, units

and represented as powers of 2

... $2^3, 2^2, 2^1, 2^0$

The logic of the binary system can be seen by studying the following numbers and their decimal equivalents.

	Binary	Decimal
	0	0
1 in the units column	1	1
1 in the twos column, 0 in the units column	10	2
1 in the twos column, 1 in the units column	11	3
1 in the fours column, 0 in the twos column, 0 in the units column	100	4
	101	5
etc.	110	6
	111	7
	1000	8
	1001	9
	1010	10
	1011	11
	1100	12
	1101	13
	1110	14
	1111	15
	10000	16

The use of the binary system in a digital computer is essential, because whereas man has ten fingers and thumbs to count on, it is inconvenient to represent this in electronic circuits. In the computer, only two electrical states are used — *on* and *off* — which represent, variously, high or low voltage, the presence or absence of an electrical pulse, the presence or absence of a magnetised force. This two-state system, on/off, present/absent, is eminently suitable for machine recognition and recording in both electronic and mechanical equipment.

(b) Integers (whole numbers)

It has already been stated that the byte is the basic unit of data held in a computer's memory. As each binary digit ('bit', to distinguish it from decimal digit) within the byte will be either 1 or 0 then it follows that the information coded within that byte will range from 00000000 to 11111111. In early computers only integer numbers were stored and, in fact, in the very cheapest of the modern microcomputers only integer numbers are handled. If the 8 bits of a byte are used to store integers then there has to be some order about the way in which the pattern of bits is to be interpreted. One bit has to be used to signify whether the number is positive or negative. 0 is used to signify positive and 1 for negative. The means that the largest possible positive integer stored in one byte will be represented by:

$$01111111$$

which is $2^7 - 1 = 127$. Negative numbers are represented by what is called 'two's complement form'. This involves writing the binary equivalent of a decimal number and then changing every 0 to a 1 and every 1 to a 0. Then 1 is added to the result. It sounds complicated but in fact is quite easy. For example: to obtain the binary equivalent of the decimal number −17 we proceed as follows:

Expressed in binary form the number 17 is 10001.

If we are going to express the number in byte form we pad it out so that there are 8 bits, that is, 00010001. Now changing 1s to 0s and 0s to 1s we get 11101110; then add 1 giving 11101111.

This bit pattern will now represent the decimal number −17 in two's complement form.

The largest negative integer which can be stored within one byte is 10000000 which is the equivalent of -2^7. In order to demonstrate that this system works let us add together the bit patterns for +20 and −17. +20 is represented by 00010100 and −17 by 11101111 as we have already seen. If we add them together we get:

$$\begin{array}{r} 00010100 \\ + \, 11101111 \\ \hline 00000011 \end{array}$$

this answer being the binary equivalent to +3, which is correct.

The rules of binary arithmetic used in this example are quite simple and are:

$$0 + 0 = 0$$
$$0 + 1 = 1$$
$$1 + 0 = 1$$
$$1 + 1 = 0 \text{ and } 1 \text{ to carry}$$

The byte can only hold a fixed number of binary digits so if there is a digit to carry when the two leading digits are added this carry digit is discarded deliberately.

In the same way we can subtract 20 from 17 using the same technique by adding the bit patterns for +17 and −20 together:

$$
\begin{array}{ll}
00010001 & (+17) \\
+\ 11101100 & (-20) \\
\hline
11111101 &
\end{array}
$$

We can see that the answer is in fact the bit pattern for −3 since if we reverse the two's complement procedure:

subtract 1: 11111100

change: 00000011 giving the bit pattern for +3

The above examples use 8 bits, but most minicomputers use 16 bits (2 bytes) to store integers and by the same conventions the largest positive integer stored would be $2^{15} - 1 = 32\,767$ and the largest negative integer would be $-2^{15} = -32\,768$.

(c) Mixed numbers

The conventional way of representing mixed numbers (numbers which contain a whole number part and a decimal part) is to use what is called *floating point format*. In order to do this the number is given three characteristics: its sign, its significant digits and its size. In order to achieve a satisfactory degree of accuracy at least 32 bits (4 bytes) are needed to store a floating point number. As with integers the sign bit is the first, or more significant, bit and 0 indicates a positive number and 1 a negative number. But before a number is stored in its 4 bytes it has to be *norma-*

lised or put into a standard form. This generally takes the form of writing the number in the form:

$$A \times 10^k$$

where A is a number in the range 1 to 9. This number is called the *mantissa* (familiar to those who struggled with logarithm tables at school). The power of 10, k, is called the exponent. If all numbers are reduced to this standard form then we can dispense with decimal points and the ten since their absolute values can always be calculated from a knowledge of the mantissa and exponent.

For example the number 135 can be written as:

$$1.35 \times 10^2$$

and the only parts of the number which need to be stored are the digits 1.35 and the exponent, which is 2. In fact, to make the storage of floating point numbers easier for the computer to handle, the exponent is usually stored in what is called an *excess* form. If it is stored in excess - 64 form then 64 is added to the exponent and the resulting number is stored. This avoids wasting a bit to give the sign of the exponent and allows exponents ranging in size from −64 to +64 to be stored. As an example, the number −0.0000005438 will be first normalised to:

$$-5.438 \times 10^{-7}$$

and the number stored as:

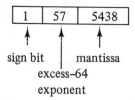

As a compromise to using the binary system — good for computers, difficult for us — much use is made in computing of both octal and hexadecimal numbers. The octal system uses the base of 8 and its numbers are expressed using the digits 0 to 7. The hexadecimal system (hex for short) uses a base of 16 and has to add the characters A, B, C, D, E, F to the usual ten digits of the decimal system. The letters stand for the numbers 10, 11, 12, 13, 14, 15. The relationship between the four systems is shown in Table 3.1.

Table 3.1

Decimal	Binary	Octal	Hex
1	1	1	1
2	10	2	2
3	11	3	3
4	100	4	4
5	101	5	5
6	110	6	6
7	111	7	7
8	1000	10	8
9	1001	11	9
10	1010	12	A
11	1011	13	B
12	1100	14	C
13	1101	15	D
14	1110	16	E
15	1111	17	F
16	10000	20	10
17	10001	21	11
18	10010	22	12
19	10011	23	13
20	10100	24	14
21	10101	25	15
22	10110	26	16
23	10111	27	17
24	11000	30	18
25	11001	31	19
26	11010	32	1A
27	11011	33	1B
28	11100	34	1C
29	11101	35	1D
30	11110	36	1E
31	11111	37	1F
32	100000	40	20

(d) Character representation

Because of the prevalence of non-numerical data in modern computing, particularly in information processing which is almost totally non-numerical, the way we store and represent what are usually known as 'characters' is of particular importance. In simple terms a character is anything that is represented by the depression of a key on a keyboard, a pattern of holes across a punched paper tape or a pattern of holes in one column of a punched card. These characters can be numeric (0 to 9), alphabetic (A to Z), symbols such as (, ? @ / " * =), or control characters. Control characters are characters which have to be sent to devices such as printers to tell them where the printing head should go next (for example to the start of the next line – the carriage-return/line-feed character). Other characters can be sent to video screens to tell the controller to clear the screen or make certain characters blink on and off.

One of the commonest codes used for transmitting characters is the 7-bit international alphabet – American Standard Code for Information Interchange (ASCII). Fig. 3.1 shows the ASCII code and the equivalents of the binary codes for the various characters in both hex and octal form.

Fig 3.1(a) *character representation in the ASCII code*

bits 7 6 5 / bits 4 3 2 1	hex	0	1	2	3	4	5	6	7
0 0 0 0	0	NUL	DLE	SP	0	@	P		p
0 0 0 1	1	SOH	DC1	!	1	A	Q	a	q
0 0 1 0	2	STX	DC2	"	2	B	R	b	r
0 0 1 1	3	ETX	DC3	#	3	C	S	c	s
0 1 0 0	4	EOT	DC4	$	4	D	T	d	t
0 1 0 1	5	ENQ	NAK	%	5	E	U	e	u
0 1 1 0	6	ACK	SYN	&	6	F	V	f	v
0 1 1 1	7	BEL	ETB	'	7	G	W	g	w
1 0 0 0	8	BS	CAN	(	8	H	X	h	x
1 0 0 1	9	HT	EM	)	9	I	Y	i	y
1 0 1 0	A	LF	SUB	*	:	J	Z	j	z
1 0 1 1	B	VT	ESC	+	;	K	[	k	{
1 1 0 0	C	FF	FS	,	<	L	\	l	|
1 1 0 1	D	CR	GS	–	=	M	]	m	}
1 1 1 0	E	SO	RS	.	>	N	^	n	~
1 1 1 1	F	SI	US	/	?	O	_	o	DEL

3 left-most bits of the ASCII Code

← Hexadecimal equivalent

Hexadecimal equivalent

4 right-most bits of ASCII Code

(*a*)

Fig 3.1(b) *character representation in the ASCII code*

Hex	7-bit Octal	ASCII	Hex	7-bit Octal	ASCII	Hex	7-bit Octal	ASCII
00	000	NUL	2B	053	+	56	126	V
01	001	SOH	2C	054	,	57	127	W
02	002	STX	2D	055	-	58	130	X
03	003	ETX	2E	056	.	59	131	Y
04	004	EOT	2F	057	/	5A	132	Z
05	005	ENQ	30	060	0	5B	133	[
06	006	ACK	31	061	1	5C	134	\
07	007	BEL	32	062	2	5D	135	]
08	010	BS	33	063	3	5E	136	↑
09	011	HT	34	064	4	5F	137	←
0A	012	LF	35	065	5	60	140	
0B	013	VT	36	066	6	61	141	a
0C	014	FF	37	067	7	62	142	b
0D	015	CR	38	070	8	63	143	c
0E	016	SO	39	071	9	64	144	d
0F	017	SI	3A	072	:	65	145	e
10	020	DLE	3B	073	;	66	146	f
11	021	DC1	3C	074	<	67	147	g
12	022	DC2	3D	075	=	68	150	h
13	023	DC3	3E	076	>	69	151	i
14	024	DC4	3F	077	?	6A	152	j
15	025	NAK	40	100	@	6B	153	k
16	026	SYN	41	101	A	6C	154	l
17	027	ETB	42	102	B	6D	155	m
18	030	CAN	43	103	C	6E	156	n
19	031	EM	44	104	D	6F	157	o
1A	032	SUB	45	105	E	70	160	p
1B	033	ESC	46	106	F	71	161	q
1C	034	FS	47	107	G	72	162	r
1D	035	GS	48	110	H	73	163	s
1E	036	RS	49	111	I	74	164	t
1F	037	US	4A	112	J	75	165	u
20	040	SP	4B	113	K	76	166	v
21	041	!	4C	114	L	77	167	w
22	042	"	4D	115	M	78	170	x
23	043	#	4E	116	N	79	171	y
24	044	$	4F	117	O	7A	172	z
25	045	%	50	120	P	7B	173	{
26	046	&	51	121	Q	7C	174		
27	047	'	52	122	R	7D	175	}
28	050	(	53	123	S	7E	176	~
29	051	)	54	124	T	7F	177	DEL
2A	052	*	55	125	U			

(*b*)

3.2 THE PROCESSOR AND PROGRAMS

(a) Program instructions

We have already seen that everything stored inside or understood by a computer must be in digital form. We have also seen earlier in this chapter that all the data which the computer is required to handle can be recorded in its storage in digital form. It then follows that the program instructions held in the computer's storage prior to their execution must be stored in a similar digital format consisting of 'packets' of binary digits. A machine-code instruction, which is the ultimate form of any program instruction before it can be acted upon by the computer, will probably consist of a set of bit patterns arranged in a series of 'fields':

Operation	Modification	Operand	Operand	. . .

The bit pattern contained in the *operation field* holds the code (*operation code*, opcode for short) that instructs the computer to perform one of its available operations such as ADD, SUBTRACT, STORE, LOAD, and so on. These operations are detailed in every computer's *instruction set*. This is the set of operations defined by the designer as being those he wants his computer to perform. The *modification field* will be dealt with in Section 3.2 (e). The *operand field* of the instruction can be one of a number of things. It could be:

– the address of a location of internal storage which contains the data to be processed or into which the results of processing are to be placed (or both);
– the number of a register, which is a special set of storage locations used to hold values or to hold data for significant purposes in a computer (see next section);
– a command to an external device in an I/O instruction;
– the number of a peripheral device (what is often called its 'logical' address, that is, the line printer may be device 12 and a particular disc drive device 76);
– the address of a storage location which contains *another* instruction.

An instruction may be referred to by the number of operands it contains, for example a two-address instruction or a three-address instruction. A three-address instruction might say 'add the contents of location 203 to the contents of location 467 and place the result in location 124'.

When loaded into internal storage ready for execution each instruction may be referred to by the address of the first storage location into which it has been loaded. This is because each instruction takes up more than 1 byte, and it is generally the bytes which are separately addressed, so that if an instruction takes up 4 bytes and the first byte is in address number 304 then we will refer to it as the instruction in 304.

The general sequence of events which takes place when a program instruction is executed is in two parts. These are called the FETCH and the EXECUTE phases of the instruction cycle.

During the FETCH phase the instruction address is computed, the instruction is fetched into an instruction register, the effective addresses of the operands are computed and the operands are fetched and placed into the appropriate registers. The EXECUTE phase consists of performing the operations denoted by the opcode on the operands, computing the effective address for storing the result, and storing the result.

(b) Registers

Registers are special storage locations within the central processing unit usually capable of storing one or two bytes at a time. The six main registers in the CPU are:

(i) *The CPU instruction register*, which holds the instruction currently being executed and has to be sufficiently long to hold a complete instruction.

(ii) *The instruction address register*, which holds the address of the next instruction to be executed. This is usually the next instruction in sequence or, if not, it will be the address of an instruction being BRANCHED to out of sequence. This address will be placed there during the EXECUTE cycle if a jump out of sequence is made. It is sometimes called the *program counter* or *sequence control register*.

(iii) *The general-purpose registers*, often called *accumulators*, which may be used to hold data for temporary storage or for intermediate results. There is always one accumulator into which data is placed after some CPU operation, usually of an arithmetic nature.

(iv) *The storage address register* and *storage data register*, which are used to hold the address and contents respectively of a storage reference instruction prior to data being placed into a location or transferred from it. They are sometimes called *buffer* registers.

(v) *The peripheral registers*. Every peripheral device contains a register which is used in the same way as the storage data register; the I/O mechanism of these devices feeds data to, or takes data from, their register which is itself operated upon by an I/O instruction — or more precisely, an I/O instruction *starts* the transfer of data into/out of a peripheral register after/before the device/mechanism fills/uses it.

(vi) *The status register*. The CPU also contains special one-bit registers, known as *flip-flops* or *flags*. They are used to indicate the state or condition of some part of the computer. Such a condition may be an emergency or unusual situation and one which may require either hardware or software action. These flags are often grouped together into a status register, whose content at any one time will indicate the aggregate condition of the CPU and its peripherals.

Fig. 3.2 shows schematically the way that registers and storage are used to control and execute the operation of program instructions in a processor.

Fig 3.2 *registers and instruction execution*

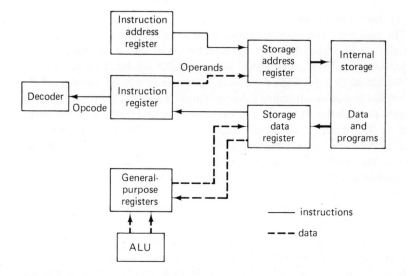

Registers and the program instruction cycle

The execution of a program stored in internal storage follows a very clearly defined pattern which is detailed as follows.

- **Step 0** – when a program is loaded and made ready for execution, the leading address of the storage locations occupied by the *first* instruction is loaded into the instruction address register (IAR);
- **Step 1** – the instruction to be found at that address is loaded into the instruction register, and the address of the *next* instruction (always assumed to be the next in sequence) is loaded into the IAR;
- **Step 2** – the instruction in the instruction register then proceeds through its fetch and execute phases, using other registers if appropriate to that instruction;
- **Step 3** – at the end of the execute phase, the program will either stop, if it is an END or STOP instruction, or it will confirm the address of the next instruction to be executed; if it is not the address already stored in the IAR (for example, if the current instruction is an unconditional branch), the contents of the IAR will be modified to show the address

of the instruction to be branched to out of linear sequence;

– **Step 4** – go to step 1.

The timing of these subsequences is controlled by time pulses issued by the system clock. The number of pulses per instruction and thus the total instruction timing, is determined by the number of separate (micro) operations in the fetch and execute phases, added to the fixed times for the rest of the cycle.

(c) Operation decoding

The computer may thus be considered as a system for routeing data movements and transfers between significant areas of storage and peripherals – for which purpose storage may also, in smaller machines particularly, be considered as a (special) peripheral device. Only a small number of the instructions in any machine's instruction set will entail the routeing of the data through the ALU as part of the detailed action required by the operation. The exact sequence of functions required by each instruction is determined by passing the operation code to a decoder, for which purpose the construction of the opcode sometimes contains bit patterns to indicate whether for instance, an opcode is a register–register or storage–register instruction.

The physical implementation of an operation may be *either* by 'hard' electronics, or by the generation of the appropriate set of lower-level instructions known as *micro-instructions*. In this respect, the decoder is itself designed to be rather like a CPU. In certain machines, these micro-instructions may themselves be available to a programmer who may use them to write complete programs or to compose his own equivalent of basic machine instructions. Such machines are known as microprogrammable computers, and microprograms written to implement special machine instructions are known in the trade as 'middleware' or 'firmware' because they represent a middle position between 'hardware' and 'software'. Such microprograms reside in control stores composed of read-only storage [see Section 3.3(d)].

(d) Data buses

The significant sections of a computer, both internally and externally, are linked by data buses or data highways, each register being connected to one or more buses of parallel wires or printed circuit tracks, and a CPU can be also considered to be a system of data buses. Data transfers occur by the opening of 'gates' from registers to the buses. The arrangement of registers and buses in any computer is largely the result of the 'architecture' (that is, the operational blueprint) of a particular make of computer and represents the main way in which a particular instruction set is implemented.

Internal data buses have a width usually corresponding to the word length (the number of bits of storage in one uniquely addressed location of internal storage), and there will be several buses depending on the maximum number of operands that can be contained in an instruction. In Fig. 3.3 there is a main bus connecting all the registers, and a subsidiary bus from the storage data registers to the ALU. The storage bus connects the storage registers to internal storage.

(e) Address generation

The contents of the operand field(s) are of course one of the significant pieces of data that are transferred from storage to registers along the data buses, and the length of the fields therefore needs to conform to the common structure. Thus it is very unusual for an operand field to be greater than 16 bits wide. Nevertheless it has to 'contain' the numerical value of any storage address location and of any register and peripheral device address.

Since there are usually no more than 16 registers, 4 bits are enough to contain a *register address*, so that a storage–register or register–storage instruction is sometimes known as a $1\frac{1}{2}$ address instruction. Eight bits will be adequate for a device address. However, even 16 bits will not be enough to contain directly the whole range of storage address values. The maximum value that can be held in 16 bits is $2^{16} - 1$ (assuming all values to be positive), which is well below the storage capacity of most computers today. In fact, all addresses start from the value 0 upwards so that a 16-bit register can directly address the full complement of 2^{16} locations.

There are, therefore, several ways in which the operand field can indirectly contain the information which will enable the real or 'effective' address of an operand to be generated (by using other values contained in one or more registers, or even in other storage locations) outside the range which it can directly address itself. These methods are of interest to computer programmers writing programs in machine-code instructions. The use of the modification field in an instruction is to indicate which type of address generation is to be used (usually by hardware) to calculate the effective address.

(f) The processor and the ALU

From these descriptions of how program instructions are performed, it is evident that the significant parts of a processor are:
- registers and gates;
- data buses;
- instruction or micro-instruction decoder;
- ALU.

Fig. 3.3 shows a highly simplified structure of a processor linking all these features. The list of features shows the ALU as only one of the functional

Fig 3.3 *a simple processor*

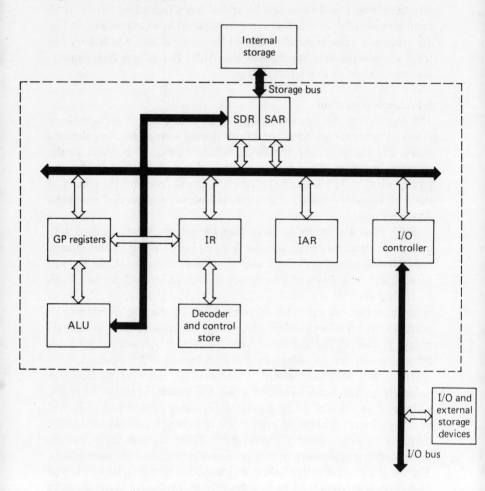

subunits of a processor, through which only a proportion of instructions are routed. Additional subunits may be provided for particular purposes, for instance hardware floating point arithmetic, and even fast array (non-serial) arithmetic units for enhanced arithmetical work. The ALU is however the most complex unit in the processor, and computer arithmetic is one of the most difficult tasks for the processor because of the range of number types, and because of the conditions which may occur during arithmetic, for example, rounding, justification, overflow or underflow, or attempting to divide by zero. The ALU therefore uses the condition flags [see Section 3.2 (b) (vi) above] to signify error conditions occurring in the course of arithmetical and logical operations.

Other significant hardware features of the processor are concerned with the organisation of external input and output, and will be described in the next chapter.

3.3 INTERNAL STORAGE

Internal storage, as has been mentioned several times, is used to store programs that are currently active, and the I/O data that is about to be or has just been processed by one of those programs. For this purpose, internal storage must be:
- capable of recording bit values in two states;
- capable of maintaining the strength of those values until a change of state is required;
- capable of transferring those values to the processor without erasing them (without 'destructive readout');
- addressable; that is, composed of uniquely identified locations each containing the same number of bits (8, 16, 24, 32, or even more).

(a) Performance criteria
Several different forms of electronic technology are used as internal storage in computers. They have some important operational criteria — principally speed, retention of data, size and cost.

(i) Speed
The *access time* of a storage system is the interval between receipt of a request for a storage reference from the command decoder and the completion of the placing of the data in the storage data register. The *access* '*width*' is the number of bits retrieved in a storage reference request and together with the access time forms the speed in bytes etc. per second. The *cycle time* of a storage system is the similar minimum interval between two such operations on the same storage location. Access time is less than or the same as cycle time, depending on the mechanism, and is in the order of 10 to 500 ns. It is also inherent in what is sometimes confusingly called random access storage (RAS) that this time is the same regardless of the location address, even in very large computers with 4 megabytes of storage or more. The access time of a storage system has to match the internal processor speed (regulated by the processor clock) and computer designers have a range of speeds available from different forms of storage technology, particularly with semiconductor storage [see Section 3.3 (c)].

(ii) Retention of data
It is obviously necessary for storage to retain the data recorded within it

while a computer is in use, and desirable during a brief shutdown or loss of power. Storage that loses its data immediately power is lost is known as *volatile*, while storage that can retain its data indefinitely is known as *permanent* or *non-volatile*. Another form of classification related to this is static/dynamic. *Static* storage retains its data once set but requires a higher power level, while *dynamic* storage has to be frequently and regularly refreshed (several times per millisecond) but uses less power and also has other desirable characteristics.

(*iii*) Size

The reduction in size which micro-miniaturisation has produced in microelectronics has been a significant feature in several aspects of internal storage. A decrease in size means, with electronic pulses moving up to their feasible limit of the speed of light, that data travels shorter distances and therefore that access times are correspondingly reduced. Lower distances travelled also result in lower power consumption and lower heat output. Finally, the automated production which is possible for microelectronic units gives higher reliability and fewer errors – Japanese manufacturers being able to deliver guaranteed zero-defect components for internal storage.

(*iv*) Cost

The most dramatic consequence, however, of the reduction in size of storage through LSI is the corresponding reduction in cost, again primarily because production can be automated on such very small components. It is this cost reduction which makes it possible to provide even microcomputers today with the volume of storage (up to 64 K bytes) that were typical of mainframe computers which cost one hundred times as much in actual terms (that is, without allowing for inflation) fifteen years ago. A significant proportion of 'conventional' computing techniques were founded in the days of low-volume storage computers from which the current high-volume machines have liberated computer users. Fig. 4.2 shows some costs for some types of internal storage.

(b) Magnetic core

Magnetic core is an array of small hollow ferrite rings threaded on a wire grid, each interconnected by four wires passing through its centre. A core can be made to represent two state values by setting different directions of magnetism around the ring, clockwise or anticlockwise. The values can be changed by reversing the direction of magnetisation by an opposite polarity current on one of the wires. Each core represents 1 bit of information, and arrays are thus constructed in byte or word dimensions.

Magnetic core storage is the type of storage which has been in use longer than any other, and its reliability is correspondingly high but its potential for miniaturisation is very limited. In addition, the cycle of events needed to read a piece of data is always longer than for other forms of storage. This is because a *read* operation always destroys the data read from the core. This means that every read must be followed by a *write-back* cycle if the data is not to be lost for ever. The complete read cycle time is therefore twice the time to access the data and will be of the order of 0.5 to 1 μs.

(c) Semiconductor storage

Semiconductor storage is composed of multiples of two-state electronic devices based on the same technology as microprocessors, that is, on transistors etched on to silicon chips in very high densities. Silicon chips are approximately 5 mm square and the density of storage on them contributes to their principal operating characteristics of speed, reliability and low cost, all of which have been advancing steadily during the last ten years. For the user and system designer, semiconductor storage provides a variety of types and technological forms (referred to by acronyms such as ECL and NMOS) which give a similar range of characteristics of performance. Access time varies from about that of magnetic core down to about 10 ns in the fastest form. This variety also provides the means for hardware designers to provide storage of the appropriate characteristics in devices other than computers – see 'intelligent devices' in the next chapter.

The following lists summarise the important characteristics of core and semiconductor memories:

Core
 destructive readout
 non-volatile
 limited range of cycle and access times (around 1 μs)
 relatively large and heavy
 high power consumption
 moderately priced
 available only in large blocks
 best for large memories

Semiconductor
 non-destructive readout
 volatile (sometimes also dynamic)
 wide range of cycle and access times (10 ns to 2 μs)
 relatively small and light
 low power consumption (depends on technology)
 low to moderately priced (depends on technology)
 available in a wide variety of sizes up to 64 K bits
 best for small- or medium-sized memories.

General purpose (that is, read/write) semiconductor storage is known as *random access storage* (RAS) or more usually *random access memory* (RAM), primarily to distinguish it from storage which allows computer programs only to access it for usage purposes, known as *read-only storage* (ROS) or *memory* (ROM).

(d) Read-only storage

The process of transferring a piece of data from internal storage into one of the registers is known as READing. When a piece of data is moved from a register to a location in storage the operation is known as WRITEing. Particularly when two or more programs are currently active in a computer, and thus cohabiting in internal storage, it is necessary to protect areas of storage against misuse, accidental destruction or interference, and some quite elaborate schemes of storage protection have been and are still used. These schemes can be avoided by the use of ROS, which is semiconductor storage. ROS is permanently programmed with information during manufacture, by imprinting the appropriate pattern of two-state values through a mask, and cannot be changed subsequently by a normal WRITE. It is thus completely non-volatile.

It is used to hold, primarily, programs which are required permanently or indestructibly, particularly compilers for high-level languages and other system software programs, and also microprograms.

Several intermediate forms of ROM storage are also available to the system designer:

(i) *Programmable read-only memory* (PROM)

PROM is ROS in which programming is available to the programmer with the use of special electronic equipment itself known as a PROM programmer, but still cannot be changed subsequently — a process known as 'blasting' because it involves blowing 'fuses' to represent one of two values in each bit location.

(ii) *Erasable-PROM* (EPROM)

EPROM is PROM which is reversible by exposure to an intense ultraviolet light source. The device may then be reprogrammed, and re-erased indefinitely. *Electrically alterable PROM* (EAROM) and *electrically erasable PROM* (EEROM) both allow complete or selective writing of bits electrically, but are more difficult to use and are slower in operation.

(e) The organisation of internal storage

Whatever the form of technology used, over which the customer has little control within an individual machine (that is, it comes as part of the black box), internal storage will have its own set of electronics to control the processes of READing and WRITEing, particularly for the purposes of decoding an address directed to it, via the storage address register, from the processor. The way in which the unit or units of internal storage are organised relative to the processor may have as significant an effect on the total access capability as the technology involved, and since this is one of the most important design features affecting computer performance, a number of significant alternative forms are used in computers. The arrangement as shown in Fig. 3.3 is common in mainframe computers and has internal storage directly under the control of the processor, which means that *all* data transfer passes through the processor between internal and external storage. This can both degrade the performance of the processor and limit transfer rates. The alternative arrangements shown in Fig. 3.4 (a) and (b) permit direct transfer of data between internal and external storage — a feature known as *direct memory access* (DMA) though this is also achievable by special mechanisms in the previous structure.

The range of addresses which can be used in storage depends on the size of the address registers (see p. 44). In its simplest form this means that if an address register consists of, say, eight bits the lowest address would be 00000000 and the highest address would be

$$11111111 = 2^8 - 1$$
$$= 256 - 1$$
$$= 255$$

This means that an 8-bit address register can address memory locations numbered from 0 to 255. However, this restricted range of addresses can be increased by organising storage in separate modules, with the first n bits of the address field of an operand representing block number and the remainder the address within block. Such a feature can also improve the transfer capability in the form of *interleaved storage*, in which the total storage capacity is provided in two or four modules, with the storage addresses spread across them rather than within them. In two-way interleaved storage, the odd addresses are in one module and the even in the other, thus providing simultaneous access to two more adjacent addresses.

Sometimes special ultra-high-speed storage is provided in small volume to hold the most frequently used data and program instructions. Internal storage may be seen as part of a hierarchy of storage in a computer system, and high-speed storage, known as *cache* or *scratchpad*, bears the same logical relationship to internal storage as internal to external. Similarly, special-purpose storage areas known as *stacks* are sometimes used to control software; stacks are groups of locations with the characteristic that they can be filled only from the bottom up, and read from the top down, and the top of the stack is the only location that is available to a READ;

it is similar to a conventional queue, and has the same kind of uses in a computer.

The most difficult concept to explain in respect of internal storage in large computer systems is that of *virtual storage*. 'Virtual' means that it appears to be there to the user, but is not actually (all) there; as a descrip-

Fig 3.4 *alternative arrangements of internal storage*

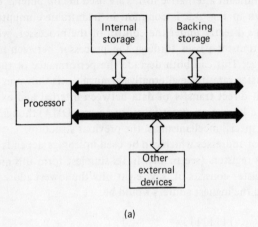

(a)

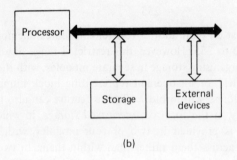

(b)

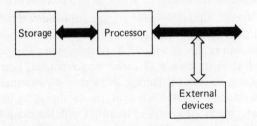

(c)

tion it can be applied to whole machines as well as to part of one. Virtual storage gives the programmer very much more apparent storage than in his 'real' machine. This illusion is achieved by both hardware and software mechanisms which load programs only in small sections ('pages') from backing storage, and translate, or map, address locations used in a program into the actual addresses of the section of storage into which it is currently loaded. These mechanisms will detect a storage reference to an area of the program which is not currently loaded, and will cause that page to be loaded after previously unloading another page.

The need for virtual storage, even in the face of widely available cheap storage technology, is one indication of the dependence of computer power on the immediate availability of very large volumes of information. The total volume of internal storage is one of the few aspects of this part of a computer system that the user can specify, usually in units of 8 K, 16 K, 32 K, etc., up to the addressable limit available on a machine. If this is not sufficient, add-on or extended storage is often available, with cost and performance intermediate between internal and external, and with special electronic control circuits. Finally, the various developments under way in backing storage (see Section 4.1) may mean that the distinction between internal and external storage are becoming somewhat blurred.

SPECIMEN QUESTIONS

1. (a) Express the decimal integer 1234 as a 12-bit binary number. Convert the binary number into octal and hexadecimal form.
(b) Distinguish between fixed point and floating point representations of numbers, and give the advantages and disadvantages of each form. Why is floating point representation of little interest to a commercial programmer? *

2. What is meant by two's complement representation? State an alternative form with the aid of an annotated example. What are the benefits of the two's complement representation? *

3. (a) Explain, with the aid of an annotated diagram, the interrelationship between the control unit, the arithmetical and logical unit and the main memory within a modern computer.
(b) Describe the fundamental steps involved in the fetch–decode–execute cycle by considering instructions which:
  (i) transfer control unconditionally;
  (ii) perform input or output;
  (iii) access the main memory. *

4. In a microcomputer, distinguish between ROM, RAM and PROM. *

5. Distinguish between direct and other forms of addressing, and show how different forms of addressing affect the range of addressable storage. Give one example each of (i) one address, (ii) two address instructions, and indicate the consequences of each type of instruction. *

CHAPTER 4

HOW PERIPHERALS PUT THE COMPUTER TO WORK

The final reason why a computer can be tailored, or 'configured', to satisfy so many diverse needs is the range of devices which can be attached to the processor as 'peripheral' devices. The term peripheral is misleading, first because these devices are *essential* to the use of a computer, and secondly because there are two distinct classes, with different characteristics and functions, subsumed within it. One class is that of *backing storage devices*, the other *input/output devices*. Backing storage devices are:

- usually local to the processor;
- connected to it by high-speed parallel communication lines;
- high-capacity, high-transfer-rate machines.
- more autonomous in operation.

I/O devices are:

- very often remote from the processor;
- connected to it by slower serial data communication facilities;
- usually low-capacity, slower-speed machines;
- more tightly controlled in operation.

As a result, backing storage can usually be considered as part of the central computer, particularly as it bears a relationship to internal storage, while I/O devices can be considered a conceptually separate subsystem related as much to the user and his world as to the computer itself [with the sole exception of one I/O device which is always close to the processor and is used as the operator console by the (human) machine operator].

This only way in which peripherals can be considered as one class is that their control by the processor, and their use by a program, is again through a READ or WRITE operation instigated by an I/O instruction which initiates the data transfer in the appropriate direction. The form of the instruction, and the way that it is handled, will in most cases be different.

Fig. 4.1 shows how these two classes of peripheral devices are usually (except in the very smallest computers) connected to the processor, and

Fig 4.1 *connection of external devices*

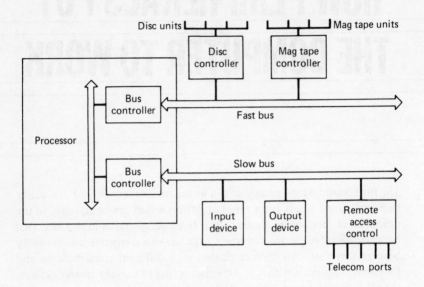

also shows the logical structure of external connections with data buses, bus controllers, device controllers and the devices themselves in a highly organised and differentiated arrangement.

4.1 BACKING STORAGE

Backing storage devices are designed to provide permanent storage for large volumes of data, and to permit retrieval of that data by the processor ('access') when required.

They can be classified into three groups according to the recording principle or media employed — magnetic, optical (video) and semiconductor states respectively — giving a range of cost and performance characteristics from which the system designer, and to a lesser extent the customer, may select. Figure 4.2 shows how different types of storage device, to be described below, offer significant combinations of capacity and access. The exercise of choice is limited by the normally processor-specific interface that is required, but there is a growing movement towards standard interfaces giving increased interchangeability of storage devices with the same processor.

(a) Magnetic storage
All forms of magnetic storage use the same or similar principles of record-

Fig 4.2 *relationship between storage capacity and access time for different forms of storage*

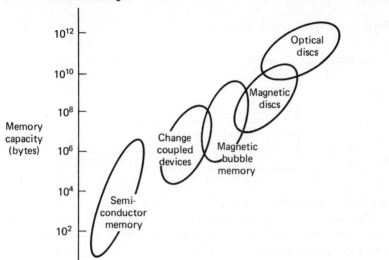

ing two-state values as are used in magnetic core. A small magnetic spot is deposited on a magnetisable material in one direction or another, depending on the direction of the electric current in a coil in a *read/write* (R/W) head, and its state is determined by switching off the current and using the head as a magnetic detector. In all magnetic storage devices the recording medium is mobile, and is passed through or under a fixed or stationary head. The R/W head either touches the surface or floats immediately above it. These principles, and the mechanisms themselves, will be familiar through the domestic equivalent of magnetic storage – audio or video cassettes, recording tape, video and audio disc records.

(i) Magnetic discs
Magnetic disc storage devices use these recording principles on a wide range of magnetic disc media. The devices vary in size from the equivalent of a small box on a desk top to a large composite device occupying significant space in a computer room (such as that which can be identified in Fig. 1.6). A disc storage device, however large or small, will contain one or more *drives*; each drive can accommodate a disc volume rotating on a spindle driven by the drive motor, with a retractable or fixed R/W mechanism containing (at least) one head per recording surface of the volume. The

drive operates under a hardware controller which usually contains micro-processor units as well as hard circuits. Fig. 4.3 shows these components

Fig 4.3 *a small magnetic disc unit*

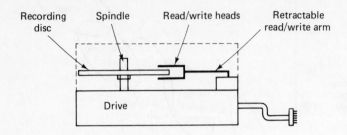

in a small disc unit the size of a domestic record player.

The discs themselves are made either of a light alloy or a polyester plastics material coated with a magnetisable layer of ferrite, and data is stored in concentric tracks on the surface(s) of the disc, serially bit by bit around the track. The R/W head or heads 'float' a few micrometres or less above the surface of the disc as it rotates at high speed — up to 5000 revolutions per minute — for which reason it is known as *rotating storage*. The technology required to make disc drives capable of reliable operation at such demanding precision is one of the most remarkable in computing, and is one of the reasons why it is necessary for high-performance disc drives to operate in sealed or environmentally controlled conditions.

Disc volumes (that is, individual disc media) come in a variety of shapes, sizes and characteristics:
- single/multiple recording surfaces;
- hard or soft;
- fixed or removable;
- formatted or unformatted.

Hard (rigid)/floppy Traditionally discs have been composed of rigid material in order to provide the required clearance for the R/W heads. One of the most remarkable developments that occurred simultaneously with the microcomputer, and indeed may be even more significant, is the appearance of soft floppy disc devices, of lower operating characteristics but nevertheless capable of full backing storage work. Floppy discs were originally invented as flexible data input media (see next chapter) capable of surviving the rigours of the postal system, containing both user data and special software from computer manufacturers. There is now a range of floppy and mini-floppy disc devices mainly used with smaller computers.
Recording surfaces There may be up to ten distinct discs ('platters')

connected into a single volume (known as a disc pack or storage module) by a central spindle. The outside surfaces of the pack will generally not be used; the top surface, known as the servo surface, is used to control the precision of the R/W operation. Ten-platter and three-platter packs are standard for removable discs. Cartridges are two-platter discs usually within an almost-sealed cover. Single platter discs may be used on one side (single-sided) or both (double-sided). Discs may be from 3–14 inches in diameter.

In a multi-platter volume, the set of tracks on each surface with the same track number (that is, those vertically above each other) constitute a *cylinder*, numbered in the same way 0 to n. An individual track will thus be identified by cylinder number and surface number within cylinder. A cylinder is also that set of tracks which can be accessed by a set of R/W heads when it is in one position, and related data is stored cylinder by cylinder on such a disc for reasons of faster overall access. (See Fig. 4.4.)

If the drive number, track number and cylinder number of a particular piece of data are known then it has a unique address, just as a piece of data in internal storage has a unique address, and this is used by the device controller to position the R/W mechanism directly to that address – a concept known as direct access (also, but most confusingly, as random access). Discs, and some other storage devices which allow the same facility, are sometimes known as *direct access storage devices* (DASDs). Note that direct access only takes the head to the addressable location; the data required may be anywhere on that track and has to be sought.

Fig 4.4 *multi-platter discs and the cylinder*

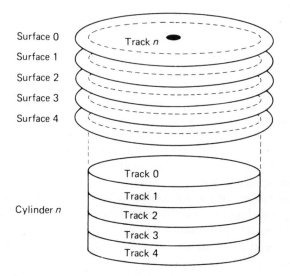

Surface 0 — Track n
Surface 1
Surface 2
Surface 3
Surface 4

Cylinder n

Track 0
Track 1
Track 2
Track 3
Track 4

Fixed/removable Some disc devices contain both a drive and a disc volume as one integral unit in which the disc volume is fixed and irremovable. The total capacity of such a unit is limited to the capacity of that single volume. Removable discs can support unlimited total storage, but the amount of data available to the computer at any one time is limited to the volume(s) currently loaded in the device's drive(s). There are two types of fixed disc: *head-per-track* discs in which there is one R/W head per track on each recording surface, and *Winchester* discs (so called after the IBM code used in their development) which have the normal retractable head per surface but are sealed units to permit greater reliable recording density. Head-per-track discs give a reduced access time (see below), but are much less used now than in the past because removable discs and Winchester discs have themselves improved their access times. The main disadvantage of fixed or sealed discs is that you need another storage device on which to take a copy of the data stored on a fixed disc, as a security against the disastrous situation which happens when the R/W heads actually come into contact with the surface of the disc. Normally the heads 'float' a few millionths of an inch above the surface and when contact occurs we have the situation known as a 'head crash'.

Removable discs are, as their name suggests, devices in which the discs can be removed and reloaded. Removable discs can support only one R/W head per surface, which has to be disengaged into a safe position before a disc volume can be removed. The operation of moving a retractable head to a track for reading/writing adds to the access time for that device.

Formatted/unformatted Each recording surface of a disc contains a number (up to 1000) of numbered concentric tracks, packed at a density of up to 1000 tracks per inch, in the outermost area of the surface. Although the innermost track of the recording area is shorter than the outside track, each track is used to store the same quantity of data (up to 30 K characters or bytes), the timing of each operation being identically controlled (by the servo surface track in a multi-platter disc) regardless of the track number. Each track is therefore used for data storage as a fixed length storage location (see Fig. 4.7). Recording density is up to 15 000 bpi.

Discs in which the entire length of the track is available for data storage are known as *unformatted* discs. Some discs units have a subdivision of the tracks, known as a segment or sector, as the lowest-level addressable unit of storage, numbered sequentially round a track and from track 0 to track *n*, and are known as *formatted* discs (see Fig. 4.5). Formatting may be performed by software or by notches or holes in the disc. It reduces the searching operation for data. An intermediate form, known as *self-formatting*, is where the disc controller packs data into a special format which aids the operation of data retrieval but reduces the amount of storage available.

Fig 4.5 *recording surface layouts*

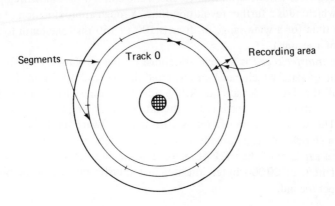

(ii) Magnetic disc storage – performance

Total storage capacity The storage capacity of a disc volume will vary from about 1 megabyte to 500 megabytes; currently the upper limit is 150 megabytes per disc surface. This means that if we use the fact that 1 byte of storage can hold one character – one letter, digit or punctuation mark – then such a disc volume could store the contents of fifty novels each of 300 pages. Capacity per device depends upon the number of volumes/ drives. On-line capacity depends upon the number of devices installed; the largest available disc has a capacity of 2.8 gigabytes. As with other equipment, there is a trade-off between capacity and speed of access. The nominal capacity of a disc may not all be available to the user, mainly because it consists of multiples of fixed-length locations, in each of which there may well be unused space which cannot be aggregated.

Speed The *access time* is defined as the time taken to locate and then transfer data from a disc into internal storage. It includes three elements:
- movement of R/W head to required cylinder/track ('seek');
- scan of track to find data record ('search');
- transfer of data.
On average, the search time will be half the revolution time ('latency'), and the transfer time will be the appropriate fraction of revolution time depending on how much data is transferred. A revolution speed of 2000 rpm would give an average search time of 15 ms and a full track transfer time of 30 ms.

The seek time is typically the largest element (0 to 250 ms) and is avoided through the use of head-per-track discs. In practice the *write access time* is longer than the *read access time*, as defined above, because of a read-after-write convention to check the correctness of a write operation, which adds a further revolution time. A rough approximation of read access time for a wide range of discs is 100 to 150 ms (one-tenth to one-sixth of a second).

The *transfer speed* is in general defined by the revolution time and the amount of data which can be transferred in one read operation. In principle all the data under a set of R/W heads at one time (that is, a cylinder) can be continuously transferred at the rate of track-length per revolution time. The actual unit transferred is ultimately software-specified, the unit being a 'block' of data, usually a multiple of data records of up to the physical capacity of the track or sector. For the unit defined above, with a track length of 20 000 bytes, the nominal transfer rate would be 660 K bytes per second.

(iii) Magnetic tape

Magnetic tape storage uses reels of half-inch Mylar tape, 600, 1 200 or 2400 feet in length as industry standards, on which one or two characters of data have been recorded across the width of the tape by a tape drive into which the magnetic tape has been threaded. Magnetic tape drives hold one working reel at a time on a 7 or 10 in. spool, but a number of drives (usually up to eight) can operate under one controller. The reels are removable, and total off-line storage is limitless.

Tape drives operate in bursts as the tape is unwound from one spool and wound on to another, past the R/W head, at speeds of up to 200 inches per second. Reel-to-reel (Fig. 4.6) drives operate directly, with high-precision tensioning mechanisms, but for higher speeds vacuum buffer drives are used, in which tape is moved into a buffer column in loops. It is then moved from one loop past the R/W head into an output buffer, also in loops, from which it is rewound on to the output spool. The loops in the buffer columns are controlled separately, by sensors, from the capstan drives which move the tape past the R/W head in response to a R/W command. The drives are capable of virtually instantaneous starting and stopping, but a space, called an inter-block gap (IBG) has to be left to allow for acceleration to full tape drive speed/deceleration to stop, data being transferred only when the tape is moving at full speed. The unit of a read/write operation is thus a block of data, whose length is ultimately software specified, each block preceded and followed by an IBG of about half an inch (see Fig. 4.7).

The data recording density comes in one of a series of industry standards: 800 bpi, 1600 bpi or the latest models at 6250 bpi. Bits per inch (bpi) here refers to the bit width of a frame (seven or nine tracks across the tape width) and thus means characters per inch; this is not so with all

Fig 4.6 *magnetic tape units*

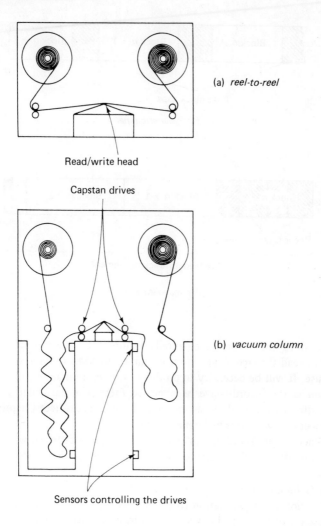

(a) *reel-to-reel*

Read/write head

Capstan drives

(b) *vacuum column*

Sensors controlling the drives

other tape-like media (see next section). Fig. 4.7 shows the layout of data on a magnetic tape.

Unlike magnetic disc, the areas of storage on a magnetic tape reel are continuous (at least within a data block defined by the computer programmer) and are not addressable. Data blocks are written to a tape in serial order (one after another) and are read in serial order from the beginning of the tape. The beginning and end of the used area of a tape will be physically signalled by reflective marks, and there may also be header and trailer records to indicate the contents and date of use. These ensure that a reel

Fig 4.7 *layout of data on magnetic media*

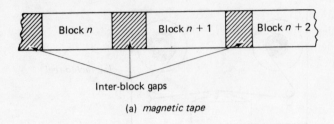

Inter-block gaps

(a) *magnetic tape*

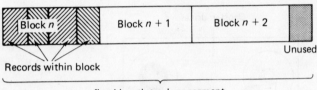

Records within block

Unused

fixed length track or segment

(b) *magnetic disc*

of tape does not become accidentally unthreaded. The normal mode of use is to read through a tape from beginning to end and then to rewind it for reuse. It will be necessary to do this to find more than one record on a tape *unless* the records have been placed there in a particular sequence which allows *sequential* rather than merely *serial* access (see Chapter 5 for a discussion of what this difference means).

Magnetic tape recording can be effected in several different ways whose initials are often used to characterise devices — the standard ones are NRZI and PE.

NRZI (*non-return to zero incremental*) is a recording mode in which the direction of magnetisation (the 'flux') changes only to signify a 1 bit, the absence of a change between bit positions indicating a 0 value. This is economic and reliable but demands high precision of speed movement, or a track to clock the pulse (that is, to separate one bit value from another).

PE (*phase encoding*) uses a positive flux change to represent a 1 value and a negative change to represent a 0 value. PE can support the greater packing density but requires a fluctuation-free drive speed.

The continued popularity of magnetic tape storage rests on its unchallenged position in cost per character stored, at the low end of the capacity/speed trade-off. A tape reel (2400 feet) costs a few pounds, and assuming only 50 per cent space utilisation at 1600 bpi density can hold 25 million characters. It is ideal for long-life storage, and for data, a high proportion of which is required in any run of a computer program, such as employees' accumulated pay and tax paid information needed in every weekly or monthly payroll run. The transfer rate depends on tape speed and recording density; for example, a unit with a tape speed of 125 ips and a recording density of 1600 bpi will transfer a block at 200 K bytes per second. Access time depends on search time, which for one record will be approximately equal to the block read time multiplied by half the number of blocks on the file; the block read time being block transfer time plus start and stop time. For the same unit and a block of 1000 bytes, the block read time will be about 25 ms.

(iv) Magnetic tape cassettes and data cartridges
Full-scale magnetic tape drives, however, are storage devices available only to medium and large computer users. For smaller computers, modified (or at the lowest level, unmodified) forms of domestic audio cassettes and tape recorders are used, with lower capacities but still surprisingly high performances. (Occasionally minitapes are also found.) *Digital cassettes* contain up to 300 feet of 0.15 in. computer grade tape, storing one track of data at 800 bpi serially, on both sides of the tape. *Data cartridges* hold up to 450 feet of 0.25 in. tape, at densities of up to 6400 bpi in four tracks, up to 16 megabytes per reel. Transfer rates are up to 200 K bits per second. In both cases data is stored in fixed length blocks.

Most data cartridges (and some small versions of magnetic tape) operate in 'streaming' mode rather than 'start-stop' mode. Streamers are not capable of stopping in an IBG, but operate from the processor at a rate which will keep it constantly in motion. When it is necessary to stop, a streaming drive repositions itself by coasting to a stop, backing up over a section of tape previously processed, awaiting the next command and accelerating to a running start.

Cassettes and cartridges are used primarily as back-up devices to fixed/sealed Winchester discs, and also for long-life storage. They are also used as data input media (see next chapter), and on the smallest home computers may be the only form of external storage available. The cost of the media (£4 approximately for a digital cassette, about £15 for a data cartridge) makes them extremely cost-effective storage devices for small computers.

(v) Mass storage
Mass storage devices offer very high ('archival') on-line storage capacities of the order of tens of gigabytes, with access times of a few hundred milliseconds. Such systems are essentially made up of complexes of small sections of magnetic tape or card strips arranged in cells. Cells or cell groups are addressable, data then being retrieved serially within the tape or card strip. Their function is likely to be taken over by optical storage devices in the very near future.

(b) Semiconductor storage

The standard magnetic recording devices have just been joined by the first of a series of semiconductor storage devices that will be appearing on the market during the 1980s. The most significant of these developments are *magnetic bubble memory* (MBM) and *charge-coupled devices* (CCD).

(*i*) Magnetic bubble memory

This type of storage is already on the market and devices are available in chip form. This is a form of non-volatile storage based on iron garnet (a crystalline material) which has the property of creating magnetic domains known as bubbles when a magnetic field is applied. These tiny domains can actually be created, destroyed and moved about tracks on the chip by variations in the magnetic field. The presence of a bubble represents the presence of a bit (1) and absence means a zero (0). If the magnetic field is rotated the bubble will collapse and disappear, thus giving the propensity for 1 and 0 values. Magnetic bubbles are now available in 64 K bit chips organised on to memory boards. The total organised capacity is limited, at the moment, making it suitable for microcomputers and intelligent terminals, but there is no doubt that it has a magnificent future; it is non-mechanical, non-volatile, consumes very little power, is compact, very reliable and will, in mass production, be very cheap (the 1 megabit MBM chip being already under development). Access time is 1 to 4 ms to the first bit, but is serial within a module. Transfer rate is about 150 K bytes per second; as such, it will not yet rival magnetic tape or disc, but it is at the very beginning of product-life.

(*ii*) Charge-coupled devices

These are similar to bubble memories with electric charges replacing magnetic bubbles. Although they have their place as storage devices their common use at present is in TV cameras where a pattern is used to build up a picture.

Access to the data depends on the data circulation rate, but can be as low as 100 μs to the first bit, subsequent access being serial. Because of the simpler organisation of the minute cells, CCD chips can be constructed several times *more* densely than the conceptually similar RAM chips, but several times *less* densely than magnetic bubbles. Access times and transfer rates are much faster than magnetic bubbles, and CCD is seen as a potential rival to both disc and cache memories where direct access is not a prime requirement. A cache storage is a very fast serial storage device forming part of internal storage. Its great use is when large blocks of data are to be read from internal storage and processed serially.

(c) Optical storage

Optical disc systems have many features in common with magnetic storage systems; both use revolving discs, on to the surfaces of which data is recorded via a retractable read-write head. An optical disc system, however, uses a laser beam to induce changes on the medium that can be detected later as differences in reflected light. Several different medium coatings are currently in use or under investigation – photographic film, polymer coating in which a bubble is induced, thin metal film in which a hole is burnt. It is not clear which of these techniques will emerge as the preferred. One current disadvantage of all optical methods is a higher error rate on reading than in magnetic storage devices, which, for the same encoding methods, will require treatment in the drive electronics or in the disc software. Once this problem has been solved, the benefits are immense:

(a) vastly increased storage capacity – up to 5000Mb/surface, 20 000 tracks/inch, 10 to 100 times that of magnetic storage, for the same access characteristics,

(b) greatly increased robustness – optical discs are inerasable;

(c) better removability and fewer head crashes, because Winchester disc heads fly about 1/4 microns over the surface, optical discs about 1000 microns,

(d) optical discs can be copied as record albums, by stamping out from a master.

When freely available, optical discs could revolutionise our methods of storing and accessing data and programs.

Fig 4.8 *optical disc format and read/write head*

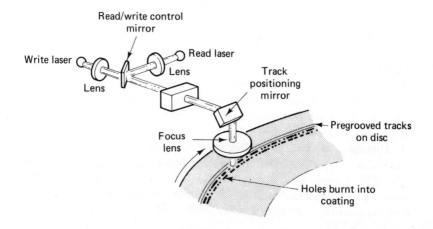

4.2 INPUT/OUTPUT DEVICES

I/O devices are the immediate interfaces to the computer — the ways that the user gets his data in and results out — in fact, how he uses the computer. The operative stages of Input are data capture, (optional) temporary data storage, and machine recognition/data conversion; and of Output, data generation, (optional) temporary data storage and data display. Data capture and data display respectively can operate from/to a variety of sources and media.

(a) Data capture

(i) Keyboards
Keyboard devices such as typewriters, teleprinters and flexowriters date back 100 years. Electronic impact or touch keyboards are now the most widely used form of data capture, both into recording media (punched cards or tape, magnetic discs or tape) and by direct data entry into the processor via a slow I/O bus [see Section 3.2(d)].

Most keyboards still contain:
- *alphabetical* keys in the original layout known as the QWERTY layout, along with
- *numerical* keys, both above the alphabet and in a separate optional group;
- *special character* keys;
- *control* keys, for example, shift keys, return key, cursor control on a VDU (the position of the cursor, usually a blinking marker, indicating where the next character will be printed);
- *function* keys, to invoke processing functions that may be continuously used by a program (e.g. a Delete Line function in Word Processing software).

Since keyboards of some type are provided with virtually all computers and on most terminals, keyboard skill is a necessity for all computer users. Keyboard skill is easily transferrable from typewriters (at least from those with electric or electronic keyboards). To those of us without nimble fingers they are an unavoidable burden — until they are replaced by an input method more appropriate to the rest of a computer system. Fig. 4.9 shows a typical layout. Standard layouts exist for most of these keys, but there are infuriating differences between the placing of the control keys on different devices.

Alternative layouts for full key content can also be found, designed to permit faster keying rates, but the vast proportion still use the conventional QWERTY layout. Special reduced-scale keyboards (keypads) also exist, mostly in small-scale portable terminals, such as those used with videotex terminals, usually a numeric key only with a few character keys. A revolu-

Fig 4.9 *fullscale and restricted keyboards for data input*

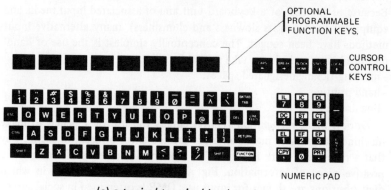

(a) *a typical terminal keyboard*

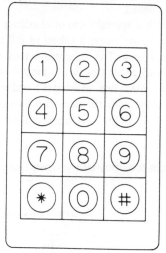

(b) *a videotex keypad*

tionary device known as a Microwriter permits full alphanumeric input (that is, all the 10 digits and 26 alphabetic characters) with five figure keys.

The universality of keyboard input means that keyboard skill is a prime requirement for most users; since electronic impact has virtually replaced physical impact on all but the older card and paper tape punches, this should not be a physically onerous demand. The logical conclusion is to remove moving keys altogether, and *touch keyboards* are available, particularly on microcomputers (where the keyboard is usually the sole input device), doubling as control console and data input.

(ii) Handproduced input

Because of the cost of a keyboard unit and of associated input media and equipment (and also its slowness and clumsiness), many alternative input methods have been sought. The conceptually simplest is the use of hand-produced input, which can take several forms
- marking/ticking designated spaces;
- hand printing;
- line drawing.

Optical mark recognition (OMR) entails the use of a pencil to make machine-recognisable marks on a pre-printed sheet or card, in such a way that a recognised mark in a specified position indicates to the computer a positive piece of information. Fig. 4.10 shows a typical form in which digit positions are shown for input use. OMR is often used in social survey work, or in sales recording, and generally in situations where it is possible to use only paper and pencil.

Handprinted input is a special form of character recognition with input devices which will recognise either a subset or full set of handwritten (but not yet cursive) characters. The processing required in the recognition process has until recently made this form of input relatively expensive, but the use of LSI components is now making it a realistic proposition.

Line drawing devices provide the user with a special pen or stylus whose movements are recorded as the pen is moved along a line or is used to

Fig 4.10 *an OMR form (courtesy of the Open University) (see also Fig 4.13)*

make any drawing on a special 'tablet'. The co-ordinates of the pen movement are recorded continuously and can then be used either to produce a graphic display or they can be stored away for future use. Also known as digitisers, these devices are particularly used for inputting maps and engineering drawings for subsequent manipulation or output. Special forms of pressure-sensitive tablets are also in experimental use for signature validation — it has been found that although visual signature forgeries are possible, the profile of signature pressure is usually unique to the owner of the signature.

(iii) Printed input

Business documents such as invoices, credit notes and sales orders are a universal vehicle for business data. Such documents contain a mixture of fixed information and variable information that the user has to originate. To avoid other forms of inputting the fixed information it is possible to print or code characters in such a way that they are uniquely machine-recognisable either by the optical or magnetic waveform that they produce under a scanner, or by other measurements of shape and characteristic features.

Mark recognition is merely the same principle as used in hand-originated OMR, but with pre-printed digit selection. Documents can be printed from a computer with fixed information pre-selected in this way, and variable data can then be marked in and the whole document re-input — called a 'turnaround' document.

Character recognition is the use of specially designed printing fonts that can be recognised optically (OCR – *optical character recognition*) or magnetically (MICR – *magnetic ink character recognition*). The latter is universally used on cheques, the former in a wide variety of applications. MICR and OCR input can be read by fixed and mobile devices; in the case of MICR there is also a range of combined reader/sorters and other large machines, designed for and used by banks for cheque handling. OCR is more flexible, since OCR fonts can be printed by some printer terminals, and some document readers can handle both OCR characters and OMR marks for variable input on the same form. Fig. 4.11 shows some uses of MICR and OCR.

Bar-codes are sequences of bars and spaces, each of 1, 2, 3 or 4 units width, in which a space unit is treated as a 0 and a bar unit as a 1. The sequence is optically interpreted as a bit sequence, in which successive groups of 4 bits are logically treated as BCD or other numeric codes. There are two very significant applications of bar-codes — on retail products sold in shops and supermarkets, and inside book covers for use in computer-based library systems. In both cases the bar-code can be scanned by a small mobile 'wand' or 'light pen', connected to the controls by a lead. For full-scale supermarket use, bar-codes can also be used with low-

Fig 4.11 *some computer-readable characters on financial documents*

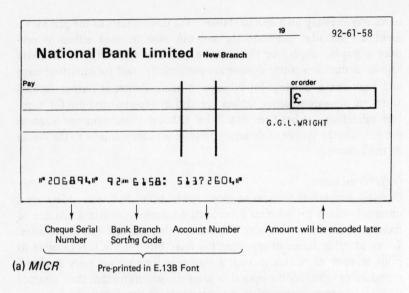

National Bank Limited New Branch

19   92-61-58

Pay   or order

G.G.L.WRIGHT

£

⑈"206894"⑈ 92⑈ 6158: 51372604⑈"

↓ Cheque Serial Number
↓ Bank Branch Sorting Code
↓ Account Number
↑ Amount will be encoded later

(a) *MICR*   Pre-printed in E.13B Font

T FILL IN PAYEE'S NAME
RE PARTING WITH ORDER

92123 831540

POSTAL ORDER

'ffice

TY PENCE

'ce)

20p

onths from last day of month of issue

OCR.A (see also Fig. 4.13)

Amount due: £9.95

Amount £

Credit
Giro a/c
number   205 5503   ← OCR.B (see also Fig. 4.12)

01 039 132 0 2 1 0557   PC06667
MR G G L WRIGHT

Signature

2572047310 0019 009954

Date   19
Please leave space below clear for use by National Giro

A72055503 ◄

(b) *OCR*

power laser beams through which the products are passed at the checkouts. In both applications, international standards apply: in the retail market a European Article Number (EAN) code contains fields for manufacturer and product, for libraries there is an international standard book number (ISBN). Fig. 4.12 shows these bar-codes and an optical wand.

Other pre-printed data may be in the form of punched/perforated *cards or tags*, or on short strips of magnetic tape stuck on to the back of *plastics cards or badges*, or on *merchandise tickets* (see Fig. 4.13). Plastic cards or badge cards are used to input personal data that can be checked against stored data in order to authorise some action that has personal or security implications; for example, payment of cash at a 'Cashpoint' terminal, entry to a restricted zone (such as a computer room), or crediting production and therefore pay to a factory worker. Pre-punched ('Kimball') cards or tags are widely used in shoe and clothing shops, as a way of inputting sales. The card or tag associated with a pair of shoes or clothing is detached at the point of sale and sent to a computer for processing or read by a portable reader attached to a point-of-sale terminal [see Section 4.3(c)].

Fig 4.12 *bar-codes*

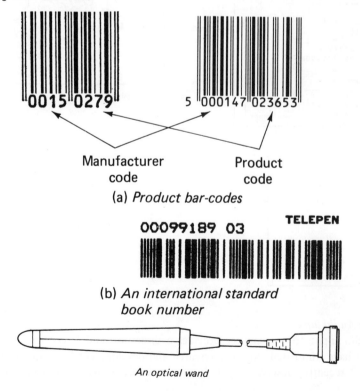

Manufacturer code   Product code

(a) *Product bar-codes*

TELEPEN

00099189 03

(b) *An international standard book number*

An optical wand

Fig 4.13 *pre-printed cards and tags*

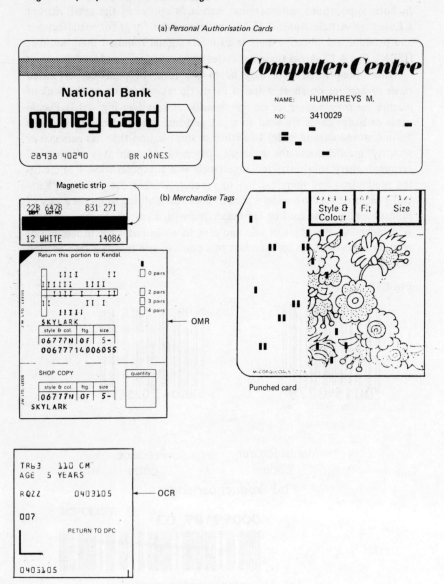

(a) *Personal Authorisation Cards*

Magnetic strip

(b) *Merchandise Tags*

OMR

Punched card

OCR

(iv) Audio input

Audio input to a computer provides a directness and 'user-friendliness' that have stimulated extensive research and development for many years. Until recently, however, the only commercially available form of audio input was *multi-tone input* (not officially permitted in the UK under previous regulations). Multi-tone hand sets generate both dialling code and number data on the same circuit as voice signals in the form of unique audible tones, one for each digit in a clearly distinguishable sequence. The tones are produced electrically by generating sound waves of different frequencies. Just as they can be deciphered by switching devices to set up a telephone call, they can also be converted to digital form in direct or indirect connection to a computer.

More recently however, true *voice input* has become available. The advantages to be derived from voice input include both ease of use and efficiency, since a person can speak faster than he can type or write. It works by digitising the waveform produced by a spoken word and storing the sampled values as a bit pattern. This is matched against stored bit patterns associated with coded representations of the words which the computer has been programmed to recognise. The principal problem still remains that the waveform produced by one person pronouncing a word will differ from that generated by another person's pronunciation, and since a voiceprint is nearly as unique as a person's fingerprints, voice input machines often have to be customised to one individual's voice patterns.

The consequential demands on storage and processing mean that voice input machines are mostly only capable of recognising a few hundred words, but vocabularies of several thousand words, sufficient for all normal speech, are around the corner. Voice input is widely considered to be an essential ingredient of the final breakthrough of computers, and we may be assured that it will become a common form of input in the near future.

(v) Direct data input

Most forms of physical data that are measured and recorded on instruments, such as temperature or weight-recording instruments, can be converted into a form that is suitable for handling in a computer. For this purpose the instrument, or 'sensor', is connected to a device which converts the data in its original, or analog form, into digital form; the device is therefore known as an *analog–digital converter* (ADC) or *digitiser*.

An illustration of the two forms is best given by reference to a thermometer; the analog value is the level of the mercury and the digital value is read from the scale of 0 to 100 °C (for normal domestic use). In order to make the conversion possible, it is necessary that the instrument presents an electrical signal to the ADC. This form of input is often known as signal input, and its processes as signal processing. It is of course the form of input used primarily in process and machine-control and in laboratory and patient-monitoring systems, and in data-logging generally. Signal processing, and the use of ADCs with sensors [and the corresponding output stage – see Section 4.2 (c) (iv)] require expert systems engineering skills.

(b) Input media

The results of data capture are in many devices transcribed in the first place on to a temporary recording medium which then acts as an input medium into a further device. The reasons for doing this are partly histori- cal and partly for efficient use of the computer since secondary input from a recording medium is very much faster than primary input from a key- board, and much less demanding of the processor. Against this must be set the time-delay in processing the data, since data temporarily stored in this way represents a batch of input data accumulated over a period of time. The process of keying input on to a recording/input medium for re-reading was originally known as data preparation. The alternative, of entering data directly into the computer at the stage of capture, is known as direct data entry.

(i) Paper media

The original and widespread input media was paper in the form of discrete punched cards and continuous paper tape, into which data is punched in the form of small rectangular or round holes, with a variety of codes used to convey numeric, alphabetic and special characters. These holes were then recognised mechanically by brushes or by photo-electric cells, in card/ tape readers which could operate at high read rates from card hoppers or tape spools. Punched cards are now found in two standard sizes – 80- column card and the smaller 96-column card – and miscellaneous tag and ticket sizes (see page 76). Mechanical card punches (e.g. the IBM 029) had no buffer memory and their speed was limited by the operation of the keyboard, to about 8000 key depressions/hour. It was also necessary to check the correctness of the punching by a repeat operation (known as 'verification') on a verifying punch. Modern card punches are buffered and retain the data entered for a visual check before the operator finally commits the data to be physically punched.

Paper tape is between 5/8 and 1 in wide, and data is recorded in frames of 5, 6 or 7 bits across the width of the tape, in a 'frame'. The importance of paper tape rested on its automatic by-production in telex and other business machines.

Figure 4.14 shows conventional punched cards and paper tape input media.

(ii) Magnetic media

Data preparation using punched cards and paper tape have been almost totally replaced by equipment systems in which data is keyed directly onto magnetic media – usually known as 'key-disc' or 'key-tape' systems.

Fig 4.14 *punched cards and paper tape as input media*

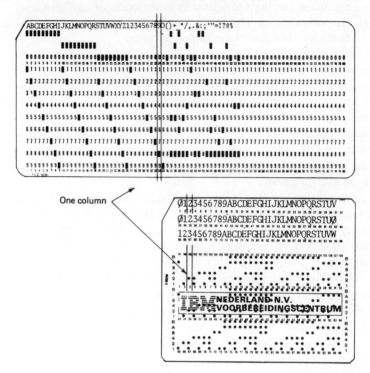

One column

Sprocket hole

One frame

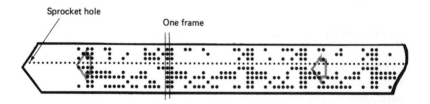

There are several impelling reasons for this change:

(a) the keyboards are all-electronic and permit the operator to work at his or her full keying speed;

(b) the storage media is more compact and secure;

(c) data can be re-read from magnetic media, or transmitted over a data communications line, faster and more reliably;

(d) the decreasing cost of microelectronics-based hardware provided real financial savings over existing punches, even before allowing for additional functions permitted by microprocessor intelligence;

(e) the reliability of electronic devices makes their maintenance cost much less than that of mechanical punches.

A wide range of key-disc systems is now to be found, from one-one replacement single workstations to multiple workstations sharing a single output station. In the latter case, the system is usually built around a mini-computer, whose power allows all the input stations to operate simultaneously at their full key rate of about 12 000 key depressions/hr while outputting to a shared disc. This arrangement is sometimes known as Processor Controlled Keying. Software may also be provided for formatting and editing the data before the file is manually or directly transferred to the main processor.

An even further stage in the revolution in data preparation is to make it a function of the main processor itself (usually in a small business computer) in which data entry software can operate in parallel with other tasks, if it is a multi-tasking machine, or in a sequence of data entry → validation → processing tasks in a single-shot machine.

Meanwhile data capture has been expanding in other directions; we now have a range of portable, microprocessor-powered and hand-held terminals, with a reduced keyboard tailored to the particular needs of the job, and data output onto a cassette or non-volatile bubble memory, from which it can subsequently be output to a full computer for processing.

(c) Data display

(i) Printed output

Printed output is the only permanent output, or 'hard copy' from a computer, and all but the smallest home computer is likely to have one, or more, from the variety of types available. Printers may be characterised as:
- impact or non-impact;
- serial, line or page;
- character or matrix.

Their common characteristic is that an electric drive moves paper by pinch-roller, as in a typewriter, or more generally by sprockets engaging sprocket holes on the sides of the paper, past a horizontal printing mechanism. Continuous pages or discrete sheets of paper (blank or as pre-printed forms) may be used, with a linespace of between 80 and 144 characters, and generally 66 single-spaced lines per page.

Impact printers create images by physical contact on to the paper through a ribbon (on to the top copy) and via carbon sheets interleaved or treated no-carbon paper for the other copies. The physical impact creates noise — a major nuisance and even a health hazard.

Non-impact printers create images only on one copy, by various processes including ink-jets, thermal effect on treated heat-sensitive paper, xerographic and laser beam printing. They are much quieter than impact printers.

Serial printers print one character at a time, *line* printers one line, and *page* printers one page at a time. Line and page printers require line and page buffers to be filled from the processor before printing.

Character printers have unique print keys for each character (like typewriters); *matrix* printers build up a character by printing dots in a matrix of 5 x 7 on dot positions (see Fig. 4.15) on the same principle as is used in most visual displays (see next section).

Serial printers tend to be slower and use matrix processes; the conventional fast printers are line printers and use impact printing with character keys. The fastest page printers use non-impact techniques, as do very slow and cheap printers installed as integral hard copy in other terminals.

The *character set* of a printer is the range of characters that can be printed on it. Character printers may have reduced character sets, for economy and efficiency; matrix printers will generally have a full ASCII set. Lower-case characters are a particular advantage, especially in any

Fig 4.15 *a matrix printer*

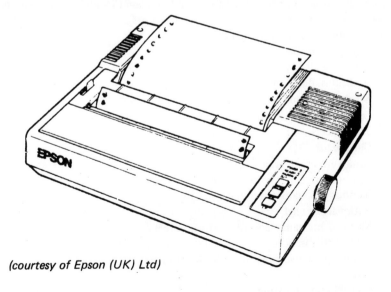

(courtesy of Epson (UK) Ltd)

printed output going to external or domestic customers, but few fast printers afford them (look at your electricity and gas bills!).

Foreign (for example, Russian or Greek) character sets are also available, but different alphabets such as Arabic or Japanese require special devices. A wide range of print fonts is also available; one particular advantage of intelligent printers which form their characters according to a matrix of dots is that by their own internal software they can cause non-standard characters to be generated. A similar example is a VDU now on the market which not only generates Hebrew characters but also prints them from right to left!

Measures of performance include *speed*, from about 10 characters per second (teletypes) to 20 000 lines per minute (page printer). Print image *quality* on fast printers is not as good as normal slower printing, except when 'golfball' typewriter devices or 'daisy-wheel' (so-called because of the shape of the print head circulating about a central hub) are used specifically to give typewriter-equivalent style and quality (for example, in word processing) and also to produce machine-readable OCR print. The fastest laser printers produce very high-quality print on a 300 × 300 matrix.

The most important characteristics of a printer are its sheer versatility and utility. The *volume* and *variety* of reports and forms printed by the computer can be illustrated by the following list of items printed in a typical well-developed payroll system, weekly and monthly except where indicated (a payroll system being normally considered as one of the first and easiest of a company's procedures to be computerised). The list includes output on pre-printed forms and on plain ('listing') paper, reports for internal and external use, reference reports and action reports, and some statutory and quasi-legal returns.

Adjustments listing.
Payroll record cards.
Additions, deletions and amendments list.
Salary advice and coin analyses.
Salary advice (industrial) and coin analyses
Time sheets.
Cheque list.
Bank Giro credit transfers.
List of Bank Giro credit transfers.
Summary of Bank Giro credit transfers.
National Giro list.
National Insurance contributions not deducted due to absence.
Summary of overtime and additional salary costs.
4-weekly SAYE listing.   Monthly

Monthly SAYE listing.	Monthly
Payroll control.	Monthly
Analysis of superannuation contributions.	Monthly
Analysis of trade union subscriptions	Monthly
Employee deductions analysis.	Monthly
Benevolent Society/HSA deduction analysis.	Monthly
National Savings control register.	Quarterly
National Savings statement of Premium Bonds/Savings Certificates.	Quarterly
National Savings substitute form	Quarterly
National Insurance card change schedule.	Quarterly
Income tax statements P9/P11 and P60.	End of year
Combined schedule of graduated pension contributions, and PAYE income tax form P35.	End of year
Cumulative superannuation contributions.	End of year
Listing of back-dated rise details for current employees.	As required by pay rises
Listing of back-dated rise details for ex-employees.	As required by pay rises

Computer listings on the familiar paper with sprocket holes are thus an inevitable part of office life, and the maintenance of a regular and reliable source of stationery is an important part of running a computer (see Section 8.6).

It is to be regretted that the speed of most normal printers is such that the computer can be comfortably used to generate much more printed output than most people need, thus contributing to the paperwork which chokes our offices and letter-boxes. One significant alternative to printed paper is *computer output on microfilm/fiche* (COM), in which semi-permanent text (for example, book references) are printed in very small form on either film strip or cards. Microfilm or microfiche can subsequently be viewed in magnifying readers which expand the text to normal size on VDU-type displays.

One further way in which computer output is already contributing to the paper explosion is via *computer-controlled typesetting*. Newspaper reports can be set to full-page layout from a terminal, and the page layout can then be either printed from the buffer or printed out to be repro-duced by a dry-printing process, in both cases bypassing the traditional hot metal process. Unfortunately the threat to our procedures from computer-generated paper may be further increased by developments in the electronic office; IBM has already introduced the *computer-controlled photocopier*, connected to a word processor through which multiple copies of printed output can be commanded.

Plotters, or graph plotters, are line-drawing devices which move a pen under computer control in such a way that continuous lines and curves can be drawn. They are known as graph plotters because the movement of the pen is directed by x and y co-ordinates from a nominal origin at the bottom left hand of a sheet of paper, as in a graph. Graph plotters are of two types: drum plotters, in which the paper is continuous and drawn across a drum, and flat bed plotters in which sheets of paper are separate.

Plotters may be regarded as hard copy graphics, and are often used in conjunction with graphic displays (see Fig. 4.16). The more sophisticated devices are capable of working to great precision, and in colour. Computer art is usually output on plotters, and any other output demanding continuous high-precision line drawings, for example maps, engineering drawings, mathematical curves. An interesting development is the production of overhead transparencies. Lower precision graphics may also be printed by some matrix printers in 'graphics mode', which requires intelligence within the printer, and even (at the level of Snoopy Dog) on line printers.

(ii) Visual output

Visual output is easy to absorb, immediate and environmentally acceptable. It is the fastest growing form of computer output, particularly in the VDU (see next section), for which reason one example is shown on the cover of this book as the single most characteristic shape associated with the computer today.

Most forms of visual display use some form of *cathode ray tube* (CRT) as the display medium, and it is the tube which gives the VDU its distinctive TV-type shape. The visual display is created on the face of the tube, which is coated with a phosphor surface which emits light when bombarded by an electron beam produced by an electronic gun. The light is either transient, in which case it has to be re-energised, or 'refreshed' by the beam scanning from top to bottom of the screen, line by line, approximately 50 times per second; or, with a special form of phosphor and electron beam arrangement, the light remains on the screen until erased. The former is known as a *raster scan display*, the latter as a *storage tube*. The type of phosphor determines the colour of the light — white, amber or green — displayed on the black surface of the screen.

The image produced on the face of the tube may either be in the form of characters (*alphanumeric* displays) or in free-line drawing (*graphics*). Characters are pre-formed on the framework of a dot matrix (see Fig. 4.17), usually 7×7, created by a character generator from data presented to it from the screen buffer store. There must therefore be a buffer store at least equal to the character capacity of the screen, and each character position on the screen is identified with a separate storage location in the buffer, from which the refreshing process originates. The form of identification is via the cursor — a square or line which moves, or is moved, to be

Fig 4.16 *graphic display and graph plotter*

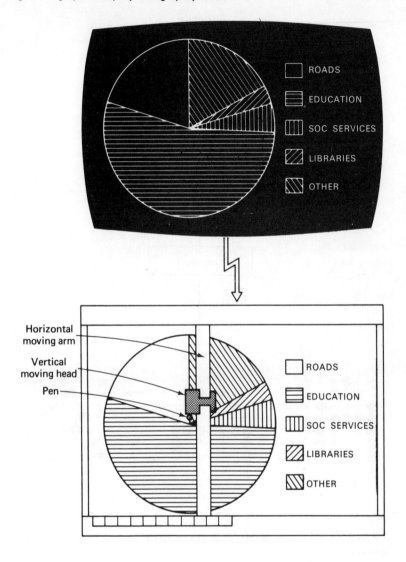

underneath or on top of the character position actually being read from/ written to.

The 'standard' screen contains either 12 lines of 80 characters or 24 lines of 80 characters (1 K and 2 K screens), but high-quality screens that display the equivalent of an A4 page (A4 screens) are being introduced in word processing systems. These lines of characters are built on

Fig 4.17 *a CRT display and character matrix*

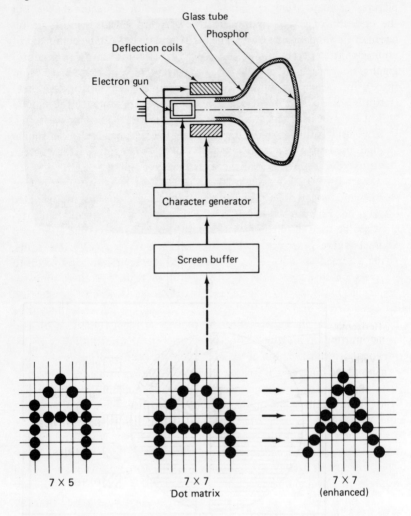

a screen of 600 scan lines. Videotex screens have a 14 × 40 character format.

Graphic displays are addressable spatially, treating the surface of the screen as a two-dimensional co-ordinate graph. The vertical scale may contain up to 800 points, the horizontal screen up to 1000, and any point may be referenced by a pair of x (horizontal) and y (vertical) co-ordinate values. The scale is detailed enough to produce a continuous line composed of very small points. Many alphanumeric screens may also be used in graphics mode but with much cruder scales (e.g. 100 × 80).

Alphanumeric displays may also be used to draw representative pictures or maps using combinations of a set of character shapes, but the precision of graphic shapes on true graphics screens is much greater because the fundamental unit is the point, and images can be composed of arrangement of points known as 'pixels', (in much the same way as photographs are printed in newspapers or transmitted and reproduced from space). In 'memory-mapped' displays the current contents of each pixel (including the colour code in a colour display) are stored in an unique area of the processor's memory or in a data buffer in the display itself.

The raster scan method of creating and refreshing displays is similar to that used in TV screens, except that the standard (UK) TV screen contains 625 lines and uses a lower-persistence phosphor.

The cheapness of TV sets makes them attractive as computer output devices, and they are used as such in small microcomputers, and as slave video displays copying the screen content of the master video screen. Similarly, they can be used in teletext services with appropriate decoding interfaces. Characters are generated in a sequence of about ten (TV) line scans, giving a screen capacity, after allowing for character–line gaps, of up to 48 lines of characters. Their other attractive feature is their slimness, which accounts for their popularity as business videotex terminals on crowded office desks, but such sets have specially engineered flicker-free screens – flicker being a consequence of the different phosphor used to avoid blurring on *moving* TV pictures). The other major influence of TV on visual displays has been in the introduction of colour displays.

The sheer bulk of CRT-based display has led to attempts to produce flat displays. The only commercial form is *gas plasma* display, which contains an arrangement of character cells, each cell filled with neon gas, and with an arrangement of wires running through it on which can be traced, by a selection process, any character outline. When a current is applied, the selected character shape glows like a miniature neon light. The principle is widely applied in some calculator displays and in the displays on petrol pumps.

For small visual displays, such as the single-line displays used in many input and data preparation devices, *light-emitting diodes* (LED) or *liquid crystal displays* (LCD) are used. LEDs and LCDs are familiar from digital watches and calculators. An LED is a solid state equivalent of the incandescent light bulb; it emits a light, in one of several colours (red, orange, yellow or green) when a current passes through a diode. However LEDs are heavy users of current, and give a poor display in bright natural light. LCDs are constructed by sandwiching a liquid crystal between two glass plates. When an electric field is passed between electrodes at the ends of any segment, light is prevented from being transmitted which makes the segment appear black. LCDs thus also need either a reflective backing or an illuminated rear light. They have the advantage of virtually zero power requirement, but the control arrangements are more complicated.

Both devices work by selecting the appropriate combination of the seven segments which make up the full display field, as shown in Fig. 4.18, to make up an alphanumeric character. Extensive development is under way to produce full flat screens based on solid state LCD components, one for each character display position, and these will undoubtedly come on the market in the next few years.

Fig 4.18   *the basis of LCD and LED characters*

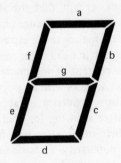

(iii) Audio output

Audio output or audio response systems have achieved a higher rate of acceptance in computer usage than has audio input. There are basically two methods used to generate speech output: the first is by converting words into digital form, by sampling the waveform, storing the bit patterns, and recalling them as required in any sentence or phase (the speaking clock works in this way). An output message is thus assembled from word equivalents stored on fast discs, converted back to the original analog waveform and amplified to a loudspeaker. This is expensive on storage, but a small number of words will suffice for a wide range of recognisable messages, usually in response to requests or enquiries over the telephone by multi-tone input. Fig. 4.19 shows a flowchart of this process, which is in commercial use.

The second method is to generate speech electronically from phonetic text. Voice parameters are computed (for amplitude, frequency and pitch) for each phonetic unit, and are fed to the synthesiser which then produces 'artificial' sound corresponding to the phonetic text. This method is much more economic in storage, and is available with several well-known micro-computers.

In a less serious vein, the same mechanisms may be used to generate other sounds: computers programmed to produce crude music, in sounds of different frequencies, have been the star attraction of many computer

Fig 4.19 *the principles of audio output*

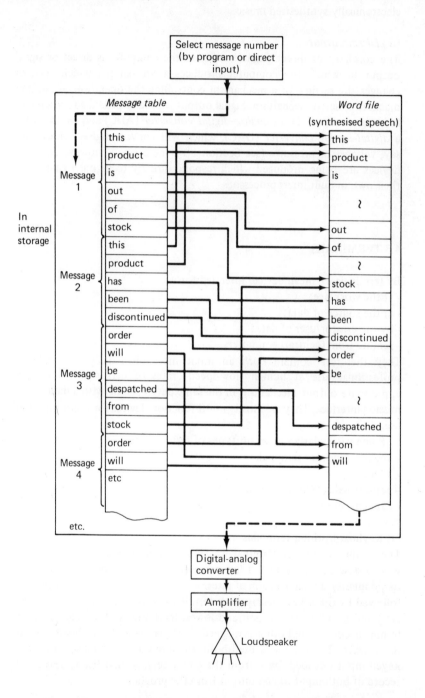

room visits, but more serious attempts are now being made in the area of electronically synthesised music.

(iv) Direct output

The corollary of direct (signal) input to the computer is direct or signal output in which the computer produces a bit pattern which sets, or changes the setting, of a mechanism controlling the operation of another machine or servo-mechanism. Signal output is usually produced subsequent to a signal input via an *analog–digital converter* (ADC) and returned via a *digital–analog converter* (DAC), which will convert digital values into, say, voltages or pressures (see Section 1.1). Increasingly, however, control devices are being produced which respond *directly* to digital signals with their own in-built microprocessor.

4.3 TERMINALS

By terminals we mean devices intended for use:
- at the workface;
- at the source of data;
- by the creator/user of data;
- remote from (central) computers.

They therefore contain *both* an input mechanism designed for 'non-professional' use at human (low-speed) rates of performance, *and* an appropriate output mechanism in the same device, along with a data transmission interface. They are mostly multi-function devices for multi-function use.

Some particularly important types of terminal are:
- keyboard/printer terminals;
- VDUs;
- point-of-sale (POS) terminals;
- data collection terminals.

(a) Keyboard/printer terminals

The original computer terminal was the teletype or teleprinter, but this was so slow and noisy that it has now become almost obsolete. However, its popularity dictated a form of interface and operation that set a standard followed by other keyboard/printer terminals (silent teletype, DECwriters, etc.) and also by the cheapest and lowest-level VDUs. A variety of other terminals containing both a low-speed serial printer and a keyboard are on the market. The printer is used both for pure output and also to record keyed input ('echoed' back from the computer), so that it contains a full record of both input to and output from the program.

(b) Visual display units

Visual display units, also called visual display terminals, contain both a display (usually a cathode ray tube) and a keyboard. The lowest levels are teletype-compatible, which means that they work in the same mode as a teletype, even to the extent of scrolling display on the screen (print lines moving up the screen and disappearing off the top), but of course with faster display speeds (usually switch-selectable according to transmission line speed). VDU's may also contain other input facilities – a light pen which can detect light emanating from a point on the screen; and touch input, in which a finger touching the screen can be positionally recognised as it breaks a grid of infra-red rays running across the screen, or causes an impedance change on a fixed conductive coating. At the top level, a VDU may incorporate a complete programmable processor and storage, in the form of a desktop microcomputer. Fig. 4.20 shows a small business computer packaged in this way.

Optional extra facilities may include:
- *line buffer(s)* so that the VDU may receive and transmit data in block rather than character units;
- *addressability* to permit linkage of more than one terminal to a line;
- non-impact printer/screen copier for *hard copy*, and interface sockets for printer and slave monitor screens;
- *split screens* to allow presentation of more than one functional output at a time;
- *processing functions* such as form display, data validation;
- *switch options* to work in different modes and to different processors ('compatibility').

Most of these options permit the VDU to be described as an intelligent terminal, effected by microprocessor and ROM storage (see below).

Fig. 4.21 shows two typical terminals; keyboard/printer terminals and VDUs are by far the most common forms of terminal.

(c) Point-of-sale terminals

Unlike teletypes and VDUs, which may be used in any environment, POS terminals are designed for use at the point of sale – in retail shops and supermarkets. They are the modern electronic equivalent of the old cash register, and still incorporate the same functions of keying-in cash received and printing customers' receipts. They also store cash and item data on a storage medium and/or transmit it centrally to a processor. They may also input sales data in other ways – optical scanning of bar-codes by a wand or laser beam is the latest method (see Fig. 4.12). It is also technically possible, but not yet socially acceptable, automatically to debit customers' accounts, such as bank accounts, by means of a credit card containing computer-readable account identification. This is one further step towards *electronic fund transfer* (EFT) and the cashless society.

Fig 4.20 *an outstanding example of a small business system built around a VDU (courtesy of Hewlett-Packard Ltd)*

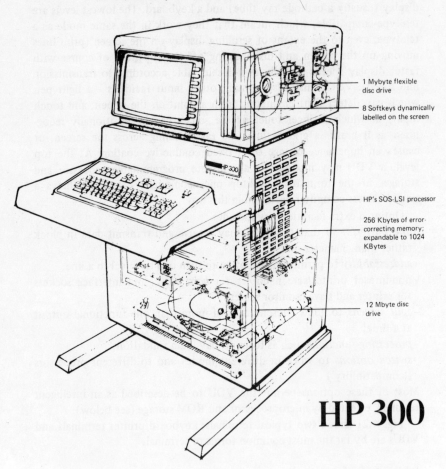

1 Mybyte flexible disc drive

8 Softkeys dynamically labelled on the screen

HP's SOS-LSI processor

256 Kbytes of error-correcting memory; expandable to 1024 KBytes

12 Mbyte disc drive

HP 300

(d) Data collection terminals

Data collection terminals are used to collect information of different types, usually in a factory or manufacturing location, where robustness and multi-function simplicity are the keys to efficient data capture and storage. They will include: keyboard functions and displays, badge readers, time recorders and pulse recorders (for automatic item counts). The environmental conditions and user requirements are among the most demanding that computing equipment face, which is one reason why the first commercial exploitation of fibre optics is to be found in this area.

The latest addition to the range of data collection terminals deployed in this, and other similar operational areas, is the battery-charged portable

Fig 4.21 *typical general-purpose terminals*

(courtesy of Digital Equipment Corporation)

terminal. This is essentially a hand-held terminal the size of a large calculator containing a simplified keyboard, an optical light wand (optional), small-scale storage (cassette or magnetic bubble) and data communications interface for subsequent downloading. It is designed for use by an operator walking or moving or driving about his normal job, in warehouses, factories, sales or wherever mobility is essential.

(e) Intelligent terminals
The continuing trend in terminal design is towards providing in-built intelligence, that is, some form of stored-program facility for processing and storage, to meet several different objectives:
- flexibility;
- connectability;
- distributed processing.

The original objective, in the face of a multiplicity of hardware and software interface arrangements (see next section) was to provide multi-source compatibility in a readily selectable mode.

The broader objective is to make terminals flexible in adjusting to users' requirements by providing a wide range of options and services – in printers for instance, to allow print size or character fonts or character density per line to be varied. Intelligence also provides *connectability*, both to allow a terminal to have its own storage media, and also to permit it to be connected to other similar terminals, to form a terminal cluster. In one manufacturer's Modular Terminal System, the components include 12 different types of keyboard, 4 floppy discs, 12 printers, 7 readers, 14 display units; each is based on a common microprocessor and therefore can be interconnected.

Intelligence for processing that is 'distributed' away from the (main) processor provides some user-programmable functions and some manufacturer-provided functions of a limited type such as some data validation, data formatting and form display to relieve the central processor of some 'housekeeping' tasks.

(f) Compatibility and interfaces
It has long been an objective of computer users to be able to connect any device to any processor. This has not been largely achieved except in the case of terminals connected by data transmission (see below).

Connectability of local high-speed devices to processors is almost entirely manufacturer-specific, except where another processor manufacturer makes his device 'plug-compatible' to IBM processors; it is not uncommon to find an IBM processor with discs and magnetic tapes from such a supplier. There are two parallel interface standards for relatively high-speed devices, but the dominant manufacturers are not enthusiastic.

Interconnectability for data transmission, and thus for low-speed devices attached via data transmission lines, has been largely achieved by CCITT (International Consultative Committee for Telephony and Telegraphy). CCITT standards are coded Vnn for equipment (eg the V24 standard for terminal/modem connection) and Xnn for procedures (eg the X25 standard for the operation of Packet-Switched Networks (see Section 4.4). A wider and integrated set of standards is now being sponsored by the ISO (International Standards Organisation), in the pursuit of Open Systems Interconnection (OSI), through which it will be possible for any terminal to connect to and use any computer, just as it is possible for any telephone user to connect and speak to (at least in the same language) any other telephone over most of the world.

4.4 DATA TRANSMISSION

One of the significant characteristics of a terminal is remoteness from a computer, which thus implies the transmission of data to and re-transmission of results from the computer. To do so requires:
- access to a data communications medium;
- selection of a data transmission service;
- provision of additional hardware and software.

(a) Data communications media
In principle any form of data communications medium used to carry voice (for example, the telephone network), pictures (for example, CCTV) or non-computer messages (for example, Telex) can also be used to carry digital data. Our freedom to use these media is limited by the scope of the public telecommunications network — landlines, land or sea cables, microwave channels, earth satellites, and switching centres and exchanges. In most countries, a national government agency (PTT) operates the public postal, telegraph and telephone services and exercises some control over the usage of an attachment of devices to the public network. Within a building or a site, however, users are not subject to any external controls over their private internal data communications.

(b) Data transmission services
Typically, data transmission services on offer over the public telecommunications network provide a range of facilities:
- line speed from 200 to 64k bits/sec;
- transmission mode — synchronous/asynchronous or block/character mode;
- traffic simultaneity — half/full duplex (one way or both ways together at a time);
- leased for private use or shared via dialling.

The services offered included a line and an interface. In services which use telephone lines as the carrying medium (currently still the general case), digital traffic has to be converted into the same *analog* form as voice traffic (for example, a fluctuating waveform). This is achieved by an interface device at the start of a line which generates a carrier (sine) wave and then superimposes on it (modulates) the bit on/off pattern coming from the digital source. A similar device at the other end works in reverse to demodulate the wave, i.e. convert it back to the original digital form (see Figure 4.22). This device is known as a *modem*, and has other important functions. For slow line speeds a much simpler device may be used at the terminal end — an acoustic coupler — which recognises the modulated waveform acoustically through a telephone handset. Portable terminals are available fitting into a business case with a built-in acoustic coupler — all you need is a telephone to connect to a remote computer.

Fig 4.22 *a modem*

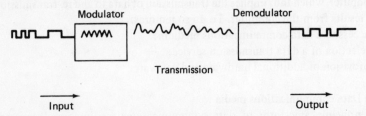

Modulation is not required for *digital data networks*, on which both voice and data are sent in digitally coded form and on which, conversely, voice traffic has to be converted to bit form, generally in the local exchange. Most countries are planning for their Integrated Digital Networks during the 1980s, in conjunction with a new generation of computer controlled exchanges and switching centres (the UK version known as System X). However it is likely that a much simpler interface will still be required. The advantage of IDNs is a much greater carrying capacity over the same physical lines, and greater line speeds in the absence of the bottleneck effect which modems impose.

The growing importance of data traffic has stimulated most PTTS to invest in services solely for data transmission, sometimes also on dedicated networks, including a faster and improved version of Telex, known as Teletex (not to be confused with Teletext).

Packet switching works on a different principle from circuit switching. In a telephone call, the circuit from source to receipt is open throughout the call; in message switching, of which packet switching is a variant, the destination need not be available at all, the message being sent via a series of switching centres which have some form of intermediate storage.

The only open circuit that is required is that between the one switching/ centre/source and the next, or the last switching centre/destination. Message switching treats an entire message as one unit; telegrams may be thought of as an example of pre-computer message switching service. In packet switching, messages are sent in a series of fixed-length packets, each packet being dispatched and handled separately.

Facsimile transmission (Fax) is a special form of data transmission originally devised to send (low-precision) pictures over telecommunications lines by scanning the image line-by-line and sending bits to signify the presence/absence of a mark in the appropriate positions along each line. It is ideally suited for the transmission of text, which it performs on the same basis. There are three international standards now available for Fax; there are regular international services between large cities, and a number of internal users, including newspapers, send copies of pages set in one location to be printed in another. In addition, several European countries are planning wide-spread internal FAX networks for electronic mail.

(c) Data transmission hardware and software

A single terminal is treated by the processor like any other slow I/O peripheral, but a distinguishing feature of most terminal-based systems is that there are many potentially connected terminals, and most of the additional hardware and software required for 'teleprocessing' is there to remedy the special problems that a multiplicity of terminals poses.

(i) A data communication controller is normally attached to the slow I/O bus, containing a fixed number of 'ports' (multiples of 8 or 16), each port being a plug-in point for one serial external line. A line may either support one slow terminal, or several more sophisticated terminals 'multidropped' on one line but with a unique logical 'address' on that line.

(ii) A device called a multiplexer may be used intermediately to pack a number of slow terminal traffics on to a faster line; the controller may also contain a demultiplexer to distribute the data back to the original terminal source.

(iii) For all asynchronous traffic (that is, character-by-character), the processor has to handle each character (by interrupting its current work) and then build up the incoming messages from each of the connected terminals. This burden may be eased by 'concentrating' characters into message blocks in an intelligent device either intermediately, or immediately prior to the processor in a subordinate processor known as a *front end processor* (FEP); this may also support some of the extra I/O software required by this type of input data.

A simpler approach that is feasible where all the system lies within one building or site is a Local Area Network (LAN). This uses low-cost cables to send small packets of data in bit form over short distances (up to 100 metres between nodes), and at very fast rates (up to 10 megabits/sec). Each terminal and processor is attached to the network by an intelligent interface ('node' or 'transceiver'), which will ultimately cost a hundred pounds or so. LANs are particularly used to connect devices in electronic office systems, and also to connect microcomputers to a shared printer/ hard disk unit. Fig 4.23 shows these alternative forms of multi-terminal network.

Fig 4.23 *multiple terminal networks*

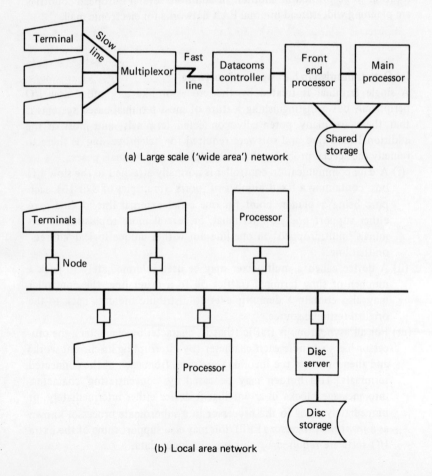

(a) Large scale ('wide area') network

(b) Local area network

CHAPTER 5

DESIGNING SYSTEMS FOR THE COMPUTER

The previous chapters have covered the basic functions of computing – input and output, processing and storage – and have described devices used to perform those functions. In order to make *profitable* use of the computer it is necessary to adapt these functions and embed them into the fabric of the commercial, industrial or governmental situation whose efficiency we wish to improve through the use of a computer. The main part of this process is known as *systems analysis*, and computer professionals who are employed for this purpose are known as *systems analysts*. The term 'systems' implies a co-ordinated set of activities, in which computer functions will perform only part of the total task, so that it is more correct, and more specific, to talk about computer-based systems, or computer-assisted systems, as an organised and integrated set of man-machine activities in the wider context of a business organisation, for example.

Developing and installing computer-based systems in these circumstances is a critical and sensitive task, calling for business judgement, personal acumen and technical ability, a combination rarely found in equal proportions. This is one reason why so many computer applications are either technically correct but don't meet their functional objectives, or are working to meet their users' needs but in a technically incompetent manner. A proper balance and compromise are required, although it must be accepted that the full capability of a computer is *not* met merely by requiring it to perform mechanical equivalents of human tasks.

5.1 SYSTEMS ANALYSIS

A computer-based system for any purposeful use, or 'computer application', will contain, as its core, a set of computer programs as its distinctive dynamic feature. It must be said, however, that the writing of these programs (computer programming) is one of the last and lowest levels of the activities in the development of a system, and only one of the interconnected activities in operating a system. (Computer programming is therefore dealt with in Chapter 6.) To use the analogy of building a house, computer programming can be seen as part of the construction work – perhaps the brickwork. Before this stage an architect has to be engaged and given his brief; the size, layout, style, contents and features of the house have to be decided on; plans and drawings and specifications of materials made; planning permission sought and approved; a site found and prepared; builders engaged; materials acquired; contracts placed, and so on.

The equivalent process of developing (or redeveloping) a computer-based system starts with some objectives for a change from the present system, triggered by problems or dissatisfactions *or* by a previously agreed longer-term plan – the *systems plan*. This is a recipe for planned original computerisation *or* redevelopment of existing systems whose equipment is about to be changed or whose useful life has otherwise expired.

Experience has taught us that this work is best approached in an orderly way through a series of stages shown in Fig. 5.1, which is sometimes known as the systems life cycle or project life cycle, since the task of developing a computer-based system is a typical project activity. It is possible, of course, to produce working computer programs without going through all these stages, but all the evidence from our previous thirty years' business use of computers is that you ignore them at the peril of wasting your time and your company's investment.

(a) What is the problem?

Although it has been repeatedly emphasised that the computer is, through the computer program and I/O devices, a highly flexible and multi-purpose machine, it cannot be assumed that it is the answer to every problem occurring in the running of a business; unfortunately no such universal panacea exists (except in the minds of computer salesmen and consultants). When a request, suggestion or command is received to computerise some business activity, it is advisable to undertake some analysis of what the fundamental difficulty is in the present set-up. Chapter 2 has itemised some business problems which may well be within the true scope of information technology, but the would-be user should be aware that there are other solutions to some of these problems – perhaps with a simple redesign of paperwork or clerical jobs that O and M or work study officers are qualified to carry out. Even inside the information handling area, there will be activities in which the computer may play a very restricted role:

(i) those requiring individual/expert skill;
(ii) those involving human counselling and advice;

Fig 5.1 *the stages of systems development*

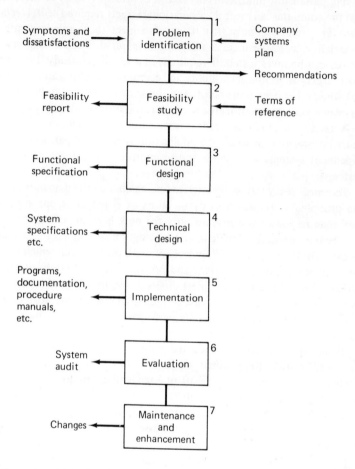

(iii) those in which the alternatives and procedures are not standardised or are enormously complex;

(iv) those involving one-off decisions;

(v) those involving complex matching and pattern recognition;

(vi) those involving very low volumes of activity.

As a consequence it may be necessary or advisable (though not necessarily politic) to reply to certain requests that the computer is not the (best) answer to this problem. Company management may however decide that for other reasons it would still be preferable to press ahead; that decision is properly a business decision taken in the full light of the best technical and professional advice.

(b) The feasibility study

Having passed this hurdle it is necessary, in principle, to be satisfied firstly that the computer can meet the operational targets required of it, (*technical feasibility*), and secondly that it can also meet those requirements in a financially acceptable manner (*economic viability*). These two interwoven factors can be investigated, if required, in a feasibility study. However, in most cases both technical feasibility and economic viability can be assumed:

(i) when it has been done before (on the same type of equipment);

(ii) when your competitors (or similar organisations) have done it.

A feasibility study is needed when completely new applications are being investigated, or when the application is critical in performance (life-dependent systems such as air traffic control, defence systems, hospital systems).

Technical feasibility is investigated by examining the demands made on the proposed systems, primarily in terms of speed of response to input (real-time response) and its capability for bulk handling of input and output, by the foreseeable traffic load. (A computer system has to be designed to cater for the maximum likely level of work on a system, which may call for statistical analysis of current and previous trends; 'system overload' is perhaps the most serious and most difficult operating problem likely to be encountered). There is obviously a trade-off between the cost of a proposed system (see below), and its performance on the one hand and its viability on the other.

Economic viability is concerned with the cost-benefit analysis of a proposed system (one which meets its operational objectives) or the relative cost-performance trade-off of a range of alternatives. The *cost* of a system is calculated from two factors:

- the initial cost (hardware plus software plus implementation/installation) written off over the period of years assessed for its operational life (less any scrap value at the end of life);
- the running costs per year (staff, materials, services).

Benefits are harder to quantify and must be sought from the following list:

- staff savings;
- speed and accuracy;
- less lost revenue through stock-outs, machine down-time, non-utilisation of plant;
- improved management;
- greater competitiveness and share of the market;
- capability of expansion and change.

The evaluation of costs must conform to the accounting standards used for the appraisal of *all* investment within a company. The *feasibility report* should contain clear conclusions and recommendations presented in a convincing manner, so that management (often the Board of Directors) can reach a decision based on the report.

(c) System definition

When it is assumed (or demonstrated) that a satisfactory application is envisaged, it is then desirable to draw up, after some investigation and discussion, a system definition or functional specification. This is a semi-legal document, which may in fact form the basis of contracts, containing a specification of what the system is to do, and the volumes and other given information. It is not a technical specification, and therefore does not specify how it is to be done unless that is particularly relevant to the case at issue.

It is at this point that some careful judgement is required by the systems analyst. He is strictly the agent of the user concerned, and must therefore have a more limited knowledge of the work area concerned, so that the user's requirements must be considered as paramount. However, most users are not fully aware of all the computer's capabilities, and will be setting out their needs in terms of their current operations. A careful synthesis of the two interests is needed. The most sacrosanct part of the specification is the output: the results are what only the users themselves can lay down, and it is then normal to work backwards from that point, to work out what input (from data input or data storage) is needed, and what are the processes to provide those results.

The system definition needs to be a document agreed by both the user (or more precisely user management) and the computer department or computer contractor, if the user company does not have its own computer department. Even if a formal contract is not entered into, it has a pseudo-contractual role and remains the ultimate and definite source document. It should contain:
- statement of objectives and scope of the system;
- performance objectives and justifications;
- brief description of the system, including main flow of data, major documents input and produced, major reports produced, and main files held;
- description and examples of output from the system;
- description and examples of input to the system;
- (additional) hardware requirements;
- master files;
- processing and calculations;
- controls;
- departmental responsibilities;
- glossary of terms;
- enhancements and potential growth.

Both feasibility studies and functional design are high-level computing tasks, often carried out by external consultants. They require a high degree of technical knowledge and experience, a full understanding of, and sympathy with, users' needs and a sound judgement in assessing standards — by profession, across industry or industrial sector, by application, etc. As do further stages of systems analysis, they will call upon fact-finding and documentation skills, dissection/analysis of findings and problem solving/ synthesis for solutions.

At the same time, the importance of joint user–computer staff work at this stage cannot be over-emphasised. In order to ensure this, a professional approach of *participative systems analysis* has recently been put forward after long exploratory studies, based on the thesis that nobody has the right to design a work system for somebody else. Participative systems analysis requires formal joint working groups at all levels (not just the user management and computer project leader), and jointly determined objectives and decisions. It clearly owes much to ideologies of industrial democracy, and while it is clearly apposite at the stage of system definition, it is harder to envisage its working successfully at the next stage, which takes off from the system definition into full-scale technical design.

It is also appropriate, particularly if the system is to be produced on contract, to accompany the functional specification with a prescription of what will constitute the acceptance test for the system, since acceptance will totally depend on specific performance of the functions and the operational targets defined in the functional specification.

(d) Technical design
The technical design stage is the detailed planning of how hardware and software are constructed and assembled in order to meet the functional specification. Like most design work in any area of work, it consists of 95 per cent perspiration and 5 per cent inspiration and proceeds through a series of technical decisions and choices made from a list of alternatives, restricted by some of the earlier functional decisions made about the system. Perhaps the most significant of these is whether to use a share of an existing hardware configuration or whether to purchase some hardware which will be dedicated to or primarily acquired for the application under way.

The decisions, which are outlined below, are also made in the light of some 'general' technical objectives (they may be thought of as the equivalent background objectives to house-building provided by building regulations):

(i) economical (that is, cost-effective) compared with alternative systems;

(ii) accurate, to ensure that all outputs are correct;

(iii) timely, to meet the schedule of outputs;
(iv) flexible, to cope with unforeseen requirements;
 (v) robust, to cope with all errors in input;
(vi) secure against loss, fraud or failures;
(vii) maintainable and intelligible (that is, well-documented);
(viii) implementable with current skills;
 (ix) compatible with existing systems;
 (x) portable over a range of hardware/software configurations;
(xi) efficient in use of hardware;
(xii) acceptable to company standards.

Detailed analyses and decisions need to be made on most of the following points:

(1) Detailed design of output formats and selection of media/devices.
(2) The same for input.
(3) The same for files (see Section 5.2).
(4) Selection of mainframe(s) (if appropriate), and centralised versus distributed processing.
(5) Selection of data communication facility.
(6) Synthesis of processing functions into programs and programs into runs.
(7) Selection of software source/programming language.
(8) Programming and testing methods to be used.

The end product of this stage is one or more system specifications, and then a series of lower-level specifications. The system specification is the ultimate technical reference, and contains detailed descriptions of all aspects of the computer system, hardware, software, and operating procedures (which is why it has sometimes to be subdivided), and may be regarded as the final plans and blueprint for the system. The lower-level specifications are for the detailed implementation work, primarily for the production of working programs and for other operational requirements.

An outline of the contents would be as follows:
- system summary; brief description, including relationship with other systems;
- system flowchart (see Section 5.4);
- data preparation and output procedures;
- data communication procedures;
- computer procedures;
- document and I/O specifications;
- file and record specifications;
- operating requirements;
- program list and software;
- references to lower-level specifications such as program specifications.

(e) Implementation

The detailed construction of the system calls for a number of parallel activities, and is the most demanding and intensive part of the project, particularly as by this time, detailed project planning to achieve the target date (see Section 5.3) is in operation. Programming is perhaps the most urgent and intensive activity (unless pre-packaged programs are used, see Section 5.5) but acquisition of hardware and particularly services such as data transmission facilities and stationery are perhaps more troublesome because they depend on outside agencies. (Subcontracting programming is also a common practice at this stage.) Fig. 5.2 shows a diagram of typical activities undertaken at this time, from which the variety of work can be seen. The processes involved in the production of working *programs* are described in the next chapter.

Another significant group of operations is concerned with final planning for the introduction of the system – (recruiting and) training staff, briefing manager and customers, producing working and informative documents – all of which, along with the final approval and acceptance of the results of the programs, also places a heavy premium on relationships with the users/customers.

The process for the final testing and introduction of the computer-based system generally moves through the following substages:

 (i) internal program and program run testing;

 (ii) conversion of permanent files into computer form;

 (iii) full-scale systems test on historical data;

 (iv) parallel running on live data *or* pilot-trial running on selected part of the organisation;

 (v) partial or total changeover.

At some stage, a formal acceptance test (which has been defined beforehand, preferably as part of the 'contract' or agreement with the systems development team) will be run and the results used to determine whether the system is contractually acceptable.

This ends the first part of systems development – with a bang not a whimper – but it should be remembered that subsequent activities of review, enhancement and maintenance may, in a system of a realistic life of say ten years, add as much content and work load as in the original phase of development.

(f) Audit and review

After the system has been taken over and run for a few months, it is common to hold an audit and review operation to consider whether the system really is working as required, and to consider whether any shortcomings can be put right. (It may be considered to be the equivalent of a warranty period.) One of the greatest problems in designing systems is that managers

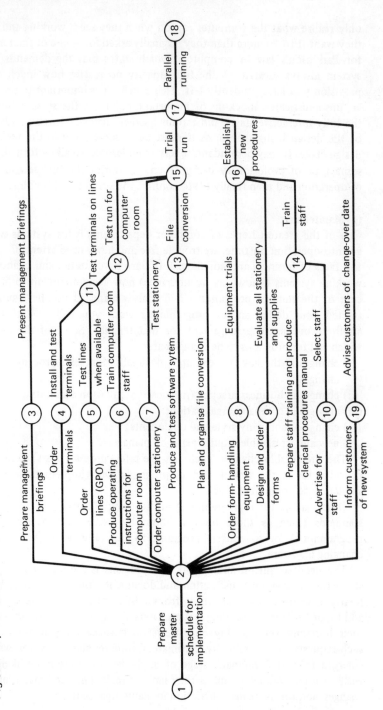

Fig 5.2 *implementation activities*

only realise what the computer can do when they see it working and then they want it to do more than they originally asked for — one of the reasons for Parkinson's law of computers, which states that the demands on a system always escalate to the full capacity no matter how much spare provision you have prudently left. That is why it is important to produce an unsophisticated mock-up of important points of the system (mostly the fully interactive stages and terminal/screen dialogues) well in advance of the design being frozen, as it must be at some point in the technical design stage. It may be prudent, if very troublesome, to allow formally for some type of evolutionary design to emerge during the first few months of operation and then finally (?) to confirm the system at this point.

(g) Maintenance

One of the greatest hopes of computer departments is for systems which go into operation on time, are trouble-free and never need attention. Alas, the facts of business and commercial life are never static, and changes to working systems (known as maintenance) now account for up to 50 per cent of the time of programmer and analyst teams. If you have subcontracted your design and/or programming work you will need to make another contractual arrangement for maintenance. Some of the factors which call for programs to be changed are:

(i) changes in the law (for example, decimalisation, EEC procedures, tax changes);

(ii) changes in business practice (metrication, inflation accounting);

(iii) changes in company organisation;

(iv) change of company style and documents;

(v) new and irresistible requirements by managers.

The predictable changes (such as wage rates, product costs) should be provided for in the sets of working programs. Only unpredictable events *should* cause program changes.

Other causes for reprogramming are to bring old programs up to new standards (such as those brought about by trends such as structured programming), or to convert programs to run on new machines when changing hardware.

The need to amend and rework old progams is the main reason why standards of program construction and documentation need to be so high. Nearly as troublesome, but arising from a different source, are requests to add to, or *'enhance'* a working system. Users change their minds, or extend their horizons, very quickly once a system is successfully working, and such requests are undoubtedly legitimate. Computer staff, however, having emerged from the traumatic stage of implementation are more likely to wish to leave well alone unless they have to make enforced maintenance changes, and this is a cause of friction in many organisations.

5.2 THE IMPORTANCE OF FILES

Most purposeful computer applications depend heavily on data permanently stored in files. A file is an organised collection of records relating to the same set of items; a personnel file contains records for each member of staff, a product file contains records relating to all company products. In fact the term 'file' is also applied to non-permanent collections of data:

- *input and output files* (for example, on cards and printer paper);
- *transaction files*, used to retain input transactions during their processing life in the computer and afterwards for legal/audit retention;
- *work files*, set up temporarily during program runs or between successive programs during a batch processing run. They act as a sort of 'scratch pad' and are deleted at the end of their useful life.

However, we are mostly concerned with the permanent on-going files, called *master files*, in the critical stages of system design.

(a) File processing

File processing is the backbone of most commercial applications, consisting of programs to:

- create a file;
- update a file (change variable data);
- maintain a file (change constant/fixed data and add/delete records);
- access and retrieve records;
- purge/compact a file;
- report on files;
- dump and recreate files.

Attention to files is therefore a key activity in systems analysis and design, and meeting operational targets of response or elapsed time depends mostly on the efficiency with which records on files can be found. This is because most commercial programs are I/O-bound, which means that they spend very much more time in I/O than in processing, because of the disparity between I/O operation times, measured in milliseconds, and other instruction timings measured in microseconds. Therefore a key issue is how to organise files to permit the most appropriate form of access, which is one of the several complex decisions to be taken in the course of file design in the technical design stage. Access methods are suitable combinations of file organisation and record search methods (see below) that are commonly supported in systems software (see Chapter 7) merely from a READ/WRITE instruction issued by a program.

(i) File organisation

This is the way that records are placed on a file either when the file is created or during file maintenance. There are basically only two forms:

ordered and unordered files. An *ordered file* is one in which records are placed in or added to a file in a specific manner:

- *Random files* (so-called) are files in which the actual or relative placement of records at an address is determined from the key of the record. This key could be a part number or even a name and the process of calculating an address from such a key is called *hash coding*. By this method a record may always be retrieved by the same derivation once in place. As a result of the operations through which key field values are transformed into an actual or relative record position, the key field values may appear to be randomly scattered throughout the file.
- *Sequential file organisation* is the placing of records on a file in ascending order of key field value both at file creation time and whenever records are added to that file during file maintenance.

Unordered files simply contain records placed there in first-come, first-served order without any pre-sorting or other record placement decision (sometimes known as serial files).

In addition to the data records, an *index* may also be created, relating record identification (key field value) to the device address in which it has been placed. Indexes may be used with any type of file, but are mostly found in conjunction with sequential files in a form of file organisation known as *indexed sequential*. Indexes can of course only be used on files loaded on disc files.

(ii) Search methods

These are procedures in programs to search for a wanted record. There are again basically two types:

- *sequential (or serial) search*, which starts at the beginning of a file and tests each record in sequence against the key field value (or other field value) which is being sought;
- *direct search*, which means moving directly to the device address at which it is known that the record will be found (if it is in on the file at all).

(iii) Access methods

Sequential access is a sequential search on a sequential file by key field value up to the point at which the value sought is equal to the value found (that is, record found), or greater than the value found (that is, record not found).

Direct access is achievable in two ways. For indexed files, a sequential search of the index is followed by a direct search of the indicated data address. For so-called random files, the same operation is used on the key field value as was used when the record was placed on the file, to provide the data address for a direct search. This method was mentioned earlier.

(iv) Selecting access methods to suit individual programs
This involves a file organisation to permit the forms of access required by all the programs likely to use the same file, and the media to support the required form of file organisation, which is a complicated and skilled activity. Some points to be remembered are noted below.

Speed and efficiency Real-time processing always needs direct access and therefore files on DASDs. Direct access by an addressing operation is faster than via an index. Sequential access is most efficient when a large batch of pre-sorted input is processed in one run.

File space Indexed and random files always take up more file space for the same amount of data than sequential files.

Devices Direct access requires the whole file to be on-line while sequential access requires only one volume at a time. Adding records and changing records on a sequential file calls for a new (carry-forward) file to be created, and therefore two on-line files at a time. Indexed sequential and random files may be updated and maintained *in situ* (that is, the new record is written over the old version). (See Fig. 5.3.) For a complete list and description of the symbols used in this diagram, see Fig. 5.8.

Flexibility Indexed sequential is the only standard file organisation which permits both direct and sequential access, and is therefore a good compromise for a multi-use file. Since indexed sequential files can only be used on DASDs, this increases the popularity of discs.

(b) Data structures
The structure of data is also an important element in designing the constituent programs. The file is the highest level, each file consisting of a number of records of the same or different types. The data on each record can also be considered at a number of levels — for example, NAME can consist of SURNAME, INITIALS, TITLE, and ADDRESS as STREET, TOWN, POSTCODE, COUNTY — down to elementary items which are non-divisible. It is also necessary to show, in a *data structure diagram*, not only the *structure* of data but also the relationship between records and data at each level. The theory of data structures makes it possible to analyse the relationships between data held in the file in three different ways. Fig. 5.4(a) shows that we can discover;
 (i) sequences of data — that a name consists of title + initial + surname;
(ii) selection of data — that a title is 'Mr', 'Mrs' or 'Miss';

112

(iii) Repetition of data – that initials can consist of one or more characters.

Fig. 5.4(b) shows the structure of a name-and-address file, showing, in
this example at least, that only commoners appear on the file.

Fig 5.3 *master file update flowcharts:*
(a) flowchart of the process of updating a record on a master file
held on disc with data input from a terminal by direct access
(note bidirectional arrows on line connecting program and file,
showing update in situ*); using the media-independent symbols of*
the NCC Standard. (b) Flowchart of the process of updating a
master file held on magnetic tape with a file of data input on
punched cards by sequential access; using BSI standard symbols

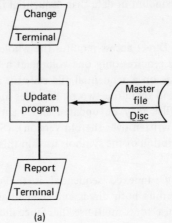

(a)

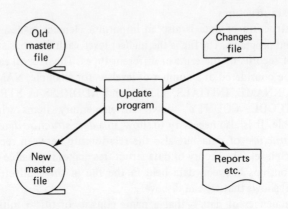

(b)

Fig 5.4 *data structure diagrams*

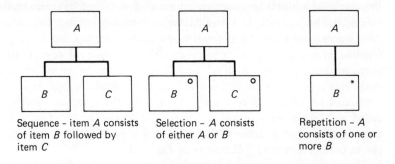

Sequence – item *A* consists of item *B* followed by item *C*

Selection – *A* consists of either *A* or *B*

Repetition – *A* consists of one or more *B*

(a) *data structure diagrams*

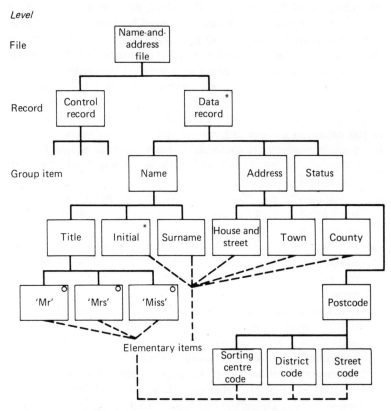

(b) *the structure of a name-and-address file*

5.3 **DATABASES**

Because most business functions are interrelated, data on files is also multi-functional; for instance, in a manufacturing company product data enters most operational areas. An alternative approach to storing data in files as required in one application is to proceed *first* to store all possible data independently, and then to develop applications using the centrally stored data. This approach is the *database* approach; the centrally/independently controlled set of data files is the database. For the computer, software called a database management system (DBMS) is needed to set up a description of the entire database ('schema') and subsets ('subschemas') that can be used in separate applications (see Fig. 5.5).

This independent approach towards a common pool of data warrants a prior investigation and analysis of all the data likely to be used in a company or a major area of it, recognising data as a strategic corporate resource. The objective of this exercise — Data Analysis — is to create a formal model, or description, of this data in its most fundamental, or canonical, form. Data analysis starts by listing the significant items, or 'entities' and their attributes, one of which is the key or identifying attribute; and then proceeds in three stages to reduce or 'normalise' the original definitions. The set of fully normalised data may then be used to create a Data Dictionary (software containing definitions of data), or proceed to the definition of a data base with a DBMS. One of the most significant parts of this definition is concerned with structural relationships between items; for example, products are composed of parts, parts are bought from suppliers. One way of categorising a DBMS is by the way in which it models these relationships:

(a) a 'hierarchical' data base is one in which data structures can be truly represented in a tree structure with a single root, for example, one product containing many unique parts;

(b) a 'network' model is more complex but more flexible in which various structures can be expressed by storing a special structure record for any relationship between two items (for example, a product/parts record);

(c) a 'relational' data base is conceptually much simpler, in which all data is represented essentially in 2-dimensional tables ('relations'). Each entry is an unique occurrence of an entity and its attributes in fully normalised form. Any relationship between two entities is contained in a separate relation-table (for example, a product/parts table).

A DBMS contains two types of facility: one to define and create a data base — a Data Definition Langauge (DDL); and the other to access data on the data base — a Data Manipulation Language (DML). Another way to categorise a DBMS is by the way in which these facilities are made available. Host language DBMS (such as the CODASYL DBTG model)

Fig 5.5 *database principles – the CODASYL model*

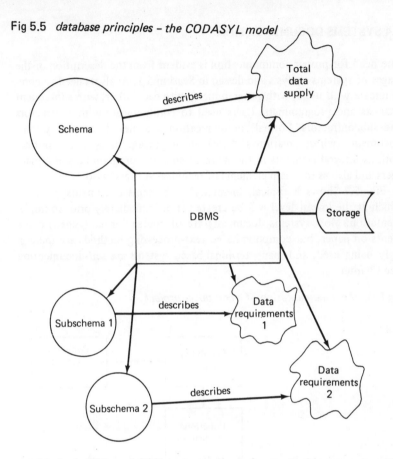

provide both DDL and DML as extensions of a standard language, usually COBOL (see section 6.4). Self-contained DBMS usually provide both in a unique form, often via a subroutine library. However, one particular benefit of a relational data base (indeed, the very objective for their invention) is that very simple, English-language-like forms of accessing the data-base can be provided. These forms are collectively known as 'Query' languages, and are mostly based on the Relational Calculus (a set of rules for operating on data items which led to the invention of the relational data base).

The data base approach to systems design calls for a high initial investment in data analysis and setting up the data base, and hopefully a lighter load in using the stored data in programs. Hierarchical and network DBMS require the power and capacity of mainframe or minicomputers, but forms of relational DBMS are to be found on microcomputers. Not all such software which claims this status is verifiably so, but intermediate forms, often described as Data Management Systems, are widespread and popular on all types of computer, and fall within a broad class of software now popularly described as Fourth Generation Languages (see section 6.4).

5.4 SYSTEMS DOCUMENTATION

The need for proper communication is evident from the description of the stages of systems analysis and design in Section 5.1. Analysts need to communicate with users, with programmers, with each other, with subsequent analysts and programmers. Users need to communicate with contractors and subcontractors. Formal communication is achieved through systems documents, whose creation and care are important parts of computing, both as integral elements in the work of analysts, programmers and managers and also as the main elements of technical authors' work.

Fig. 5.7 shows a typical 'hierarchy' of systems documents, most of which at the lowest level will be created at or immediately prior to implementation. Most systems documents are of course formal (typed) documents on paper, but computer-based text-processing methods are increasingly being used, and many terminal-based systems are self-documenting (see Chapter 7).

Fig 5.6 *the documentation of a computer project*

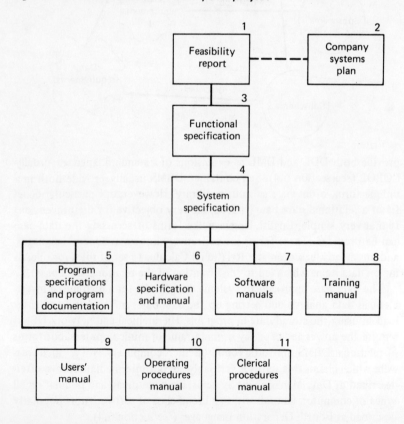

Two important features of systems documents are flowcharts and other diagrammatic aids; and system documentation standards. A *flowchart* is a graphical representation of a procedure, showing the constituent activities of the procedure within box symbols, and connections between the activities by connecting lines which may indicate flows from one activity to the next. Flowcharts of various types are widely used by engineers and work study officers. They may in particular be used to describe existing or proposed clerical and computer procedures at any level of detail down to the internal processes of computer programs. Various conventions are used, according to the particular need and occasion, some of which are prescribed in official standards and are deeply enshrined in popular practice. You will find templates to assist you in drawing them.

   (i) a block diagram shows all activities in undifferentiated block symbols — for an example see Fig. 5.1;

 (ii) a data flow diagram shows the flow of data within a system, from source to files and processes, and then to their destination; a variation is a document distribution chart. See Fig. 5.7 for a definition of terms and an example;

(iii) a system flowchart shows the flow of control (sequence of activities) within a computer-based system, generally at the level of programs, input, output and files. See Fig. 5.3 for a simple example, using the symbols shown in Fig. 5.8;

(iv) a network or arrow diagram, showing activities and events usually in a once-off job, or 'project' in general, is a common method used in the planning of all types of work involving multiple activities in parallel, and an example is shown in Fig. 5.2;

 (v) Hierarchy + Input-Process-Output (HIPO) Diagrams were introduced by IBM as part of their Improved Programming Techniques programme. A hierarchy diagram shows the internal structure of a system or program, very much like a conventional organisation chart (see also Section 6.3). Input-process-output analyses any activity solely into these three phases. Examples of HIPO diagrams are shown in Fig. 5.9.

(vi) One disadvantage of flowcharts is they depict linear and sequential processes well, but not so the parallel procedures found within computer systems. A Decision Table overcomes this difficulty in a situation where it is necessary to select one of several decisions according to the outcomes of several conditions. A DT is therefore the set of decision rules applicable, each rule consisting of those conditions which must be satisfied for that rule to apply, and those actions which must be taken to implement that rule. A decision table consists of:

- the condition stub;
- the condition entry;
- the action stub;
- the action entry.

Fig 5.7 *data flow diagram – holiday tours operations*

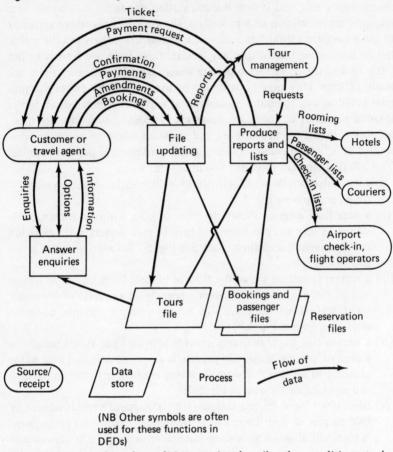

Source/receipt

Data store

Process

Flow of data

(NB Other symbols are often used for these functions in DFDs)

The condition stub and condition entries describe the conditions to be tested while the action stub and action entries describe the actions to be taken. In the decision table these four elements form quadrants, thus:

condition stub	condition entries
action stub	action entries

The conditions are listed below one another in the conditions stub, and all possible actions are similarly listed in the action stub. The condition entries' and action entries' quadrants together constitute one or more decision rules, which run vertically through the two quadrants. These rules indicate the actions that are to be taken according to particular combinations of conditions. Fig. 5.10 is a decision table composed to show the conditions under which some of the alternative systems development strategies discussed in the next section might be preferred to the orthodox

Fig 5.8 *computer system flowchart symbols*

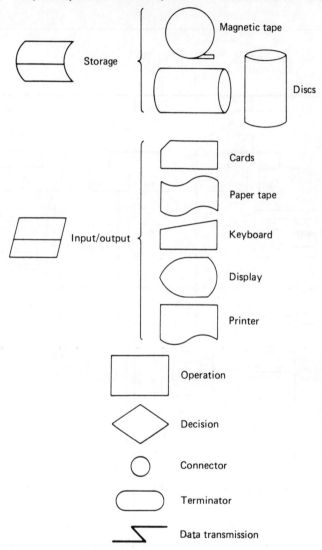

systems design and programming procedures described in Section 5.1, in
conjunction with similar choices relating to hardware, to be discussed in
Chapter 8.

A diagram is no more than a documentation aid which, like most diagrams, is worth a thousand words. Other diagrammatic rather than verbal
forms of documentation are to be found in *documentation standards*,
comprehensive guides to systems documentation content and layout. They
are available from:

120

Fig 5.9 *HIPO diagrams*

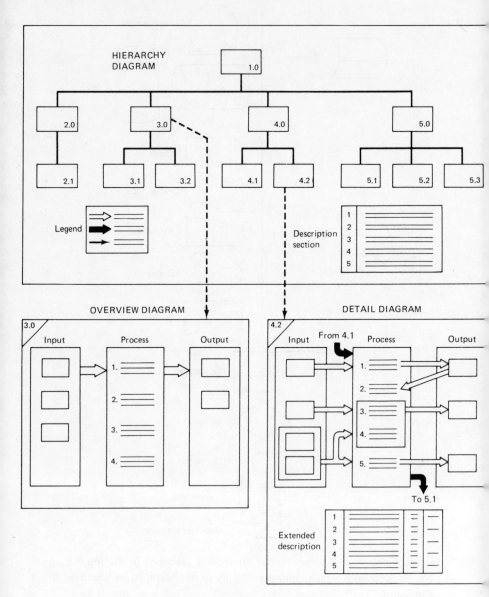

- independent computer bodies, primarily the UK National Computing Centre (NCC);
- computer manufacturers, particularly IBM and ICL;
- computer consultants and service companies;

Fig 5.10 a decision table – 'Guide to Systems Development Choices' (courtesy of NCC)

Chart Sheet NCC	Title: GUIDE TO SYSTEMS DEVELOPMENT OPTIONS	System: MASTERING COMPUTERS	Document: FIG.5.10	Name: GGLW.	Sheet

		1	2	3	4	5	6	7	8	9	10	
CONDITIONS 5												
1	Your own hardware	Y	Y	Y	N	N	N	N	N	N	N	E
2	" " Systems analysts	Y	Y	N	Y	Y	Y	Y	N	N	N	E
3	" " Programmers	Y	N	N	N	N	Y	Y	N	N	N	S
4	Want your own centre	–	–	–	Y	N	Y	N	Y	N	Y	E
5	Want single responsibility	Y	–	N	N	N	N	N	N	N	Y	
ACTIONS 8												
1	Design your own systems	X	X	–	X	X	X	X	–	–	–	
2	Use system consultants	–	–	X	–	–	–	–	X	X	–	
3	Do your own programming	X	–	–	–	–	X	X	–	–	–	
4	Buy software	–	X	X	X	X	–	–	X	X	–	
5	Buy turnkey system	–	–	–	–	–	–	–	–	–	X	
6	Buy hardware	–	–	–	X	–	X	–	X	–	–	
7	Use bureau	–	–	–	–	X	–	X	–	X	–	
8	Write to me for advice	–	–	–	–	–	–	–	–	–	X	

RULES 10

– standardising institutions, for example, the British Standards Institution (BSI) and the American National Standards Institute (ANSI);
– trade and professional bodies.

A *data record layout form* is a typical example of documentation aids found in most standards. One such form appears in Fig. 5.11 and illustrates the structure of the name-and-address file shown in Fig. 5.4 (b). It defines exactly what is to be in every field of every record and how much storage is to be taken up by the record. In addition, it states the name given to every field in that record by the programs which use the file.

5.5 USING PACKAGED SYSTEMS

The reader may well, by now, have gained an impression of the long and tedious process of systems development, and may well have wondered whether there is not a short cut or easier way. The full process as described in Section 5.1 is relevant to a company deciding to produce a system entirely from scratch and entirely to its own specifications – a 'tailor-made' or 'custom-built' system. Everybody will be aware that this is very

Fig 5.11 a record layout form (NCC Systems Documentation Standards) (courtesy of NCC)

Record description: NAME-AND-ADDRESS **System:** N-A-S **Document:** **Name:** N-ADDR-2 **Sheet:**

Medium: DISC **Record length:** Fixed ☒ Variable ☐ **Record format:** Fixed ☒ Variable ☐ **Record size:** 110 **File specification refs:** N-ADDR-1 **Lay-out chart ref.**

Ref.	Position From	Position To	Level	In system design	In program	Data Type	Size	Algt ment	Picture	Occurrence	Value Range
1	1	1	1	RECORD-TYPE	F-REC-T	C	1		9	1	2
2	2	11	1	REFERENCE NUMBER	F-REFN	C	10		A(10)	1	
3	12	43	1	NAME	F-NAME					1	MR,MRS,MISS
4	12	15	2	TITLE	F-TITL	C	4		A(4)	1	
5	16	16	2	INITIAL	F-INIT	C	1		A	4	
6	20	44	2	SURNAME	F-SURN	C	25		A(25)	1	
7	45	93	1	ADDRESS	A-ADDR					1	
8	45	59	2	STREET	F-STRT	C	15		A(15)	1	
9	60	74	2	TOWN	F-TOWN	C	15		A(15)	1	
10	75	86	2	COUNTY	F-CNTY	C	12		A(12)	1	
11	87	93	2	POSTCODE	F-PUST					1	
12	87	88	3	SORTING CENTRE	F-SORT	C	2		A(2)	1	
13	89	90	3	DISTRICT-CODE	F-DIST	C	2		9(2)	1	
14	91	93	3	STREET-CODE	F-STCD	C	3		9A(2)	1	
15	94	110	1	STATUS	F-STAT	C					

much more expensive, as a general method of acquiring goods, than taking off-the-peg or off-the-shelf standard goods. The computing equivalent of an off-the-peg solution is a *package*. A packaged system is one which comes with pre-written and documented programs for pre-defined activities, and sometimes with pre-printed input and output documents and devices, even occasionally complete with all hardware (in which case it is known as a 'turnkey system').

Packages are particularly relevant where the activity is fixed or standardised:
- by legislation (for example, PAYE and VAT);
- by industry practice (for example, accounting practices);
- by industry-type practice (for example, workshop scheduling);
- by common business functions (stock control);
- by formula (maths/stats/engineering);
- by company policy (for example, in multinationals or conglomerates).

Packages are available from a number of sources, with corresponding costs and advantages or disadvantages.

(i) Commercial packages
These are packages that have been produced specifically, or developed from an original set of programs, for the purpose of selling at such a cost, and in such quantities, that both the producer (usually a software/systems house) and the vendor/licensee make a profit. They are available primarily from software houses and service companies, and represent the major *raison d'être* of many such companies, and a major source of excellence in software.

(ii) Manufacturers' packages
These were primarily produced as a service to customers, in order to attract them to buy in the first place, and thus were sold at a nominal price or provided free, included in ('bundled' with), and disguised in the overall cost of the hardware along with system software (see Chapter 7). This practice has now largely disappeared in mainframe computers with the introduction of 'unbundling', and manufacturers' software operates at the same sort of level as commercial software, though not necessarily at the same profit levels, and not necessarily at the same level of excellence.

(iii) Program libraries
Many computer manufacturers, users' organisations, and some professional institutions have built up extensive libraries of computer programs, usually contributed on a mutual self-help basis, and usually programs written for specific purposes. The contents of libraries are described in library guides, and a program, with minimal documentation, is available for the cost of a magnetic tape, or disc, on to which the required program is copied.

Programs obtained from program libraries are mostly unguaranteed, and language/machine specific, but at the same time very cheap. For a commonly required utility function or application program you will almost certainly find what you want from these sources, provided you can accept the uncertainty associated with it.

There are, however, a very few quality-controlled libraries available, usually for a higher entrance fee. The Numerical Algorithms Group (NAG) Library and the International Mathematical and Statistical Library (IMSL) are particularly good examples, and if this is your line of business, you cannot do better than to purchase subscription rights.

(iv) Software brokers and indexes

The scope for using existing software, however, extends well beyond the capacity of organised libraries, and more organisations have been tempted to make their software available, at a fee, to external users, through the agency of commercial software brokerages and indexes. Smaller software houses also use such agencies as selling outlets. Software obtained in this way usually has a higher guarantee of reliability, and the National Computing Centre operates a carefully thought out software verification scheme for software available on its computer-held index.

(v) Small business systems

These still come as complete bundled packages, usually from systems houses who have bought in naked hardware and clothed it in their own software. Commercial deals will generally include an element of help towards the major problems of using a package, that is, *customising* it to fit your own final details, such as your own invoices and payslips. The best packages will make specific and easy provision for this; others present the same difficulties as program maintenance, particularly because computer software cannot (yet) be patented and documentation may therefore be deliberately vague.

(vi) Turnkey systems

The least-disturbance way of obtaining a full working system of hardware, system software and application software is to specify your entire requirements to a contractor (either the computer manufacturer or a software/ systems house) as a *turnkey system* — a term borrowed from the construction field which indicates exactly what you expect to do to make it work.

It will be particularly appropriate to proceed by this route if you envisage a totally dedicated (that is, single-function) computer system which you will not need to extend, change or replace during the working life of the computing equipment, and which you can effectively consider as a totally sealed 'black box'. You will, however, need to choose your contractor with care, and you will have to specify your requirements exhaustively and in detail, possibly moving through several draft stages before you can sign it away for the full implementation.

(a) Using packages

The advantages and disadvantages of using a package are hotly debated. If you have no program development staff, or not enough, then you have little choice, other than to go without or delay your project. For those users with the choice, the advantages and disadvantages are listed in Table 5.1.

Table 5.1

Advantages of package	Disadvantages
Saves staff	Requires 'customising'
Saves time	Likely to be less efficient
Provides expertise	Difficulty of buying
Should be cheaper	The 'not-invented-here' syndrome
Avoids 're-inventing the wheel'	

The appropriateness of some of these alternative forms of software (and hardware) acquisition are succinctly shown as a decision table in Fig. 5.10.

(b) Customising packages

The extent to which it is necessary to individualise a set of programs produced for general use varies according to particular circumstances and also a company's willingness to conform. It is not unreasonable, however, to expect to do this in the following areas:

(i) computer output on pre-printed documents which reflect your corporate image, for example invoices, payslips, cheques, orders;

(ii) computer-held records on your master files, to add extra items of information;

(iii) inclusion/exclusion of optional processing modules; for example, that dealing with deduction of trade union subscriptions at source in a payroll system.

You should expect to find facilities in a package that allow you to exercise these rights in a straightforward, easy manner, without requiring software knowledge of you. In my experience, however, our software ergonomics fall far short of ideal, and customising is nearly always far too demanding an exercise. The inexperienced user should always expect the software house to do this for him initially until he has developed his own expertise. Even for experienced computer users, the ease and cost of customising is usually one of the critical pro- or anti-package criteria. Both the volume of customising and the level of skill required to implement more demanding work, such as merging additional code into a packaged program, can aggregate to a point which wipes out the original cost advantage of the standard product.

(c) Buying tailor-made software

You will avoid some of this if you decide to have a software house produce a software package to your own specific requirements, for which you should, to start with, produce a functional specification in exactly the same way as you would for in-house software. From then on, however, the software will be produced through the stages of systems design, programming and testing, by some form of legal contract, by the software house.

Several standard forms of contract exist for software contracts, and such contracts should be approached on a competitive basis. The acceptance tests are again a critical part of the contract. If the package produced for you is likely to have wider applicability, you should be able to negotiate a royalty agreement with the software house for any subsequent sales.

Since most large and reputable software houses will have highly efficient software production methods, they should be able to produce packages as cheaply as the *equivalent* standard of work produced in your in-house teams. You *may*, however, find it possible to accept lower standards of work from your own staff (for which you will eventually pay the penalty); you should never accept anything but the highest standard of work from a software house.

(d) Microcomputer packages

The cost of producing custom-built software for microcomputers is quite out of scale with their low hardware cost, and packaged software is the rule rather the exception. Micrcocomputer packages sell very cheaply through mass sales, and in order to protect themselves against unauthorised copying and software piracy, most producers provide minimal technical documentation and assistance. Customisation is therefore virtually impossible, other than by selection of features — you buy the software on an as-seen, take-it-or-leave-it basis.

Under these circumstances, and given that most microcomputers contain many hardware components assembled from the same few OEMs, selection of a system is likely to depend more on the quality and usability of the software which will run on it. The great commercial success of microcomputer software is the Spreadsheet (typified by Visicalc) which allows a user to enter data on a displayed business sheet in a relatively free manner, and then allows results to be calculated on a rows-and-columns basis. No business microsystem should be without it.

CHAPTER 6

PROGRAMMING THE COMPUTER

After reading the description of computer program instructions in Chapter 3, the reader may well be approaching this chapter with trepidation, not without justification, since programming a computer at that level, in instructions drawn directly from a machine's basic instruction set, is both tedious and very detailed. In fact, for most computer users, including perhaps 95 per cent of all computer programmers, writing computer programs is a much less difficult, if still demanding, task and one that is within the grasp of a large number of people, at a certain level, who are not professional programmers.

6.1 THE PROGRAMMING TASK

The task of computer programming is in fact much wider than that of merely writing programs. It includes;

  (i) defining the function of the program (or having it defined in a program specification);

 (ii) designing the program – determining how it is to be organised (its *structure*), and what it is to perform (its *logic*);

(iii) coding the program in a programming language;

(iv) testing and debugging the program, to ensure that it is free from errors *and* does what is wanted of it;

 (v) documenting it for subsequent use by operators and modification by other programmers (and oneself).

By using the analogies referred to in Chapter 1 for computer programs – recipes or crochet patterns – the relevance of these subdivisions will become clear. Developing these analogies, one may also say that, just as few meals or few garments require only one recipe or crochet operation, few computer applications require only one computer program. The number may well be 50 or even greater, subdivided into linked programs known as *program runs*, for the reason that they are a sequence of programs run at one time. A typical system will have runs that are performed at different times of the system cycle — daily, weekly, monthly, quarterly, yearly, on demand — and runs to perform significantly different functions, most of them concerned with file processing such as an update run or a reporting run. The whole collection is known as a *program suite*. A number of the programs will be similar to the same types of programs occurring in most other program suites, including some which merely change the order, media, or format of data, and are known as 'utilities' or 'housekeeping' routines, usually provided as part of systems software (see Chapter 7).

As an example, the payroll system mentioned in Section 4.2 might contain about 50 programs, of which about 10 might be Sort programs, divided into 12 Runs as follows:

Run 1   Input to and update of the employee file and statistics summary file with adjustments to the previous week's/month's payroll.

Run 2   Input to and update of the employee file with all amendments and transfers.

Run 3   Input to and update of the employee file with details from time sheets and returns of overtime, standby, etc., and compute net pay.

Run 4   Produce all main payroll output from the employee file.

Run 5   Produce payroll statistics from the employee file.

Run 6   Print lists of Save As You Earn deductions, and clear down employee file cumulations.

Run 7   Produce month end reports from employee file and statistics summary file, and clear down the cumulative totals within these files.

Run 8   Produce the quarterly National Savings data from the employee file.

Run 9   Produce the end of quarter National Insurance card change schedule.

Run 10   Produce year end statements of data extracted from the employee file, and clear down the employee file annual cumulations.

Run 11   Compute back-dated pay rise details.

Run 12   Employee file enquiries.

Computer programming is therefore not an individual task at professional level. Programmers usually work in small teams on parts of, or related, programs, often with the support of senior technical assistance known as a *chief programmer team* (CPT). The CPT provides the technical environment, support, advice and quality control for a programming team, as part of the wider program production (sometimes called 'software engineering') task.

6.2 THE PROGRAM SPECIFICATION

Whoever is responsible for this part of the programming task, there are some essential items of information that must be determined or agreed at the outset, and collectively they form the *program specification*:

   (i) title;
  (ii) function within larger system;
 (iii) detailed description with appropriate documentation;
 (iv) files used, with reference to other documents if appropriate;
  (v) input and output, with reference to other documents if appropriate;
 (vi) controls and error messages required;
(vii) program structure method to be used;
(viii) hardware and software environment, including language to be used (see Section 6.4);
 (ix) implementation schedule;
  (x) test/acceptance data (see Section 6.5).

The accompanying documentary evidence may include:

 (xi) extract from the systems flowchart showing this program as one activity;
(xii) file/code library references, and data dictionary (list of approved data-names).

The detailed description may itself be written in a formal *program definition or design language* (PDL), a pseudo-programming language which is capable of precisely defining procedural functions (or 'schematic logic') of a program's procedural activities, and from which may be launched the subsequent design and coding or, in the longer term, possibly even automated coding — there are several such approaches under serious development and in trial use at the moment.

6.3 PROGRAM DESIGN

The objective of program design is to map out the detailed work of the program (the 'program logic') and the form that it will take ('program structure') in a way that will help to ensure the subsequent production of programs that:

  (i) meet the user's requirements;
 (ii) are error free;
(iii) require less maintenance and are easy to modify when necessary;
(iv) can be produced on time with minimum effort.

The difficulty of meeting these objectives without specifically planning for them lies in the very nature of a computer program.

A program when written down appears as a linear list of instructions; in fact, because of the JUMP/BRANCH instructions in every computer's basic instruction set, instructions are executed out of sequence, and because of the conditional BRANCH (IF . . . THEN) a program will contain alternative subsequences. This can be shown in a *program flowchart*. The principal symbols in a program flowchart are: an operations box, for unconditional instructions of all types, and a decision box for conditional instructions from which, as shown in Fig. 6.1, there can be two outcomes, or 'exits'. There will thus be a number of unique ways of following the flow of control between the beginning and end of a program; each one is known as a 'path', and is treated as a distinct entity in testing, even though there will be common sections. In theory there are 2^n separate paths in a program with n decisions.

Fig 6.1 *program flowchart symbols*

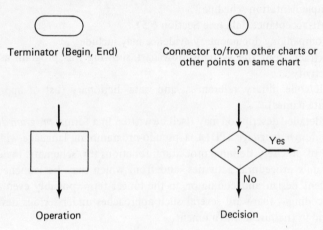

Terminator (Begin, End)

Connector to/from other charts or other points on same chart

Operation

Decision

A further element of complexity to programming is added by the length of many programs, which the growing cheapness and volume of internal (and 'virtual') storage are encouraging. These two factors create problems of quality in coding, testing and documentation which have to be countered in program design.

Modular and structured programs
In order to avoid the difficulties which surround the writing of large and complex programs in an undifferentiated, or 'monolithic' structure, it is now standard practice that program design starts from the 'top down', using the program description as a starting point. It is then the (senior)

programmer's task to map out the way that a program will work, and then progressively to split up the program into either short understandable sections (or modules), or, where the environment allows it, into a series of levels or hierarchy, so as to define a 'modular' or 'structured' program.

A modular program is one which in effect consists of a number of smaller subprograms, each subprogram being initiated by a program instruction. *A structured program* extends this by constructing modules using as components only the three basic program constructions:
- sequence (one instruction followed by another);
- selection (one instruction followed by one of two alternatives);
- repetition (one instruction repeated a number of times).

Fig. 6.2 shows these structures, which are equivalent to the basic data structures discussed in the previous chapter. It should be noted that strictly there is no place in structured programming for the GOTO instruction but in practice it is difficult to avoid using GOTOs altogether. The

Fig 6.2 *basic constructs of a program*

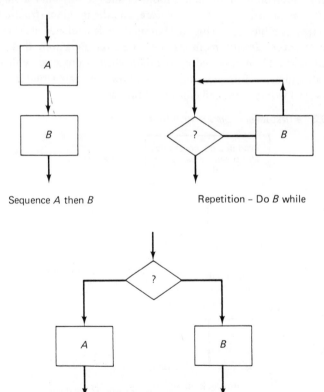

Sequence *A* then *B*

Repetition – Do *B* while

Selection – *A* or *B*

advantages of defining a program as a controlled structure of modules, of a size of no more than 50 to 100 instructions, are that the units of code can be tested thoroughly in themselves, and also that the whole program can be progressively assembled to guarantee reliability. A modular program should also be easier to understand and easier to modify. It may also be possible to identify and use common modules and so reduce the total volume of coding.

There are two methods that can be used in the process of splitting up a monolithic program into modules and fitting them into an appropriate structure: 'functional decomposition' and 'data-driven design'. *Functional decomposition* is a common-sense process of partitioning a list of program activities into separate functions, particularly by identifying them by phase and frequency of execution, and by the nature of input, output and processor function. Small programs may be subdivided into modules on one level — a simple 'functional decomposition' of most programs would produce the simple structure shown in Fig. 6.3. Larger programs will require subdivision of the inner loop, in such a way that a single level structure is turned into a tree structure, and the program structure can be illustrated as a hierarchy (Fig. 6.4) or module dependency chart (Fig. 6.5)

'Data-driven design' methods are based on an axiom that program structure should be governed by the data which it processes, either on the data structures of a program or the data flow. The data structures method is now well worked out, and consists of four steps:

Fig 6.3 *a first-level program structure*

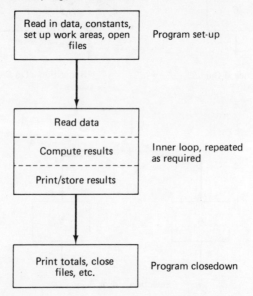

Fig 6.4 *a modular hierarchy*

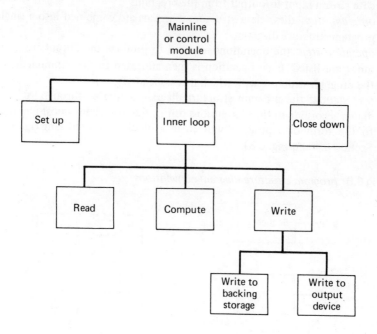

Fig 6.5 *a module dependency chart, showing the flow of control from one module to another*

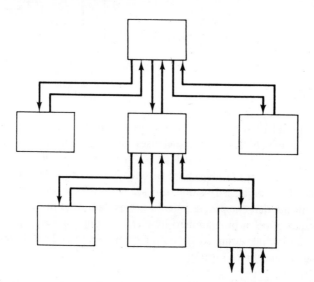

- *data step*: a data structure diagram [see Fig. 5.4(b)] is drawn for each data stream input to/output from the program;
- *program step*: these data structure diagrams are combined into a single program structure diagram;
- *operation step*: the operations required to produce the output from the input are listed. Each operation is then allocated to the components of the program structure with which it is associated;
- *text step*: if the program structure diagram is rotated through 90° and drawn according to the conventions of Fig. 6.6, it is then almost identical to the form of a program written in a block-structured language (see Section 6.4 and Fig. 6.8).

Fig 6.6   *program structure diagram conventions*

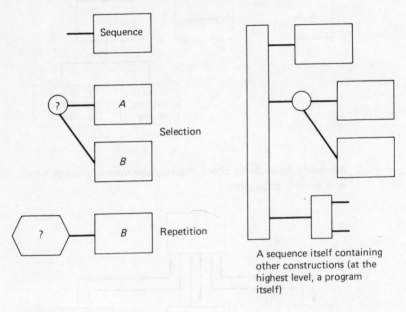

A sequence itself containing other constructions (at the highest level, a program itself)

Despite all these 'rules', program design remains a relatively subjective activity in which the programmer uses his judgement and flair, and the end product betrays individual style. The principal check used at this stage is, in effect, the judgement of one's peers, or perhaps a senior programmer, in an organised examination known as a *'structured walkthrough'*, which means that the programmer has to explain what his program will do to a group of other programmers by reference only to the program specification, and while doing so he normally has to defend his design against probing technical interrogation.

6.4 **CODING**

Coding is the writing of the program text as a set of program instructions, either on to a punching document or by direct input from a keyboard. The code is written in one of (very) many *programming languages*, and constitutes the 'source' program. Programming languages are categorised either as *high-level languages* (HLLs) or *low-level languages* (LLLs). LLLs are close to machine code (the instruction set which can be directly translated into a machine activity), while HLLs have been invented for the convenience of programmers. HLLs use English words and common symbols but require a lot of machine activity, called *compiling*, before the instructions written in an HLL can be broken down into the machine code which is actually executed by the computer. HLLs are designed for specific purposes as will be seen later in this chapter.

Only the machine code, in bit patterns, is directly executable (or via microprograms) on a computer; all other languages require translation into machine code, by software specially written for the purpose. If the translation and execution are immediate, the software is known as an 'interpreter'; if it is a distinct two- (or more) stage process, it is known as a 'compiler' (for HLLs) or 'assembler', and an 'object' program is produced which can be stored and run independently in that form. If the process of translation is performed on one machine and the object program run on another machine (usually a small computer) then it is known as 'cross-assembly' or 'cross-compiling' respectively. Fig. 6.7 shows a flowchart of these processes.

An *assembly language*, or *assembler* for short, is essentially a one-for-one version of the machine code used by the computer — see Chapter 3. The operation code (opcode) of the machine language is replaced by a mnemonic (LDA for 'load the accumulator') and the operands are replaced by *labels* or *symbolic addresses* which are usually letters of the alphabet or a letter followed by a digit (Y2, G9, etc.). The assembler program then decodes the mnemonics and allocates storage locations to the operands. Assemblers are unique to particular machines except where, for compatibility within or to other machine ranges, a semi-standardised assembler is produced, in spite of architectural differences, via microprograms. There are also machines known as 'soft machines' which (mercifully) have only micro-instructions and no machine code and therefore no assembler. Assembly language is also known as *symbolic code* and *mnemonic code*, for the reasons given above.

Most high-level languages, on the contrary, are not machine-specific but have been designed to be industry-wide machine-independent languages. (There were intermediate languages known as autocodes which were

Fig 6.7 *the process of program testing through compilation and interpretation*

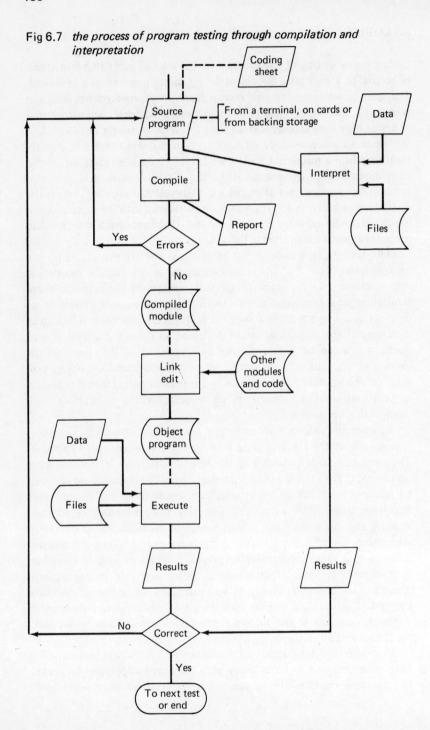

machine-specific, several-for-one, versions of assemblers, but these have almost disappeared.)

The arguments in favour of a number of *standard HLLs* are:

- languages can be written in forms related to users' environments (for example, scientific, commercial, real-time, process control, beginners);
- programs can be (hopefully) portable from one machine to another, thus permitting transfer of products and skills;
- programming can be made a less demanding task, and one that is therefore available to a wider cross-section of society (thus permitting the greater expansion of the industry);
- programming can be easier, therefore faster and less expensive.

The disadvantages are firstly that they require extra software, and secondly that the translation process very often produces machine code programs which are less efficient (in terms of storage space and execution time) than equivalent programs written in assembler. Now that hardware is cheaper, programming is a bastion of labour-intensive work. Overall efficiency, covering labour productivity as well as machine productivity. moves the balance in favour of HLLs even further. Ironically, it is the appearance of microcomputers, which at the lowest level cannot even afford the beginners' language BASIC, that has given assembler programming some resurgence. Currently, however, it is estimated that 95 per cent of programming is coded in a HLL.

(a) Some high-level languages

BASIC (most HLLs are known by acronyms) is the *b*eginner's *a*ll-purpose *s*ymbolic *i*nstruction *c*ode, and is the easiest generally available language to learn. As such, most 'Beginning Progamming' texts rely on BASIC (and the companion volume in this Mastering Series is no exception). More than this however, the size of the BASIC interpreter makes it the standard or only HLL for many micro and small computers, for which it has been extended well beyond its original objectives into a reasonably effective all-purpose programming language. It is also cost-effective for throw-away programs, and can be used to write the demonstration and mock-up programs used in the system design stages.

FORTRAN (*for*mula *tran*slation language) and ALGOL (*algo*rithmetic *l*anguage) are 'scientific' languages, which means that they have powerful mathematical and computational features suitable for use by scientists and engineers. They differ, however, in that ALGOL is a *block-structured* language, which means that it has facilities for building up a program in blocks, each block forming part of a higher level and initiated by it. Block-structured languages are therefore more suitable for 'structured' programming.

COBOL (*co*mmon *b*usiness *o*riented *l*anguage) and RPG (*r*eport *p*rogram *g*enerator) are described as commercial languages, that is, they were devised for programming in an organisational context ('commercial' in this sense applies to all purposeful organisations, whether operating strictly commercially or not). Both these languages are designed to extract and present information held on files. They are therefore low on computational ability but high in file manipulation.

RPG and other similar languages such as FILETAB rely on the commonality of structure of most commercial computer programs, so that they build around a common 'skeleton' and therefore have to provide only the significant details. In the case of RPG, originally designed as its initials suggest for report programs, the details are provided in a set of separate forms — very near to programming by questionnaire. Another description is 'filling in the blanks', indicating that some of the program is already provided in the skeleton. Languages of this type are recently labelled as Fourth Generation languages, indicating that they are increasingly relevant to today's computing because of their ease of use and higher productivity.

COBOL is not a block-structured language but is highly structured into four divisions: identification, environment, data and procedure. It has very highly developed data definition facilities, and procedure statements written in English language rather than symbolic form. It is by far the most widely used language in commercial computers. Software known as a pre-processor may be used with special versions of COBOL that have block-structure facilities added.

PL/1 (Programming Language 1) was designed to combine the best of COBOL and FORTRAN in a block-structured language that would be all-purpose and efficient. It has failed to replace COBOL even within IBM, and has not spread outside IBM except to some microcomputers. It remains as an example of an approach to a programming language that has now completely disappeared. Considerable effort is still being devoted to finding better and cheaper ways of producing programs, and programmers are warned that these efforts are sure to succeed in the not-too-distant future, either through 'natural language programming' or fixed-function programming such as that described above.

Ada is the latest standard HLL, designed by a team on contract to the US Department of Defense for use in real-time systems. It is a complex language, but its impact will be felt during the 1980s since there is no other *de facto* or *de jure* standard in this area of computing.

Beyond this list there is a host of other HLLs, of which Pascal and APL are worth mentioning. Pascal is a programmer's language, used for teaching programming in many colleges because it was designed for and eminently suited to the writing of structured programs. Its use is also spreading on microcomputers for production programs, mainly because of the existence of a portable Pascal programming sub-system, compiler with utilities, known as UCSD Pascal after its source (University College of San Diego, California).

Pascal is also the basis on which Ada was designed. By comparison, APL is a complex and cryptic interactive language with its own set of unique symbols (which requires a separate APL keyboard) but gives greater power for a small amount of code, particularly for throw-away programs.

Whatever programming language is used must be capable of expressing the specified or desired structure, logic and manipulation. Ideally the appropriate language should be used for the task in hand, but choice is restricted (mostly by the availability of the compiler, but also by installation standards: most well-organised computer departments like or require their programmers to use only one HLL).

(b) Common features of programming languages

The large number of HLLs in use, and their difference of type, make it difficult to describe them in more than very general terms, which is why most 'Introduction to Programming' texts (including *Mastering Computer Programming* in this series) illustrate only one language in detail. It is, however, true to say that all programming languages possess certain features in common.

(i) Input/output instructions

All languages need statements which cause data to be transferred from one part of the computer system to another. This could be to or from a terminal in the case of an interactive computer system, using words such as INPUT/ACCEPT or PRINT/DISPLAY which will cause data to be transferred between the terminal and main memory. The words READ and WRITE are usually associated with the transfer of data between files and main memory.

(ii) Jump instructions (transfer of control)

A jump instruction is an instruction which causes not the next instruction in sequence of the program to be executed but an instruction situated in some other part of the program. Such instructions are said to be either unconditional, a peremptory GOTO a part of the program identified by a unique label, or a conditional jump which depends on the truth or otherwise of an assertion.

A conditional jump will always involve a logical test of the form IF (some assertion) THEN (a directive). Logical assertions usually contain one of six relational operators. These are:

$$
\begin{aligned}
&= &&\text{Equal to} \\
&\neq &&\text{Not equal to} \\
&> &&\text{Greater than} \\
&< &&\text{Less than} \\
&>= &&\text{Greater than or equal to} \\
&<= &&\text{Less than or equal to}
\end{aligned}
$$

For example a conditional jump would be of the form:

IF PAY $>$ = 5000 THEN GOTO INCREASE-PAY

This means that the part of the program labelled INCREASE-PAY is the next to be executed if PAY is greater than or equal to 5000. If the test of the value of PAY fails (that is, it is less than 5000) the next instruction in sequence is executed and the jump to INCREASE-PAY is not made. In some languages the form is:

IF . . . THEN . . . ELSE . . .

Conditions may also be expressed in other forms, such as:

PERFORM . . . UNTIL

(iii) Arithmetic instructions
All HLLs allow for the performance of arithmetic on pieces of data by statements such as:

(LET) AVERAGE = TOTAL/NUMBER

but beware of the use of the = sign which has a very special meaning in this context. It is actually used here as an assignment instruction, saying that the result of the calculation performed on the right hand side is assigned to the variable on the left hand side, and in some languages is replaced by ← for this purpose. The use of the word LET is used in some versions of the BASIC HLL as a reminder of the assignment role played by the = sign. Symbols for addition and subtraction are used as normal in arithmetic but / is used for *divide* and * for *multiply*.

The up-arrow, ↑, is used for *raise to the power* (sometimes ** is used) and together with a liberal use of brackets these enable complicated formulae to be evaluated, at least in languages designed for that purpose. Any book on programming in a specific language will detail the way it performs its arithmetic functions.

(iv) Looping instructions
These allow a section of code to be repeated either a fixed number of times or until a pre-determined condition is reached. Some mechanism is provided in HLLs to define the start and finish of a loop — words such as DO, REPEAT, FOR for the start and UNDO, CONTINUE, NEXT for the end.

(v) Data definitions
These are usually statements about certain variables to be used within a program and state at the outset whether certain variables are to be treated as integers, complex numbers, lists of numbers or strings of characters, for example. The nature and extent of data definitions in a program depend

entirely on the HLL. For example, the data definitions available in a language such as BASIC are very restricted but in PASCAL they are very varied to the extent that the user can define his own data types.

(vi) Comments and remarks
See Section 6.6.

(vii) Subroutine and subprogram facilities
If a program is structured so that different parts can be executed independently of the main logical flow of the program then two mechanisms are required: a *naming mechanism* so that sections of the program can be uniquely identified and defined, and a *calling mechanism* so that one section of program can control another, known as a *subprogram*.

Subroutines are strictly separately compiled and stored programs which can be 'called' by another program and executed at that point, with a subroutine CALL statement. There may be a library of subroutines for such tasks as the calculation of square roots, evaluation of logarithms, and so on, provided by the manufacturer as part of the compiler for each language, but the programmer may also define and produce his own subroutines. An advantage is that a subroutine does not have to be written in the same language as the main program, and so, for example, a program written in a commercial language may CALL a FORTRAN subroutine for a special piece of mathematical work. The most important set of subroutines provided (in systems software, see Chapter 7) for use by application programs are subroutine packages (called 'access methods' or 'housekeeping packages') which perform (or rather initiate) READ/WRITE operations required by an I/O instruction, by a call to the system software (supervisor call). There may be separate packages to perform the different types of record access described in Chapter 5.

A similarly organised 'library' of *source code* routines is known as a *'macro' library*. Macros are consolidated into a program, either by using the macro-name as a pseudo-instruction (as for functions) or with a separate instruction such as COPY or INCLUDE. Several programming languages provide both short pre-written sections of code for common *'functions'* such as square root, and also allow the programmer to define his own functions. They are then usable just like program instructions: LET Y = SQR(X). Fig. 6.8 shows the essential difference between these forms.

6.5 PROGRAM TESTING

The only useful programs are those that work, and work every time. Errors, or bugs, prevent this happening and the object of testing and

Fig 6.8 *subroutine and subprogram facilities*

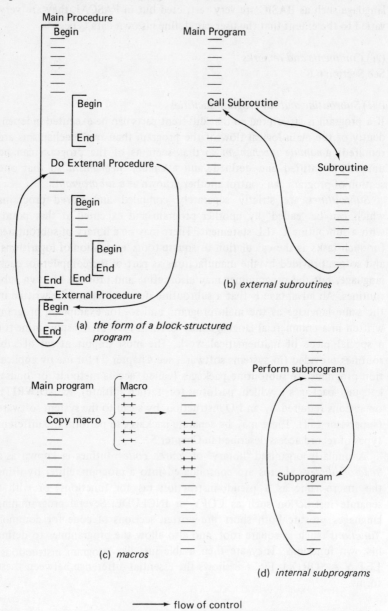

Main Procedure

Begin

Begin

End

Do External Procedure

Begin

Begin

Begin

End

End End

External Procedure

Begin

End

(a) *the form of a block-structured program*

Main Program

Call Subroutine

Subroutine

(b) *external subroutines*

Main program

Copy macro

Macro
++
++
++
++
++
++

++
++
++

(c) *macros*

Perform subprogram

Subprogram

(d) *internal subprograms*

⟶ flow of control

debugging is to eliminate errors in computer programs. There are two sources of error at this level, firstly in the formal 'syntax' (that is, grammar/spelling) of the code, and secondly through defective program logic. It is therefore necessary to plan and follow through a series of *compilations* to eliminate source code bugs, and then a series of *trial executions* (a sequence that is repeated if source code is changed after a trail run) — after, of course, the programmer has made every effort to check that his code is correct and complete, by desk-checking or dry-testing, or having a colleague check it for him.

(a) Compiling

Compiling is the process of executing a compiler (taken to mean any program which translates from an HLL into an executable machine code program) with an input file comprising part or all of a program in a programming language.

As Fig 6.7 shows, the input to the compiler can first be written on a coding sheet and then punched on to an input medium or directly from a keyboard. The output can be in printed form, or displayed on a VDU. A compiler has two functions, the first to produce error diagnostics when it finds errors in the source code submitted to it, and the second to translate correct code. Some compilers are in fact more, or solely, biased towards the first function, leaving the production of efficient code to another compiler.

Compilers which work interactively may produce an error diagnostic, if required, after every line submitted to it (known as line-by-line syntax checking). This helps because an error at an early stage in a program can cause a series of errors later on. 'Batch' compilers on the other hand produce a whole list of errors at the end of the compilation. Some examples of error diagnostics are shown below, selected from a variety of machines and languages.

```
?SRTNSS NO SUCH SWITCH AS '*SORTOU.DAT

? INITIAL PART OF STATEMENT NEITHER MATCHES A STATEMENT KEYWORD NOR HAS
 A FORM LEGAL FOR AN IMPLIED LET---CHECK FOR MISSPELLING IN LINE 110

%FILE NOT FOUND -- SOTRIN.DAT

ERROR****(267)IF-STATEMENT MUST BE TERMINATED BY "." OR "WHEN"

***** WARNING: BUFFERSIZE CALCULATED WITH MAXIMUM HEADER

OUT OF BOUNDS ERROR AT LINE 1360

STNO 166 ERR 356 LVL E PART OF STATEMENT MISSING
```

The mark of a good (error-detecting) compiler is the amount of information given in an error-message:

"Line 80 – Syntax Error" is not a professional effort.

Instructions which are incorrect have to be resubmitted. The easiest way is to have originally created a source code file on disc, and then to use another software program known as the *editor* to change the offending instruction on the file; alternatively it may be necessary to replace the incorrect instruction by submitting another version and updating the source code file. The most inconvenient way is to have to resubmit the entire source file on cards, having replaced the incorrect instruction with a new card.

(b) Testing

A program test is a trial execution of a program or program module with specially prepared input data – 'test data'.

Testing is the most time-consuming part of programming, which is probably why it is most often neglected. Since the object of writing a program is to make it work, it is essential that every path through the program is explored so that as near 100 per cent reliability as possible is obtained for the program. Without it, all the effort put into writing the program will go to waste.

Test data must be produced for every combination of circumstances that the program has been designed to meet (and perhaps also some unanticipated), and the expected results for each test run must be pre-calculated for checking against the results achieved.

Testing also has to be a planned process, particularly for a structured/ hierarchical program. Although top-down design (working from the specification towards the code) is an accepted strategy, there are two alternative testing strategies – top-down and bottom-up. Top-down testing means writing and testing the highest levels of modules first, which means making 'dummy' entries for the lower level of code 'called' by them. *Bottom-up* testing is the coding and testing of the lowest level modules first, which means testing part-programs. Special software is required to compile and test (part-program) modules – known as *module test harnesses*, or *drivers* – in the absence of the high-level modules which control them.

A programming language that provides for subroutine or function libraries, or for separate procedures to be compiled into 'load modules', will require a phase of development known as *link-editing* or *consolidation*, which is exactly as the name implies, a formal consolidation of all the object code into one named object program.

It is this object program that is the one that is finally executed by the computer and it has to contain every piece of code necessary for the implementation of the orginal specification. The job of the final link-editing phase is therefore to tie up all the subroutine calls to library subroutines, all the I/O routines which are handled by the systems software and all the separately written subroutines, which form part of the suite of programs, into a complete 'run-time' packet. This is then stored away on a disc file so that at the appropriate command this complete packet of machine code can be loaded into storage and immediately executed.

The importance of properly planned and executed tests is also indicated by the trend towards providing such software assistance, in the form of a 'programming environment', specifically along with, and as part of, a programming language – so MASCOT with CORAL, APSE with Ada, and the Programmers Work Bench in Unix (see next chapter).

6.6 PROGRAM DOCUMENTATION

Given that about 50 per cent of the total programming effort and costs are attributable to program maintenance, it is common sense to write programs for easy maintenance. Part of this objective is reached by documenting programs to make their structure and operation understandable. We have already seen some formal documentation relating to a program – its specification and design diagrams. Formal operational documentation that is, ideally, produced during the testing stage, consists of two forms: program comments and external write-ups.

Programming languages all allow the programmer to insert *comments* into the program text – lines introduced by an identifying symbol or pseudo-opcode which are bypassed by the compiler. These should be used to identify the program and sections, and to provide instructions on how to use them. In the case of interactive programs, operational instructions should be contained in the program's dialogue at the terminal, or assistance should be available if required by requesting 'HELP', which should throw up a detailed narrative on to the screen. Beyond this, the way that a programmer names his variables and his code sections should make their function clear by mnemonic names wherever possible, while indentation and layout of code should also help to clarify structure.

The programmer should also produce some additional documentation to accompany the program specification, his working documents and the program listing:
- flowcharts and other diagrams;
- operating instructions;
- test data and results.

These should all be put together as a formal program file with index, contents list and amendment list. This is the basis for further program maintenance, and must be kept up to date when changes are made to the program.

SPECIMEN QUESTIONS

1. (a) Describe the operation of key-to-disc devices. Give an example of the use of this form of data input and comment on the benefits of its introduction.

   (b) What is meant by an Optical Character Reader? Briefly discuss the benefits of an OCR device, with the aid of a relevant example.

2. Describe (i) magnetic disc and (ii) magnetic tape storage devices. In each case name two different types of device, and give one typical application for each case. Name two advantages of disc storage and two of tape storage. *

3. What is a Local Area Network? Describe how it can be of use in organising the use of microcomputers in schools.

4. What is meant by an 'application package'? Give two examples of such packages and comment on their content. Assess why packages are bought for (a) mainframe computers, (b) microcomputers. *

5. The feasibility study is one of the main stages in Systems Analysis. Name the other main stages and indicate the logical order in which they would be performed, and why. Describe what is involved in one of these stages. *

6. (a) Explain the concept of a data base.

   (b) Explain each of the following methods of organising a disc file: (i) sequential, (ii) indexed sequential, (iii) direct or random.

7. State and explain the fundamental steps involved between the definition of a problem and the execution of a computer program to solve that problem. Briefly describe how the correctness of a program may be established, and name other characteristics of a successful program. *

8. State the main purposes of program documentation. Discuss how it may be produced, and assess the potential consequences of using a program without the corresponding documentation.

9. What is meant by the term 'structured programming'?

   Why are sub-programs needed in the development of structured programs, and what are the benefits of producing programs in this way? *

CHAPTER 7

RUNNING PROGRAMS

After the process described in Chapters 5 and 6, the programs and related procedures can then be operated, hopefully for the purpose originally intended. The operation of computer-based systems will be covered in this and the following chapter. Just as a computer program comprises executable statements and data definitions, so running a program involves *initiating and controlling program execution* and the *preparation, marshalling and input of data* to that program during execution; and equally it requires the availability of a processor/storage system, set up and ready for the program, which is the subject of Chapter 8.

7.1 PREPARING DATA FOR A PROGRAM

Since the function of a computer program is to process data and produce results, it follows that either before or at the very start of a program execution, it is necessary to have prepared or have available the data required; or alternatively to ensure that the program can be run whenever, or as soon as, the data is available. Which of these two alternatives will be followed, *routine-dominated execution* or *event-dominated execution*, will depend upon the nature of the task, and the choice is also affected by the timescale and distance between the data arising and its processing.

Many business and non-business activities are performed according to a regular routine, as is the nature of organised life, and since computing assists in such work, many computer program suites are run regularly according to an operational schedule which reflects normal business patterns — weekly salaries, monthly salaries, daily warehouse dispatches, etc. For these regular runs, all the data that has occurred since the previous run will be accumulated, regardless of volume, into one or more batches, and then processed as a batch. *Batch processing* is both a continuation of previous data processing practice, and a contribution to operational efficiency, in that the delay between the data occurring and its processing provides time for carefully planned preparation for processing; it also, incidentally, makes best use of a processor in that a program is only loaded and started once for a large number of iterations of the inner loop (see Section 6.3). The time-scale will also, in most cases, allow for transportation of data from branches and other locations to a centralised computing function. The computer industry has well-developed procedures for data preparation in these circumstances (see Section 7.2).

Other business activities, like other aspects of real life, require that as soon as an event occurs and data originates, it should be processed without the delay inherent in batch processing. *Transaction processing* implies the immediacy of event-dominated computing, whether real-time, in that a reply has to be given within the time-scale of the wider activity, or pseudo-real-time, in that the immediacy is one of convenience rather than necessity. Most of the transactions of this type, such as requests, bookings and enquiries, occur at the point of sale or point of customer contact, and thus too far away to permit the direct use of centralised computing equipment except by *data transmission* (see Section 4.4) and by input and output at a *terminal* (see Section 4.3).

7.2 BATCHED DATA PREPARATION

The objectives of data preparation are to ensure that:
- all the data that the user has is submitted and processed;
- it is as error free as possible.

(a) Data control
Control over data is a joint exercise. In the department(s) where the data originates or arrives, transactions are recorded, checked and accumulated into batches. For each batch, a batch control sheet or card is produced, containing a sequentially allocated batch number, the transaction total and a check total (either a summation of a variable, such as order quantity, or a total of document numbers). Completeness may also be aided by giving each transaction a sequentially numbered identification — for internally raised documents these can be pre-printed. The data will then be recorded into the computer department by a data control clerk, and will remain as a batch through data preparation and some if not all stages of processing. The completeness of the batch by transaction counts or sequence number will be checked during processing.

(b) Error control
Errors in input data are the bane of computing (GIGO — garbage in, garbage out — applies). The *avoidance* of errors goes right back to the form of data input, avoiding copying or transcription if at all possible.

If not, then the original document containing the data needs to be specifically designed as a punching document, from which the data preparation operator will punch either on to a medium or directly into a computer file. Such documents, with boxes for characters and internal column number, will be familiar to many people who belong to consumer organisations; an example is shown in Fig. 7.1. If this is not achievable, then it may still be necessary to copy data from the original document on to a punching sheet to give the data preparation operator a clean data source. The completion of original or punching documents needs to be guided by formal instructions, the preparation of which is one of the responsibilities of the systems analyst during implementation.

The *detection* of errors starts with a repeat performance of input punching on the same cards, etc., or a visual check by the same operator before the record is released, known as *verification*. It continues in the first processing run on the batch of data along with the batch control header, in which a number of checks are performed, known as *data vet* or *data validation*:

- records read against input transaction total and computed check total against input check total;
- check digit verification — many key numbers have an extra digit attached which is produced by the result of a mathematical operation on the original digits (usually a modulus 11 operation — sum the weighted digits, divide by 11 and take remainder). The ISBN book number is one such code. Recalculating the check digit and comparing the result with the original will detect an error in that field;
- programmed checks for data type, value range and key field value on file.

Errors detected are then corrected, and re-input until the entire batch is clean before full processing begins.

The same process, up to data validation, applies to any type of input device used for batched data preparation, whether off-line on to cards or magnetic media, or on-line by direct data entry into internal storage (the terms 'off-line' and 'on-line' were discussed in detail in Section 2.2). It is also possible to input data directly for batch processing, from a remote terminal, though in most cases a batch would be created locally and then transmitted as a batch.

7.3 DATA INPUT AT A TERMINAL

It is difficult to over-emphasise the importance of terminals in computing today. They are more than just an input device, more than just a remote device — they are, to very many people, the embodiment of the computer and, if present trends continue, they will constitute, with built-in processors, the vast majority of the world's population of computers. Terminals

Fig 7.1 *computer input punching document (courtesy of the Automobile Association)*

CAR INSURANCE
CHECK-UP REQUEST

Please use BLOCK CAPITALS

About yourself   initials   Surname

Mr Mrs Miss

Membership No. (if applicable)

Address

Post Code

Telephone No. Day

Eve.

Occupation(s) .... Employer's Business ....

About your car

Make and model of car including details of modifications

....

....

Reg. No.

Engine cc .... Year of manufacture 19   Value £

When do you use your car?   *please delete the word that does not apply.*

In addition to private use, will the car be used for:

  (a) Driving to work on three or more days a week?   NO YES*

  If **YES**, name city, town or suburb where you work ....

  (b) Business use by yourself only?   NO YES*

  (c) Business use by any other person?   NO YES*

  (d) Commercial travelling?   NO YES*

What cover do you want?

Please tick type of cover you require:

Comprehensive ☐ Third Party Fire & Theft ☐ Third Party Only ☐

If you wish to reduce the premium by bearing the cost of any damage to your car indicate (√) the appropriate amount:

up to £25 ☐ up to £50 ☐ up to £100 ☐

Please indicate (√) who will drive the vehicle:

  (a) Yourself only

  (b) Yourself and wife husband only   In case of (b) and (c) please give

  (c) Yourself and one named driver only   details of other driver or in the case

  (d) Any licensed driver   of (d) of youngest known driver.

        Age   yrs.

  Length full UK Driving Licence held yrs.

When would you like cover to start?   day month year

(Indicate when your present insurance ends).

On that date:

  (a) How old will you be?   yrs.

  (b) How long will you have held a full UK driving licence?   yrs.

  (c) Will you have been resident in the UK for 3 or more years?

  (d) How many years No Claim Discount   yrs.

    will you be claiming in your own right?

Have you or any other person who will drive the car:

  (a) Been convicted or have pending any prosecutions for a motoring offence?   NO YES*

  (b) Been involved in any accident or loss regardless of blame

    in the last five years?   NO YES*

  (c) Suffer from any physical disability or infirmity e.g. heart disease etc?   NO YES*

If you have answered **YES** to (a), (b), or (c), please give details on a separate sheet.

Registered Office: Fanum House Basingstoke Hants RG21 2EA Regd. No. 912191 England.

FOR OFFICE USE ONLY

S i

948

NO OBLIGATION

can be classified according to their mode of usage, into fully interactive and semi-interactive.

By *interactive* we mean a pattern of computer use in which there is frequent interaction between the system and the user in the form of question and answer or input and response, item by item, line by line, or record by record. *Conversational* is also used with the same meaning. Interactive programming means computer programming in a language which gives a response after each instruction, interactive I/O means a program in which each piece of data is requested from the terminal user and checked item by item. The form that this interaction takes, between the system or program output on a screen or printer, and the user input on keyboard, is known as a *terminal* or *man-machine dialogue*, and is one of the most important parts of program design for terminal input.

Semi-interactive means, in the same way, a process in which there is less interaction. Output from the system only at the end of an execution, or a stream of data input at a terminal for subsequent delayed batch processing, would qualify as semi-interactive. A particularly common form of terminal use with local storage media (see data collection terminals in Section 4.3) is collecting data (interactively or not) and then submitting it to the processor at the end of a shift or day. This is known as:
- *remote job entry* (RJE) if accompanied by commands to initiate the processing;
- *remote batch entry* (RBE) if purely data;
- *conversational* RJE/RBE if there is an interaction in inputting the data only.

Data input at a terminal needs particular care because in some cases (that is, real-time or pseudo-real-time) the source of the data is lost immediately after the transaction is processed, and also because there is no time for the careful preparation of data, starting with data input instructions and through to data validation, as in the case of batched input. The same principles, however, have to be followed, and have to be built into the form of interactive dialogue between the terminal user at his keyboard and the system, via the display screen or printer.

The first objective of a *terminal dialogue* is to prompt, invite and guide the terminal user/operator to input the correct data and complete data. The terminal user will particularly need guidance if he is only an occasional user, or if the structure of the data is complex, guidance which in batch data input can be provided by instruction manuals. There are a number of different methods for providing this guidance, of which the most important are *menus* and *forms control*.

Menus are lists of options displayed or printed out from which the user has to select by typing in the appropriate number or keyword. The act of selection inputs a particular value, or causes a further menu list to be printed out, or causes output to be displayed at the terminal. A very good example of a menu-driven terminal (although primarily for output selection) is provided by the Prestel service, which at the beginning of an enquiry provides an option list covering *all* the information available. Entering a number from 1 to 9 then provides a further list of options, and so on, depending on the information required, until the bottom level of classification is reached and the full data page is displayed. Fig. 7.2 shows such a menu-driven search for information about cinema shows in Cardiff.

Menu-driven input is particularly important in some sales/order input systems in which different materials or products have significantly different characteristics, options or alternatives. Not all data, however, can be selected from lists of alternatives, and the prompting for such data can best be performed by either a straight printed *request/instruction*:

ENTER SURNAME

or a straight *keyword* prompt:

SURNAME?

perhaps with format or dimension instruction:

SURNAME (UP TO 20 CHARACTERS)?

Forms control is the displaying on to the screen of the blank outline of a form (of the type which could be used if the information were being input on a form of convenient batch data preparation). The cursor is then moved, by program control, into the first data field position to await input, and from there to the next, again guiding the terminal user to provide all the data necessary. Fig. 7.3 shows an example of a form-driven input procedure for sales order input.

Whatever the form of the dialogue, it is essential that the data input under the guidance of the instructions is rigorously checked for validity *at that point*, and errors sent back to the terminal to initiate a re-input. Equally it is important for the terminal user to know that his input has been accepted as valid. If the terminal is not intelligent, error checking will require a transmission to the remote computer, a process which may induce errors from the transmission process and cause a re-transmission or even a re-input request.

Unless the terminal is being used as a direct data entry station, in which the same procedures apply as for batch, it is more difficult to ensure completeness of all data transactions, but it is usual for the computer to allocate a sequential transaction number to each set of data submitted to it and to use that number for subsequent throughput checking.

7.4 PROGRAM EXECUTION AND SYSTEMS SOFTWARE

(a) Systems software
When data is ready or available for processing, a program can be started up,

Fig. 7.2 *a menu driven terminal dialogue: X indicates user selection by pressing the appropriate key on a Prestel keypad (see Fig. 4.9). In the Prestel service it is also possible to look up the detailed page numbers directly in the manual classified directory or to use an alphabetical index*

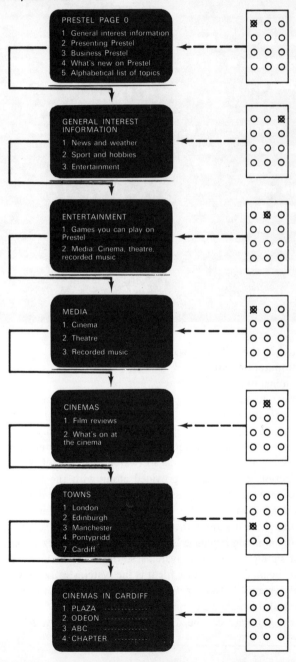

Fig 7.3   *forms control display* □ − *cursor;* [ ] − *data input fields*

```
OUR ORDER NO.      000022        CUSTOMER       FOR AMENDMENTS  :-

CUSTOMER ORDER NO [█        ]     ORDER FORM     TYPE '1' = CANCEL

ACCOUNT NO.        [        ]    -- PAGE 1. --   TYPE '2' = NEW QUANTITY

                                ----------------  TYPE '3' = NEW DELIVERY

     DESCRIPTION     STOCK NO.  QUANTITY REQUIRED  TYPE OF AMEND.   NEW WEEK NO.

  DEVON TOFFEES      ABC1      [        ]          [ ]              [ ]

  BARLEY SUGAR       ABC2      [        ]          [ ]              [ ]

  WINE GUMS          ABC3      [        ]          [ ]              [ ]

  BUTTER SCOTCH      ABC4      [        ]          [ ]              [ ]

  JELLY BABIES       ABC5      [        ]          [ ]              [ ]

  LIQUORICE ALLSORTS ABC6      [        ]          [ ]              [ ]

  SYSTEM MESSAGE AREA [F1]                         LAST ORDER NO. 000021
```

or initiated, in the following ways:

- by a computer operator;
- by a terminal user;
- by commands fed into it along with the program, or from another program;
- by an external signal.

The process of initiating a program does not involve only the data source, the program and the computer, it primarily requires interaction with, and through, some aspect of 'systems software'. Systems software is an organised collection of programs, provided along with the 'naked' processor, which collectively make it possible for programs to be developed, stored, changed, loaded and run. It is the systems software which handles all the I/O routines and organises the access of data within disc or tape files. In fact a programming language is locked into an operating system, except in the most simple of computer systems, so that when an instruction causes a READ to be made from a disc file it is the systems software which handles this. The systems software acts as an interface between the programming language and the 'naked' computer.

Systems software can be divided into two types: *systems service* and *systems control*. The term 'operating system' is also widely used, sometimes to include both types of function, sometimes restricted to the second, and will be used in this book in the *latter* sense.

Systems service routines are those which have already been mentioned earlier in this book: compilers/assemblers, libraries, editors, testers and utility programs. Their function is to provide service and support for programmers and other users. They need not necessarily be provided by the computer manufacturer, and are often available from software houses and other software sources (see Chapter 8).

Systems control routines, usually called a monitor or supervisor, are concerned with program initiation and execution, and with system management in the context of most computers today which run more than one program concurrently ('multi-programming' – see below). There is a wide range in the scale and type of functions included, and no commonly agreed terms or structure. One common way of looking at systems software is to consider it as a hierarchical structure, each 'layer' moving progressively further away from the naked machine. The lower-level routines are as much a part of the machine as the hardware, and are almost always provided with it. Fig. 7.4 illustrates this view of systems software. There is an increasing trend to implement systems software in firmware, that is, permanently 'blown' on to some form of ROM.

(b) Systems commands – job control and operator commands
The facilities of systems software are used in two ways: firstly by *systems commands* which are explicitly issued by operators, by terminal users and by programmers, and secondly by involuntary *controls* on, and *calls* made by, programs during execution, which the operators, terminal user or programmer cannot see, and of which they may not be aware.

Systems commands are equivalent, at a higher (systems) level, to instructions in an applications programming language, except that their execution, by a systems software routine variously known as the reader/interpreter, or command handler affects either individual (sets of) programs or the whole set of programs currently active in the processor. *Job control commands* relate to jobs, a job being a set of programs (or program-steps) run as one task at one time; *systems control commands* refer to the complete working system and therefore to any or all active jobs. On microcomputers, where only one job is active at a time, normally, the distinction disappears.

(i) Job control commands
These are written in *job control language* (JCL) and effectively form a higher-level program in which the names of application programs and datafiles appear as the operands, as will become clear from the examples which

Fig 7.4 *systems software — the bare machine and its software superstructure*

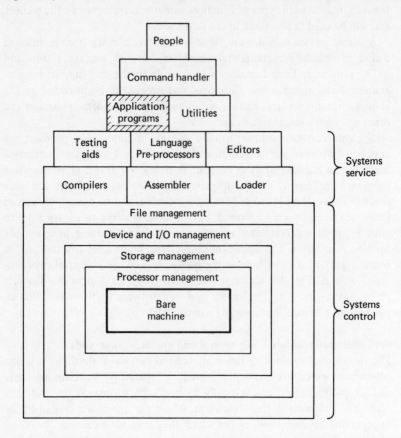

follow. Since there is no standard form of JCL, except in one significant case (those supplied with the BASIC programming language), the examples given are merely representative forms.

(i) To compile a source program

```
COMPILE        prog-name WITH COBOL
EXECUTE        COBOL with prog-name
RUN BASIC
COBOL
```

(ii) To store a program on a library, and remove

```
SAVE   ⎫
STORE  ⎬  prog-name
COMPILE   prog-name TO LIBRARY
```

DELETE }
REMOVE } prog-name or file-name

(iii) To load and run program

GET }
LOAD } prog-name

START }
GO   } prog-name

EXECUTE }
RUN   } prog-name (equivalent to LOAD and START)

CHAIN   prog-name from another program.

(iv) To use utility programs

SORT   file-name on sort-key
LIST }
TYPE } file-name or prog-name
MAIL   file-name to user-name
DUMP   file-name to device-name

(v) To create/change a file

EDIT   }
CREATE } file-name

(vi) To identify input data in files and assign to devices

DATA   file-name (or symbol indicating data in card reader)
ASSIGN   file-name to device-name
FILE   file-name

(vii) To identify a job and password (see below)

JOBNAME . . . PASSWORD . . . ACCOUNT-NO . . .

(viii) To start and end a terminal session

LOGIN, LOGOUT

(ix) To delimit the operation of a previous command

ENDJOB, EOD
(a standard symbol may also be used for END)

The stand-alone commands, for example EXECUTE, may also be qualified, for instance giving a priority to a job, giving a program a time-limit or stating its resource requirements. Also, very important, either as a qualification or as a separate command, conditions may be stated, for example:

> EX prog-name-1 BEFORE prog-name-2
> IF FAIL . . .

Job control commands issued by terminal users, *terminal commands*, are usually simple and clear, influenced by the commands which, uniquely in BASIC, are supplied with the programming language itself, distinguished from program statements only in that you do not require a statement number. In other cases commands are issued whenever the system software prints an invitation symbol on the screen such as @ or *. Terminal commands are normally issued at the time they are needed, and it is in the nature of terminal use that these needs are relatively unpredictable. It is part of the dialogue between a terminal user and the system that a response will be given by the system after each command. The following example shows a typical sequence of commands and responses for a terminal session in which a program is loaded, run and then changed and re-run (the operator input is underlined).

```
@LOGIN GGL-WRIGHT
 Job 20 on TTY52 23-Sep-80 10:26:26

@RUN BASIC

READY, FOR HELP TYPE HELP.
OLD NADADD

READY
RUN

NADADD          10:27          23-SEP-80


                    NAME-AND-ADDRESS FILE ADDITIONS
ENTER YOUR CODE WORD                        ?MACSDH4

ENTER YOUR DATA RECORD ITEM BY ITEM AS REQUESTED

CODE NUMBER         ?45632
SURNAME             ?EVANS
INITIALS            ?NH
TITLE               ?MR
HOUSE AND STREET    ?THE MANSE
TOWN                ?TREHARRIS
COUNTY              ?MID-GLAM
POSTCODE            ?CF469ZZ


RECORD 45632 ACCEPTED ON FILE

ANY MORE RECORDS? ENTER 1 FOR YES, 2 FOR NO    ?2
SIGNING OFF 34 RECORDS ON FILE


TIME:  0.61 SECS.

READY
LIST


NADADD          10:30          23-SEP-80
```

```
5 PRINT TAB(18);"NAME-AND-ADDRESS FILE ADDITIONS"
10 PRINT "ENTER YOUR CODE WORD"; TAB(45);
20 INPUT Z$
   {
   {
1000 END

READY
25 IF Z$="2254" THEN 60
SAVE

? DUPLICATE FILE NAME, REPLACE OR RENAME
READY
REPLACE

READY
RUN

NADADD        10:32        23-SEP-80
```

For batch processing (for example, jobs input from a card-reader), job control commands are prepared in advance, and submitted to a computer either along with a source program or object program, and data, or stored away in a library as a command file ('stored procedure'). Job control commands are prefixed with a special symbol such as // or ?, to distinguish them from program instructions. A typical set of job control commands submitted, along with a source program and test data, to compile and test a COBOL program, could be:

£JOB ... ACCOUNT-NO ... PASSWORD ... (Defines a specific job and references it to a particular programmer)

£COBOL ⎫
       ⎬ source program (Enters program in HLL and compiles it)
       ⎭

£IF FAIL THEN EOJ (Terminate run if program does not work. EOJ = End of Job)

£EXECUTE
£DATA ⎫
      ⎬ (Test data)
      ⎭

£EOD (End of Data)
£EOJ (End of Job)

Job control for routine work would normally operate from stored procedures, with references to a command-file and to data also, usually, stored as a data-file, for example:

```
£JOB . . .
£EXECUTE        £proc-name
£DATA           data-file name
£ EOJ
```

Such stored procedures would normally be very much more complicated than simple commands that application programmers would generate themselves, particularly on large mainframe computers. Their preparation would be the responsibility of a 'systems programmer' whose role is to maintain and use systems software. In such cases the job control language may well be more similar in form to an assembler language, rather than to the high-level language forms illustrated above.

(ii) System control commands

In batch-processing operations jobs are prepared in advance and fed continuously to the system by the operator. System control commands enable the operator to maintain control over the system and *all* the jobs running on it at any one time. They will be typed in at the operator console, and will elicit responses from the system, and may well be prompted by initial error messages or warnings on requests from the system itself. In this case the dialogue is between the system and the operator.

System control commands, for ease of use, are usually simple and clear, and may well be abbreviated as the operator can quickly become accustomed to them. Their use is, however, a key part of the operator's job which, as will be discussed in the next chapter, is concerned with the efficient running of the entire system. System control commands will therefore mostly not be available to a programmer or terminal user except in small business systems where the system is not so complex and where there may be no full-time specialist operator. Typical operator commands will be:

$$\left.\begin{array}{l}\text{START} \\ \text{STOP} \\ \text{HALT} \\ \text{CONTINUE} \\ \text{DISCONTINUE} \\ \text{CANCEL} \\ \text{SET or CHANGE PRIORITIES}\end{array}\right\} \begin{array}{l}\text{individual job or streams of jobs,} \\ \text{or entire system}\end{array}$$

SET TIME and DATE and other options
START the system and CLOSE it down

DISPLAY various items and status

ASSIGN and REMOVE on-line devices
process the system LOG

(c) Operating system functions

One of the operator's first functions at system start-up is to start up the operating system by what is known as a 'bootstrap', usually now automatically from a ROM when power is switched on. The operating system then runs all the time, intermittently between, and in the middle of, application programs. It performs certain functions as the result of job control or system control commands input when a job is loaded or terminated, or whenever the command is received, and other functions according to 'calls' made to it as the result of events occurring during the course of programs' running. These functions can be classified as:

- *processor management* − deciding which jobs are to run and in what way ('scheduling');
- *storage management* − allocating internal storage to programs;
- *I/O management* − controlling the use of devices;
- *file management* − controlling files on backing storage and supporting I/O operations on those files.

The scope and complexity of these functions, and the volume of the software provided to perform them, vary according to the degree of multiple activity in a computer. The task of internal management is one created by specialisation and co-ordination, so that the greater the level of activity inside the computer, the greater is the requirement for it to be centrally controlled. The smallest monitors are those required by single-program computers, and by embedded or dedicated real-time systems; in the first case because the sequence of activities is relatively straightforward, and in the second case because the alternatives are restricted by the environment.

(i) *Processor management and multi-programming*

Complexity is unavoidably generated in most other types of computers by the operating regime of '*multi-programming*'. Multi-programming means multiple program operations on one computer, in which there will be more than one applications program resident in internal storage (along with storage reserved for the use of the operating system). This gives the impression that the computer is executing more than one program at a time. Its prime objective is to ensure that the processor is as continuously in use as possible, by enabling another program to use it when one program has (temporarily) to discontinue using it. (In a single-processor computer, only one program can actually be in control of the processor at any one time.)

Reasons why a program may be unable to use the processor continuously and/or have to relinquish control of it, include:

- it issues a READ/WRITE request to a peripheral which operates independently of the processor, thus causing a call to I/O software;
- another program's READ/WRITE request is completed and that program is ready to continue;
- a hardware or software fault;
- a normal halt or termination;
- a higher priority program, or a previously suspended program, is ready to (re-) use it.

(ii) The interrupt

When more than one program resides in storage at any one time the switching of control is by a simple but extremely powerful mechanism known as the 'interrupt'. It is primarily a hardware feature which:
- recognises the occurrence of certain events;
- stops the processor from continuing with a program after the current instructions have been completed;
- stores away information related to that program, mainly the contents of the IAR (that is, the address of the next instruction to be performed) in the status register or a specially reserved area in internal storage;
- causes a branch to a systems software routine which determines the cause of the interrupt and the next action to be taken – usually the passing of control to another program whose status information is reloaded in the IAR, etc., from the stored area.

Originally the interrupt was provided to enable a high-priority program to be initiated when required by an external signal (an *external* interrupt) indicating that data is incoming and has to be processed immediately. This is how a program is loaded and run in an interactive system. The interrupt is caused by the person at a terminal typing a command such as RUN.

The combination of internal and external interrupts allows for the highest priority to be given to real-time programs, normal priority to I/O-intensive programs, and low priority to compute-bound programs. Interrupts can also be generated deliberately, for instance to cause a timer to interrupt a program if it has been running without a break for longer than a fixed time-slice of a few milliseconds. This permits the sharing of a processor among multi-access users. Fig. 7.5 shows how interrupts operate to effect multi-programming.

(iii) Distributed computing

Multi-programming also requires the other resources of the computer either to be shared among the concurrently active or to be allocated to one (group) of them. It is common practice to segregate common programs by their resource requirements and load them for execution in streams or queues accordingly. In fact, the demands of storage, device and file manage-

Fig 7.5 *multi-programming and interrupts*

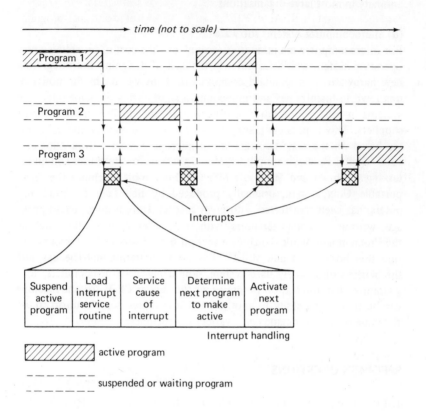

ment are very much more demanding than those of processor switching and allocation, and collectively contribute to the situation that the time and space on the machine taken up by operating systems routines almost wipe out the gains in machine efficiency which multi-programming contributes. The inescapable size and complexity of large machine software are reasons why systems designers are deliberately exploiting the lower costs of hardware by moving away from central mainframes into linked groups of smaller machines with simpler software – a process known as *'distributed computing'*.

The related process of putting processing power into terminals and other devices also contributes to the simplification of the work of 'proper' processors. *Distributed* systems, incorporating both distributed computers linked by data transmission, and distributed intelligence, finally enable computing power to be provided at the user's elbow, in keeping with the organisational trend of decentralised company operations. Centralised computing, incurring heavy data transmission costs, has long been an anomaly in most large organisations.

(d) Microcomputer systems software

For microcomputer manufacturers/assemblers, the cost of providing a new operating system would far outstrip the cost of designing and integrating new hardware from standard components. Thus we are in the position, unknown in mainframes and minicomputers, of having the same operating systems in use on a number of otherwise distinct models from different suppliers. This is possible mainly because most commercial microsystems are based on the same two families of microprocessors – from Zilog and Intel. Digital Research supply CP/M and versions for multi-user and multi-tasking machines and Microsoft MSDOS. For 16-bit machines the semi-portable Unix system, originally produced by Bell Labs for minicomputers, has been transferred with great success. Unix is an excellent package, written by computer users, with some interesting utilities, such as the Programmers Work Bench (see section 6.5). Users of 8-bit micros will find that both CP/M and MSDOS have some irritating inefficiences, but the benefits of a widely used system, supporting the same compilers, does guarantee that application programs written under CP/M for one machine can be transferred easily to another, and it is at least some comfort to use the same system commands on a variety of machines.

SPECIMEN QUESTIONS

1. (a) State three of the aims of an operating system and briefly describe how each of them are achieved in a system known to you.
   (b) What is the purpose of a bootstrap loader and why is it so called?
   (c) Briefly describe the design and functions of a job scheduler. *

2. (a) Distinguish between multi-programming and multi-access. Outline the methods by which each is achieved by an operating system and indicate the effects of the user.
   (b) Give four examples of interrupts.
   (c) Give two examples of utilities that are provided with a modern operating system and show how a programmer could take advantage of them. *

3. Whatever form of data processing is employed, the design of source documents is of prime importance. What are the features of good source document design, and how else should these features be observed in operating a computer-based business procedure?

CHAPTER 8

ACQUIRING COMPUTER HARDWARE AND SOFTWARE

Whether for an individual or an organisation, a computer represents a sizeable financial outlay, and one which is complicated by several factors: the need to obtain both hardware and software before the computer can be used, the need to secure services to keep it going, a high rate of technical obsolescence, and last but not least a supplying industry which is one of the last refuges of the hard sell. In the entire manufacturing and service sectors of the industry, the salesman is king, and it is not surprising therefore that *caveat emptor* applies very strongly. At the same time this gives an advantage to a buyer who operates from a position of strength and knowledge.

8.1 SOURCES OF HARDWARE

The intending purchaser today is in a much stronger position than his predecessor of fifteen years ago, in that he can select from a wide variety of machines offered for sale by a range of different types of organisations:
- computer manufacturers;
- independent terminal and peripheral manufacturers;
- selling companies;
- systems builders;
- brokers;
- leasing companies;
- retail shops.

(a) Computer manufacturers
The mainframe computer manufacturers and some of the larger minicomputer manufacturers maintain national and regional marketing organisations (and in some cases agents), and their marketing costs are reputed to be a high proportion of their selling prices. However, computer marketing traditionally requires a high degree of pre- and post-sales support, without

which the spread of computing would have been very much slower. Computing has grown on the backs of these manufacturers, and the assurance of their support is still one of the main reasons why companies choose one machine rather than another.

No potential user is likely to be unaware of these companies; their marketing database is usually very thorough on current and potential customers, and their approach is both personal and direct.

The smaller minicomputer manufacturers, and some of the specialist mainframe manufacturers operate with national sales forces only, often operating in specialist areas. For instance, there is a sub-sector of the industry, in both computer and terminal/mainframe sales, which specialises in making equipment identical to IBM, and supporting IBM software, but with a better cost–performance ratio; this is known as the plug-compatible market.

(b) Terminal and peripheral manufacturers

The relatively high prices and profit margins of the mainframe manufacturers also provided the opening for independent manufacturers of terminals and peripherals, many of whom also supplied their products as system components for larger companies. These manufacturers work on a 'high volume equals low cost' basis, and bring their products to the notice of potential customers by trade publicity, and particularly through annual trade exhibitions. The proliferation of terminals is, to an outsider, bewildering; a current trade index lists over 250 models of VDU terminals alone, and prices and services are highly competitive. By virtue of their size, and the easier connectability to any computer, their products are more easily demonstrable, and salesmen are more than willing to bring them to your front door when asked.

With some exceptions (which time and 'production under licence' are continuously removing), customers have a wide choice of suppliers in this area, particularly as many of these products are also sold by selling agencies.

(c) Selling agencies

These companies operate solely as retailing organisations, and are a relatively new addition to the hardware-supplier scene, some specifically formed and others getting into the business from related sectors such as office equipment. They are particularly rewarding in that it is often possible to buy products from them at a lower cost than from the original manufacturer. They also operate principally through trade advertising. However, they rarely offer mainframes or minicomputers; for alternative suppliers of computers, a customer has to go to one of three sources — the systems builders, the brokers or the leasing companies.

(d) System builders

This term identifies a group of related hardware sources, whose particular distinction is that they buy-in processors and other hardware from original equipment manufacturers (OEMs) and build additional hardware and software into an added-value product. In some cases this product retains the identity of the OEM; in other cases the label changes and the product is sold entirely under the new title. DEC and Texas Instruments computers form the basis for a host of small business systems, and also of key–disc systems, and microcomputers and other MPUs are at the heart of most word processing systems. Equally many turnkey systems (complete working packages of hardware and software) are sold without such badge engineering, and it is often very helpful for a customer to know the origin of the essential components of such a system.

Most microcomputers and personal computers also appear as built systems, on the foundation of Zilog, Intel or Motorola chips, and the economics of micro-electronics mean that all except the largest companies are buying in MPUs to build into their products.

(e) Brokers

The selling policies of the mainframe computer manufacturers, and the ever-improving cheapness and performance of their products, have fostered a mystique of newness among most computer users. When IBM announced their 303X models, the rush of orders virtually overnight would have doubled the world's computing capacity. The trend away from direct purchase has also meant that there are fewer computer users with second-hand machines to sell (part-exchange is not much in practice at the moment).

There is therefore, a very under-developed second-hand market, and computer brokers form the bulk of this supply sector, operating much as brokers do in any business, by inside knowledge and business expertise. For any customer who does not have to possess the latest glossy model, a second-hand machine is usually priced as an absolute bargain, but there are few companies who will openly admit to using them. It is something of a mystery, in fact, as to where all the displaced 360s and 1900s end up; many schools have benefited from low-price second-hand machines or even give-aways, and there have been rumours of remote and mysterious graveyards and dumping grounds.

It should not be a disadvantage to be using second-hand machines for most straightforward computing, since the obstacle of obtaining maintenance for them has now been overcome (see later sections of this chapter).

(f) Leasing companies

Leasing of computers was a phenomenon that first appeared in the late 1960s, although leasing of other capital equipment such as aircraft is widespread. Leasing companies are financial organisations who will buy computers directly from manufacturers and then lease them to customers, and in general represent the only way of acquiring a new mainframe computer other than directly from the manufacturer. At the end of the lease of course, the machine reverts to the leasing company who then has to dispose' of it as a second-hand machine. Many computer manufacturers operate leasing themselves, and most independent leasing works with IBM equipment.

(g) Retail shops

Retail shops are the latest phenomenon to appear, associated with the arrival of personal and home computers, simply because these machines are too cheap to support separate marketing organisations. They are a growth business in our towns and cities, over one hundred now operate in the United Kingdom with little publicity, word passing quickly among the *cognoscenti*. Post-sales support is a problem, particularly as the movement is so new and appears to work on a shoestring.

8.2 FINANCING HARDWARE – PURCHASE, RENTAL AND LEASING

This is one of the major controversial areas in computing at the moment, and the potential purchaser is warned to beware of entrenched positions. Straightforward *direct purchase* is, in principle, the cheapest way to pay for equipment: all the rights of ownership, including tax allowances and investment grants go with it. The disadvantages of purchasing are both the need to dispose of second-hand equipment, and the cost of financing your own purchase, either by tying up cash instead of using it productively in your business, or by borrowing it from banks or elsewhere, in which case you are at the mercy of fluctuating interest rates and overdraft recalls. Originally, also, the very high cost of computers, in an area of a company not used to capital investment, meant that financial directors were unwilling to authorise outright purchase.

The first alternative to purchase was *rental*. Rental gives usage rights, but not tax advantages (though some companies will pass on special regional investment grants in lower rentals), and rental charges can be disguised as revenue operating costs. Manufacturers have traditionally fixed their monthly rental charges in a way which brought large profits to them; currently mainframe rentals are about 1/36 of purchase price, and terminal/peripheral rentals about 1/30. Rental is an advantage therefore for usage periods of up to three years, and is flexible in that rental agreements work on one or three month's notice.

Most companies will plan to keep their equipment for much longer periods than this, even though manufacturers are tending to bring out new models at about this frequency, and the introduction of *leasing* was an enterprising bid to break the grip which the large companies exerted on their customers. The economics of leasing are based on a fixed-term legal agreement under which most of the benefits of ownership and usage pass to the lessee, in return for fixed annual or monthly leasing charges, though the lessee can usually re-lease at very low rates. At the end of the fixed period the equipment reverts to the lessor. Tenancies of up to seven years are normally available. As the principal owner, the lessor can claim the full capital allowances, but the lessee can also claim leasing charges as operating expenses deductible against tax.

Two forms of lease are currently available: an *operating lease*, in which the lessor does not cover his initial outlay over the period of the lease, and has to consider the residual value of the equipment at the end of the lease, and the *financial lease*, in which the full outlay, plus profit, is recovered. Operating leases are more risky but offer better financial terms to the lessee, and it is this form which has gained wide support from computer managers and their financial directors. More recently, however, customers have become more wary of signing fixed-term leases which would not enable them to take advantage of new products in the meantime, and some of the leasing companies have introduced what is known as *flexible leasing*. This allows a lessee to escape from a leasing agreement at certain points, provided that he takes out a new lease for replacement equipment with the same company, and also recompenses the lessor for any shortfall between his original leasing revenue and his revenue from a re-lease of the replaced equipment.

Hire Purchase is not widely used at the moment, partly because of restrictions on the length of the HP period, which result in relatively higher payments, and also because HP controls are a favourite weapon of governments in our stop/go economy. We may expect HP to become a standard method of financing the acquisition of personal computers.

In conclusion, the financing of hardware acquisition is altogether a complex subject, and one in which an intending purchaser should seek local, independent, expert and up-to-date advice.

8.3 SELECTING A COMPUTER

The selection of a computer system, whether for the first time in a company or as a replacement for an existing system, can be both lengthy and very complex. As the effect of the use of a computer system can be far-reaching, especially on a company which has previously existed without one, much time, expertise and just plain common sense needs to be expended.

The selection procedure can be divided into eight stages (see Fig. 8.1).

(a) Stage 1 — decide what you want it to do

The need for a computer is, in the first case, usually triggered off by an operational problem, or a dissatisfaction with current methods and the wish to do better or to compete successfully — a basic business drive, in fact. A *first-time user* is faced with two pitfalls: either he does not know what a computer is capable of, or he thinks it can solve everything. The first can be overcome by informed advice from organisations such as:

- trade associations;
- other computer users;
- polytechnic or university computer departments;
- the National Computing Centre;
- computer manufacturers;
- computer consultants;
- management consultants.

Many companies will have a natural reluctance to resort to the bottom of the list, but may seek some assurance from the consultancy branch of their auditing company, from members of the Management Consultants' Association and Computing Services Association (both of whom operate Codes of Conduct for their members), or companies included in other approved lists (such as MAPCON, or those operated by some computer manufacturers).

An *existing computer user*, on the other hand, will probably have an on-going systems or computerisation plan, and will need to acquire new equipment either to replace existing machinery or to provide extra power to support a new application.

(b) Stage 2 — the feasibility study

In most cases a would-be computer user can be confident that a computer can do the work required of it, in principle at least. There are very few computer applications that have not been tried successfully, somewhere, and although the fine details are always unique, generally a computer application qualifies for a 're-inventing the wheel' label. (This is one reason therefore, for buying-in that experience by using packaged software; see next section). There are, however, always pioneers: there was a first holiday company to use a computerised reservation system, a first traffic authority to install a traffic light control system, a first washing machine manufacturer to replace a relay timer with a chip. In such rare cases, it is advisable

Fig 8.1 *the process of acquiring hardware*

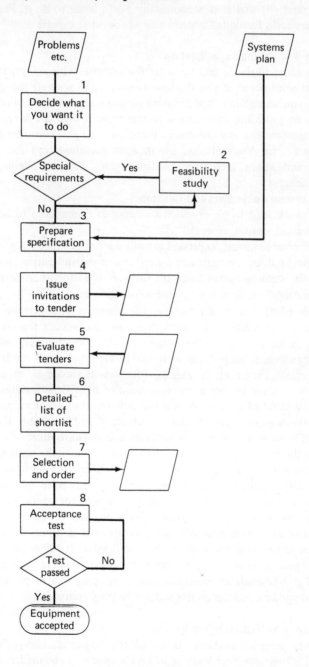

to perform a detailed technical study to ensure (i) that it is technically possible and (ii) that it is economically worth while to do it. Feasibility studies are tasks for skilled systems analysts or other experts.

(c) Stage 3 – writing a specification

You are more likely to end up, after the exercise, with a computer that will meet your needs, if you produce a detailed and accurate specification of what you want. Such a specification performs several other functions in addition to providing information to tenderers: it acts as a blueprint for further systems analysis and design work, and can also form the basis of acceptance tests. You will find specification guidelines and checklists in various publications, including Standards guides, but at a minimum you should include:

(i) the system's objectives and functions;

(ii) the work load to be executed (volumes of transactions to be input, processed, output, stored);

(iii) performance targets, expressed in units per hour of batched processing throughput, or response time for terminal input and output;

(iv) special requirements in hardware, software and support services;

(v) operational requirements (availability targets, etc.).

At this point you should consider the necessary arrangements which will have to be made to accommodate, man and service the computer system you are envisaging. The installation of a computer, depending on its size, can include such things as special power supplies, air conditioning and structural alterations to existing premises. It should be made clear that tenders should include a precise account of any special features which need to be supplied by you. A clear indication of the cost of maintenance outside the warranty period must be obtained and remember that this often will include maintenance of hardware and software alike.

A specification of this type does force you to undertake some elementary business systems analysis, of a type which calls for business understanding rather than technical knowledge, but this is preferable to giving potential suppliers something of a blank cheque (for example, 'Please supply a system to run my payroll') which provides a basis neither for comparative evaluation nor objective measurement. Beware of giving an indication of the expected cost on the specification. If you do, the quotations will always be at or slightly below the price you have suggested and you will give yourself an additional task in deciding what is put into the tenders as padding and the quotes will not be truly competitive.

(d) Stage 4 – invitations to tender

To identify potential tenderers, trade indexes and publications such as the invaluable *Computer Year Book* or *Which Computer* can be used, and there

will usually be no shortage of contenders. Valid factors to be used in pre-selection can include:
- nationality of machine (not always very easy to identify, even when you know the source);
- reputation of supplier, particularly in your line of business;
- locality of supplier (you want service from a local base, and you may well wish to favour local companies particularly in development areas).

The specification is issued along with tender documents and instructions, and in order to get back what you want, it is useful to send a pre-printed questionnaire as well. Most suppliers will subsequently want to discuss your needs and clarify obscurities in your specification before delivering to you a formal quotation and presenting a formal briefing.

(e)Stages 5/6/7 — evaluation, test and selection

Your difficulties begin when the tender documents from each invited supplier are delivered to your door. The task of selecting one only of these calls for some extensive and tedious work, which is best approached in three stages: reduction to a short-list, detailed testing of the short-listed alternatives, and the final selection.

Short-listing is based on the tender documents and the mandatory briefing session, and candidates can be assessed by a number of subjective factors; mostly hinging on the global credibility of their proposals and their sales effort:
- are you impressed by their salesmen?
- do you believe that the system can do what it claims?
- have they included everything that was asked?
- does the proposal meet your cost target and delivery dates?
- what (free) support and guarantees will they offer?

This judgemental process should leave you with a short list of, say, 3 to 5 proposals, which are outwardly satisfactory, in that they appear to meet the specification, from companies with whom you would be happy to enjoy the intimate relationship which computer usage engenders.

Detailed evaluation relies on some analytical investigation of comparative performance to be weighted against comparative costs of the contenders. Performance assessment or performance evaluation techniques broadly fall into the following classes:
- comparison of machine characteristics, such as instruction timings or weighted combinations of them, known as mixes;
- power measurement *vis-à-vis* certain 'scalar' machines (usually a comparable IBM computer);
- actual, artificial or simulated tests on each system of representative work loads, by the time taken or response achieved.

There really is nothing better than a full test on each machine configuration offered, of an actual work load (known as benchmarking) but this is not always possible, and is certainly never easy, particularly in terminal-based systems, and some form of artificial or simulated test may be all that can be achieved. There are, however, some useful professional aids — the Auerbach Corporation test every new machine announced on a series of typical computer routines ('kernels') and offer their results, on which reliance can be placed, to subscribers to their service. Many large computer users with purchasing muscle, such as the government agencies, will at a minimum insist on a set of standard representative programs ('synthetics') being run on as near a working configuration as possible.

The *final selection* has to be a weighting of test results against cost, and finally moderated by one personal or collective judgement both of the equipment offered and the company itself.

It is arguably only the most experienced, or most foolhardy, who will consider a model which they cannot test in any way, which has not been produced even as a prototype. It is, however, a fact of life that when IBM announce a new model, with new deliveries a year or more away, it immediately attracts massive orders merely on the basis of the manufacturer's own estimates of cost and performance, and one *may* take this as a measure of that company's reputation for delivering the goods.

Consultants are widely used during this stage, but it would be a mistake for a company to rely entirely on outside technical advice and ignore the expertise which exists in their own organisation.

(f) Stage 8 — acceptance tests
It is essential that you lay down acceptance tests as part of the conditions of purchase, and that you strictly adhere to them when the time comes. This is the final opportunity to ensure that you are getting what you asked for, but unfortunately the normal circumstances in which they can take place (at the final test stage in the factory, and after installation on your premises) put pressure on both sides to cut corners. You will need patience to hold the supplier to demonstrating formally that his machine can meet the performance targets and operational requirements which you laid down in your specification. Only when you are convinced that these are all met should you sign for the machine.

8.4 ACQUIRING OTHER EQUIPMENT

The same type of procedure should also be followed when selecting additional peripheral or terminal units, or when enhancing or replacing an existing computer. In these cases, however, you need to specify the computer currently in use, to ensure compatibility of physical and logical connection or ease of replacement and conversion. In addition support for the conversion process ought to be specifically requested and should form a major criterion of choice. It is also advisable to specify trial usage of any terminals put on the short-list, for full-scale operational and user trials with your existing machine.

The purchase of *personal computers* ought to be approached with particular care, the selling and systems companies still being in something of an unsettled state and the market bedevilled by rapid change and badge engineering, giving all the appearance of an Oriental bazaar.

Inevitably, many buyers are going to find themselves with machines which they cannot get serviced, whose manufacturer has gone out of business or has abandoned the model, or that the rapid rate of obsolescence has condemned to a premature disuse.

You should give particular attention to the following precautions:
- ensure that the machine of your choice can receive local maintenance;
- beware of short-life and obsolescent products with no development prospects;
- avoid manufacturers and retailers whose survival is in doubt;
- examine and avoid potential weak points in the machine (for example the keyboard, which is often the weakest part of a machine, and messy connections in the form of trailing wires, loose sockets, etc.);
- look closely at the frame of your machine if you intend it to be moved about frequently, since flimsy plastics packaging may fracture connections;
- don't pay excessive prices for brand-name peripherals such as videos or cassette equipment which you can buy more cheaply as ordinary domestic TV sets or audio-cassette equipment from a High Street store;
- make sure that you are able to add more storage and devices when you can afford to (Parkinson's law of computing – see Section 5.1 (f) – applies strongly to personal computers).

Software is a particular problem. You will be more likely to acquire software if your computer is based on a microprocessor from one of the big three manufacturers – Intel, Motorola or Zilog.

Your best source of advice is one of the computer clubs that are springing up about the country, and the occasional review articles in personal computing magazines. Ultimately the customers' interests are going to be better served when personal computers no longer merit special retail outlets but take their place along with other electronic items in High Street chain stores, as has happened to electronic games.

8.5 USING SOMEONE ELSE'S COMPUTER

The drawback of the exercise of selecting your own computer is not usually one of the reasons for deciding to use somebody else's computer

in preference to obtaining your own. If you fall into one or more of the following categories, however, you should be seriously interested in one of the various forms of proposition that are itemised below:
- your computer usage is occasional or sporadic or one-off;
- your computer usage is regular but very small;
- your computer usage is regular but has extreme and infrequent peaks;
- you wish to keep your computer costs as low as possible;
- you don't want to bother with the hassle of obtaining and running your own computer;
- you are approaching your first experience with a computer;
- you wish to use some specialised software which you haven't got on your machine;
- you wish to arrange standby facilities in case of accidental or deliberate failure of your machine.

(a) Computer bureaux

The most widespread method of obtaining the services of a computer, without directly or indirectly owning it, is to become a customer of a computer bureau. This is a commercial organisation whose sole function is to sell its computer services at a profit — punching and verifying (data preparation), systems and programming, and computer operations.

Typical customers of a computer bureau can include first-time users, who may soon develop the need and confidence to acquire their own machine; existing computer users with excessive peak loads or abnormal one-off requirements (such as file conversion or program conversion); computer users with infrequent needs; and, finally, large and sophisticated customers who have decided as a matter of policy to leave the whole business in the hands of experts.

Computer bureaux cover the whole spectrum of computer work, from batch to interactive mode (which needs a terminal on customer premises), and from general-purpose to specialised application areas. Most computer bureaux are well-established companies of substance, and you will probably want the additional safeguard of choosing one that is a member of the appropriate trade association such as the CSA in the United Kingdom or ADAPSO in the United States. Fees are generally work-content (x pence per sheet of printer output) or time-related (y pence per kilobyte of disc storage used per week), but you may get a fixed-price quotation for systems and programming work.

(b) Time-selling

Most computer departments will sell time on their machines to outside users: usually spare time on an evening, night or weekend shift, with or without operators in support. Contractual arrangements can take various forms, and in some cases can be permanent agreements, such as exist in a number of places in the United Kingdom between a county council and its constituent district councils, or in the University Regional Computer Centres.

(c) Consortia

A consortium is a permanent agreement by two or more organisations jointly to purchase and operate one computer. The objectives of a consortium are two-fold: firstly to concentrate scarce manpower resources, and secondly to achieve the benefits of scale that larger machines are thought to deliver (see Grosch's law in Chapter 1). It has to be admitted that experience in computer consortia and co-operatives is not uniformly favourable, and you need to be convinced that you can work in harmony with another organisation in matters that intimately concern your own organisation, over a period of years, before considering such a proposition.

(d) Facilities management

This term is used to describe an activity which very many companies support in their catering or transport operations; you provide the equipment and accommodation, and contract an outside specialist organisation to run it for you, at a fee, under your broad directions. Most large computer service companies will offer an FM contract, and there is usually an added benefit that an FM outfit will use spare time either for time-selling or for their other activities, passing on a contribution of the income to the contracted company.

8.6 ACQUIRING SOFTWARE AND SERVICES

One of the difficulties of computer selection is that even with the smallest computer you are purchasing a mix of hardware and systems software, and, as described in Chapter 7, you may not be sure where the dividing line occurs, nor whether performance is due to one or the other. Beyond the irreducible minimum of systems software, you will eventually be requiring other software, whose total cost will almost certainly over-run the initial purchase cost of the hardware plus bundled software (that is, the essential systems software included at no extra cost) in the life of a machine, and whose operational life will exceed that of the machine for which it was first produced. This software will include:

- utilities; sorts/merge, media/format conversion programs;
- applications software;
- database management system and data dictionary software;
- data communications software;
- programming aids; compilers, automatic flowcharters, testing aids, etc., decision tables and language pre-processors;
- additional systems software.

This software can be obtained from a number of different sources in addition to the computer manufacturers (from whom it is now almost always 'unbundled'), and to get the best value for money, in terms of costs (purchase or rental) and quality, you should shop around.

As a packaged product, software suffers primarily from the drawback that it is (i) *invisible* and (ii) *unverifiable*. For information about the *content* of a package you must rely on documentation, and a major problem for pre-sales examination is that in the United Kingdom and most other countries, software does not enjoy patent or copyright protection under the law and package salesmen may be loath to reveal too much of their professional wares. Ultimately you should expect to receive:

- systems specification;
- program specifications;
- operating manual;

that is, the same documentation as you would, or should, produce if you wrote the software yourself. You should also expect to receive the source coding.

Verification requires your being able to test the package either in-house or at the supplier's premises, but you are unlikely to be able to test all the paths of all the programs. You should therefore protect yourself against errors in the code through a guarantee or maintenance contract not only involving the salesman but the original producer of the package. This should also cover you against changes in the interface between the package and your machine's system software (which the computer manufacturer may wish to modify from time to time). More importantly, however, you should seek confidence by buying only well-used packages from well-established and reputable companies.

(a) Software for microcomputers

The potential deficiencies in software for personal and microcomputers have already been mentioned; generally such machines are the least well provided with software, or most 'naked', and the conventional sources of software are unlikely to be satisfactory for a mass, low-cost, hardware market. The problem is heightened by the lack of standards in the programming languages generally available on small machines, BASIC and PASCAL in particular. There is a gap which the following sources are attempting to remedy:

  (i) computer clubs;

 (ii) free software, printed in personal computing magazines or in catalogues produced by the original microprocessor manufacturers;

(iii) low-cost software houses; but beware of cheap plastics software which matches the flimsy hardware packaging;

(iv) telesoftware; a software 'hire' service to be provided on Prestel.

In principle, however, there should be no insuperable problem. Proper software is expensive — of the order of £5 per instruction for fully tested, debugged, documented and delivered software — but the large market should be able to spread the initial high cost over a larger number of users. What we are lacking is a credible marketing and distribution vehicle — perhaps a universal software catalogue — 'Send £5 and an audio cassette tape . . .', working through public libraries.

(b) Other computer services

Your procurement needs, of course, are not satisfied only by hardware and software. You will need various materials and services to run your computer installation, for which you will find no shortage of willing suppliers. Stationery is the most essential consumable item, and from time to time shortages and long lead-times appear, so that it is essential to keep a high level of stock in hand. Running out of computer stationery would be an operational disaster, the sort of nightmare that haunts DP managers.

By far the most critical operational source is *hardware maintenance*, a service until recently exclusively provided by computer manufacturers, at an annual charge of up to 25 per cent of your annual rental or its equivalent. It is already possible, however, to obtain servicing from one of several independent computer maintenance companies. These companies have a less extensive repair network, and you will also need to check that they have the requisite machine knowledge and spares availability.

A maintenance contract should cover the following points:
  (i) scope of cover: for example, weekdays, morning and afternoon shifts only, continuous;
 (ii) callout response on machine faults: for example, within two hours of call;
(iii) availability of spares: for example, on-site or at nearest maintenance centre;
(iv) back-up facilities to local service: particularly for faults diagnosed as software-generated;
 (v) preventive maintenance: frequency, time and length;
(vi) availability of your company's facilities: engineer's room/work desk storage.

The overall level of service from your maintenance engineer is critical to the level of availability of the computer to its users, and the preventive maintenance session is often a bone of contention. The engineer will need to run diagnostic tests to detect actual or incipient faults, and then remedy them. He will thus require the system for this period, which will be unavailable to the user. This poses some difficulties if you are running a computer application of a real-time or continuous service nature, and in this situation you will in any case probably afford a duplicate/standby machine to provide cover in case of scheduled *or* unscheduled breakdown.

In general the reliability of computing equipment is high, and with the move towards electronics inside the electro-mechanical media-handling peripherals, we may expect further improvements. We are at the point where it is no longer economic to take out a preventive maintenance contract on low-cost VDUs, for instance, but merely to repair on call. Your computer manufacturer may also offer an on-line diagnostic service, in which the diagnostic program and other tests are run remotely without requiring the engineer to be present or the machine to be taken out of service.

SPECIMEN QUESTIONS

1. 'The advent of mini and microcomputers represents a threat to both the business of computer bureaux and to the sales of larger computers.' Discuss this statement and compare the relative advantages and disadvantages for the smaller company of owning a small computer or of using a computer bureau.

2. Draw up an organisation chart showing the staff and their interrelationships in a typical commercial data processing department. State typical job specifications of three different grades of staff.   *

3. Assess the likely impact of microcomputers in companies with large data processing installations.

4. Discuss control procedures which are available to a data processing manager to ensure (a) the security of data held within the installation, and (b) the validity of data to be processed.   *

5. Discuss three of the factors that have led to the increase in computer crime. Comment briefly on the people that could be involved in computer crime. How can a company prevent such occurrences?   *

CHAPTER 9

ORGANISING A COMPUTER

Having obtained a computer with the necessary software and programs to run on it, the would-be user must then proceed to organise its use and operation so that he may enjoy dependable and satisfying service from it. The general needs are merely those of a proper and purposeful arrangement, similar to those called for by any business using any machine, and I would guess, for instance, that organising a transport department calls for the same type of arrangements. Because of the particular needs of computers, there are some particular considerations, treated under the following headings:

- staffing;
- accommodation;
- work organisation;
- security.

9.1 THE COMPUTER DEPARTMENT

The most important factor in organising a computer for use is, paradoxically, people. They are required:

- to operate it;
- to develop/maintain programs and systems for it;
- to maintain and service it;
- to manage it.

(a) Computer operations

(i) Computer operators
These are the people who physically control a computer, by starting it up, feeding it with input, removing output and responding to messages from the operating system with commands. That description does not, and cannot, convey the full nature of the job. The computer is not a simple

machine, and the speed and complexity of its operation, particularly with large mainframes operating under multi-programming and with tele-communication links, make heavy demands on the operator's speed of reaction and technical understanding. It is thus a technician's job and requires a technician's skills and education.

Most organised computers work either round the clock (particularly embedded or real-time systems) or over two shifts, and most operators at some time will work on shifts, in shift teams.

(ii) Data preparation

This is the operation of data preparation or data entry equipment on data provided to them by the users via data control. Still essentially a keyboard task, it requires bright clerical staff with keyboard training, as do the related tasks of specialist terminal operator and word processor operator.

(iii) Data control

This is the interface between the user and the computer department, often a very busy registry. Data control may also be responsible for operating any of the post-printer ancillary machines still in use — collators, folders, envelope stuffers, franking machines — in computer departments with a direct-mail output role. Data controllers play an important role in scheduling the work of an operations section, and may also be increasingly involved in data administration for database systems.

(iv) Media library

In any large data-handling computer department, the circulation and use of disc and tape volumes are under the care of a media librarian. These volumes will contain master file, transaction files, history files, program libraries, etc., and there will be separate rules covering their security (see Section 9.4) and retention.

(b) Computer development

(i) Systems analysts

Systems analysis (see Chapter 5) is the most important function in making a computer work effectively for the organisation, and a job requiring both business knowledge and technical knowledge. There have been moves to split the role into two — with a Problem Analyst and a Systems Designer — and to vary the location in which they are organisationally placed, in order to improve their effectiveness as the liaison and interpreting function on the boundary between the computer department and the user.

(ii) Systems programmers

These are concerned with systems software, as defined in Section 7.4, and also with other delivered software and packages, such as database management systems (Section 5.2) and data transmission software (Section 4.4). They also perform some work directly concerned with computer operations – the maintenance of stored procedures and computer performance studies – and some or all may be responsible to the operations manager.

(iii) Applications programmers

They may also have a split role, in that about a half of their work, on average, is taken up, not in developing new work, but maintaining existing programs. Commentators have been predicting their gradual disappearance, as the industry finds less labour-intensive and more productive ways of producing programs, and there is now just a little evidence to suggest that this may be happening.

(iv) Project teams

Because of the project nature of systems development, most analysts and programmers will work together in mixed project teams under a (temporary) project leader who may be either a senior systems analyst or senior programmer. Project teams may be assisted by support teams of specialists, either a chief programmer team (see Section 6.1) or a technical support section containing, for instance, database and/or telecommunications specialists.

(c) Maintenance

Hardware maintenance is almost always performed under contract by engineers working either for the equipment manufacturer or retailers, or from specialist maintenance companies. Their function is divided between breakdown repairs, for which they must be on call, and preventive maintenance carried out on a regular monthly basis.

(d) Computer management

It goes without saying that any organised activity requires co-ordination, control and responsibility for it, vested in management. There is some justification for an opinion that computer management is an undervalued activity, perhaps arising from the early days of organised computing when a computer manager was often the senior technical person in post rather than a true manager, and when a company treated its computer as it treated, say, its transport department. Computer management also includes the arrangements made for board-level reporting; originally many computer managers themselves reported to the finance director because of their original preoccupation with financial systems, but it is now more common for them to report to a board member with sole responsibility for computing (and perhaps management services), reflecting the dependence which many companies have on their computer systems. It is also common for the computer manager to report to a computer steering committee consisting of other senior staff whose work also depends on the efficiency of the computer department.

There are several different models on which the formal organisation of these groups of people are based. In the first, as shown in Fig. 9.1, all groups of staff are responsible to one person and organised in one department called, usually, the data processing department. Such a department is an active and executive part of a company, an organisational 'empire' in its own right and very much part of the *status quo*. At the moment it is under attack because it tends to be mainframe-oriented, and thus antipathetic, and even resistant, to the recent technological trends in computing, most of which refer to smaller computers and decentralised operations.

The second model separates responsibility for the day-to-day operations of the computer from that of developing new work for it. The dividing line varies: the systems analysts are always on the other side from computer operations, but the systems and application programmers may be on either side. In the extreme, systems analysts will be found in user departments only.

Under pressure from the new technological trends and the maturity of the computer industry, there is some evidence that the central organisation of computers and computing staff may be changing. There is a strong move towards dispersing or *distributing* a central unit into smaller units in decentralised company branches, leaving a central computer manager responsible only for a co-ordinating/advisory function, and perhaps a small pool of staff.

Alternatively, or additionally, some companies have applied to their computing departments the same management philosophy which is widely applied to operating departments, turning them into actual or quasi-independent companies with their own boards of directors but with shares fully owned by the parent group/holding company. Such companies are now well represented in the growing computer services market.

Smaller companies, with small machines, will not of course need to apply any of these models. What they must do is recognise the validity of the four functions of operations, development, maintenance and management, and allocate them somewhere even if, at the beginning, three of them devolve upon the same person.

Purchasers of personal or home computers may have to remember only two lessons: firstly that all machines require some servicing, and secondly that new software and programs are expensive and possibly difficult to

Fig 9.1 *the organisation of a typical data processing department (common alternative titles are shown in parentheses)*

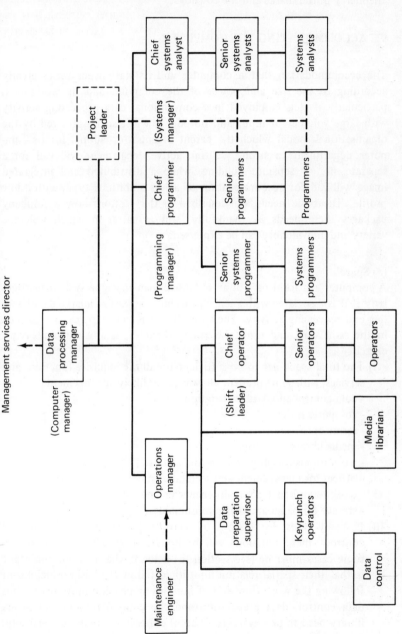

acquire. Owning a machine without any programming ability puts you at the mercy of the sharks and the cowboys.

9.2 ACCOMMODATING THE COMPUTER

The accommodation that a computer and its staff needs varies greatly according to the size and power of the computer and its work load, particularly if it is employed in a conventional data processing activity with large volumes of input and output. It will also be affected by the organisational model which the parent organisation adopts for its computer department: a strong, central, active department will call for a separate site or separate building, while a distributed and integrated image will call for accommodation of a less ambitious type, with a low profile. The basic needs are described in this section: how a company packages these needs is, thankfully, still a matter in which welcome variety and individuality can be expressed.

(a) Space
A computer can form part of an extensive man–machine system, particularly if it is associated with ancillary machines as part of a large data handling and processing activity. The space that it is to occupy can be planned in the same way, and using the same principles, as any machine-layout exercise.
 (i) The total space has to be sufficient for all the requisite functions and services, with some prudent allowance for likely enhancements:
 - data control and data preparation;
 - computer room;
 - terminal room(s);
 - media library and storage;
 - work rooms for programmers and analysts;
 - offices for management and secretarial staff;
 - work room/bench for maintenance engineers;
 - storage for paper and other consumables.
 (ii) In many cases, for reasons of security, privacy and environmental controls, these functions will be housed in separate rooms, and in some cases must be (see section (b) below); what is more important is that their spatial relationship should follow the basic principles of following the work flow and of minimising physical movement. Thus data control, data preparation and the computer room and media library need to be physically adjacent either horizontally or vertically. For development staff, the physical proximity to the computer room is not so urgent, particularly if program development is via terminals,

but the spatial organisation of work-rooms to facilitate supervision is more important.

(iii) Within each room the space and layout are defined by operational criteria: for *equipment*, to permit easy access for normal use and for maintenance; and for *staff*, to meet work requirements and at least any minimum legal stipulations. There is no typical or preferred layout, except that in a computer room it is usual to have the processor and operator's console in the middle of the room, and the I/O and backing storage devices arranged around it in a circle or half-circle, or around the walls, both to minimise cable runs and to permit easy observation and monitoring by the console operator. This may also be true in a data preparation room, particularly one equipped with key-to-disc equipment in which there is again a control console. Fig. 1.6 showed a large computer arranged in this way.

(b) Special requirements

Of these rooms or sections, it is only the machine rooms which call for special facilities, and then only in the case of large computers. For smaller computers it is often a matter of policy to make them as unobtrusive a part of the office furniture as possible (see Fig. 1.9).

(i) Power requirements

Large computers (mainframes and some minicomputers) require a high-voltage power supply and a transformer to boost the voltage from the normal power supply. Computer systems with demanding operational reliability criteria will also justify standby generating equipment, both as a precaution against total power failure and against temporary fluctuations in the public power supply which can cause brief but potentially serious failures in processing.

(ii) Floor requirements

Most large computers with stand-alone units will require either a false floor or special ducting to carry the connecting cables between them and the processor. Trailing cables may well be illegal under safety regulations. Large computers and storage devices may also need specially strengthened floors to support their weight.

(iii) Environmental requirements

Many large computers require an operating environment in which ambient temperature, humidity and dust are controlled by air conditioning equipment. Processors still generate considerable heat, and some large processors are water-cooled, which calls for special plumbing. Others are fan-cooled, blowing heat into the room for disposal by air-conditioning. Dust particularly affects storage media, discs and tape drives where the precision of the gaps between read/write heads and the recording media is critical – one reason for the move towards sealed Winchester discs.

Most smaller computers are intended to work in normal business environments – but be careful because in some countries 'normal' implies some air-conditioning in any case (for staff comfort). The need for full air-conditioning, in sealed computer rooms is, in my opinion, one of the factors fostering the mystique of the all-powerful and unapproachable machine, and the sooner they are dispensed with the better for user-computer understanding.

(iv) Access requirements
It is surprising how many times large and heavy equipment has to be delivered by crane, or hoisted through the roof, because the necessary access via doors and corridors has not been available. Access to rooms for stationery supplies is also advisable.

(v) Data transmission lines
Terminal-oriented computer systems will require the installation of cables for internal use, and Datel-type external services. Restrictions, for example on the maximum length of local cable lengths, may affect room-layouts, and it will also be necessary to avoid potential sources of 'noise'. There are further constraints on using external data transmission services; for instance there are restrictions on the layout of some terminal networks in which multiple terminals are connected to one line. The availability of some services, for example wideband or packet-switched services, are also geographically limited and, at an international level, the whole range of services and costs applicable in any one country may influence the choice of location for a supra-national centre.

(vi) Sound insulation
Teletypes, impact printers, some card/tape readers and some ancillary equipment (card and cheque sorters) create excessive noise and even vibration. It is advisable to install sound insulation or buffering to minimise nuisance to adjoining rooms. There may well be legal requirements which have to be satisfied.

(vii) Rubbish disposal
Another problem, often overlooked, is that a large-scale data processing computer department creates a lot of waste paper for disposal or burning. Waste listing-paper is, however, often of value either as scrap paper for recycling or for use in schools.

(*viii*) *Fire precautions*
Part of physical security, see Section 9.4.

(*ix*) *VDU accommodation*
There is now reliable evidence that particular care has to be taken in the provision of the working environment for VDU operators who, more than any other working group in computing, will be sitting down and working in a fairly static manner throughout a working day. The normal ergonomic problems of seating and operating a keyboard are in this case intensified by the effects on the eyes of staring at a screen, and the room lighting and screen quality are particularly important in minimising the effects of glare. In fact working conditions for VDU operators often include regular (two-hourly) breaks for this purpose.

9.3 ORGANISING THE WORK

A computer department is in the position, similar to some other functions but unique in its intensity, of being both a service company in that its work is the workload of other operating departments, and an operating company in that it is directly in the line of execution of other operating departments' work. Those departments depend very largely, if not entirely, for the volume, timing and quality of their own performance, on the computer department – a factor accounting for some ambivalent feelings inside such a company. The organisation of workloads is therefore a particularly important aspect of computer operations management.

(a) Authorisation of use
Because it is an operational department on whose services people depend, and for which they have effectively subcontracted, it is necessary for both regular and *ad hoc* use of a computer to be authorised, either by the computer management or by the computer steering committee, one of whose functions must be to determine priorities if the machine's capacity is potentially over-committed. Routine work is authorised by its incorporation into a work schedule, and takes priority. *Ad hoc* work, including terminal users (except full-time terminal operators) therefore need authorisation up to the level at which the total capacity will meet demand, but no more. Authorisation in some accounting methods will also entail allocation of the appropriate costs to other budgets, so that a computer department's running costs may be recovered from the other company functions who make use of it. Finally, authorisation of use is one method of fostering security (see Section 9.4).

(b) Work scheduling

(i) Most routine *batch* work performed by a computer has a target deadline or response time largely dictated by the wider company system: for example, salary cheques to be ready by Wednesday midday, monthly accounts to be produced by the end of the first working week of the next month. To meet all the different targets it is necessary to have a work schedule showing the jobs to be run, their promised delivery time and a loading time that will make some allowance for fluctuations in the volume of input data. The preparation of this schedule, and the organisation of routine and one-off jobs on the computer as required by it, is still largely a human operation task, using work boards or lists in liaison with data control and data preparation to ensure that the data is ready for the time that the job has to be loaded into the appropriate queue. Some operating systems, however, can accept a DEADLINE command as a qualification for an EXECUTE command, and adjust priorities according to the relative differences between the deadlines of loaded jobs and the current clock time. Gaps in a work schedule will show if and when other time-critical work can be fitted in.

(ii) A computer system running a *mixed work load* of terminal and scheduled batch work will have to adjust the amount of time available for terminals according to the state of the work schedule. This may permit some program testing to be performed during the working day, but most large-scale systems testing will have to be performed out of the normal working day. Most systems analysts and programmers will have to work occasional irregular hours for this reason, and flexitime is now common in data processing departments.

(iii) Computer systems entirely devoted to *terminal users* will of course not have a work schedule, and should in any case have been designed to accommodate all predictable levels of demand. It is in the nature of many types of terminal-oriented systems that they are subject to occasional peak demands, at which time either a degraded service has to be accepted or the level of demand artificially reduced by either automatically logging out some connected terminals on some order of priority, or by refusing to accept any further LOGINs. Most operating systems designed for such applications will have facilities for monitoring performance levels and taking such action.

(c) Reliability

Computer users have every right to expect a service from the computer which is totally and utterly dependable. Reliability (or machine availability) is an aspect of computer system performance that becomes critical in the case of real-time and/or life-dependent systems, but is implicitly assumed in all computer work.

At the same time computers are machines which, like all machines, are subject to wear and tear and therefore occasional and unpredictable failures, and reliability to provide uninterrupted machine availability when needed has to be specifically planned for and built into a computer department's operations. This planning starts with the selection of equipment with reliability as a primary criterion — both by type and by reputation, avoiding equipment with a poor reliability rating, and also by seeking written guarantees in contracts.

Subsequent precautions include:

- preventive maintenance whose objective is to anticipate faults that might otherwise cause random failures;
- the replication of critical equipment either *in situ* or by holding standby/ spares;
- arrangements for rapid call-out and repair in case of faults;
- and in the last event, standby arrangements to transfer data, programs and files to another identical installation not too far distant (usually under some reciprocal arrangement).

With nearly 100 per cent of the components in most computers made from electronic elements, availability of 98 or 99 per cent of uptime (that is, downtime of 1 or 2 per cent) should be achievable with normal general-purpose hardware, leaving software as the main source of processing failures. Guaranteed fault-free applications can be sought through properly designed and tested programs, which are achievable with the latest programming methodology. The most persistent and deep-rooted faults still occur in systems software which by its complex nature defies comprehensive testing of every path and every combination of events. It is a sensible precaution, therefore, to arrange a hot-line to a manufacturer's software team, and strictly to log software failures in particular so that evidence of failures may be used to support some recovery of charges out of rental or maintenance payments.

(d) Quality control

Both the computer department and the immediate user of computer output have a common interest in checking the quality of output before it is ultimately released. Most of the computer errors that reach the popular press arise from errors in programming that in the first place should have been detected during program development or even earlier at the specification stage, and in the second place should have been picked up by a quality-control inspection of output. It is, regrettably, unwise to let any output be automatically transmitted without such a check, since excessive payments made through a computer error may not be recoverable at law, and sending out demands for £0.00, while not financially serious, reflects no credit on any organisation.

Inspection is also recommended for excessive input rejection rates at validation or during processing, which may indicate either a falling off in the accuracy of data origination or preparation, or a more serious condition in the relevant programs.

9.4 SECURITY

A computer department is the custodian of two valuable, rare and strategic properties: the computer equipment and its processing capabilities, and the information contained on its files. The security of these properties is one of the most important responsibilities of a computer manager, against damage or loss, and unauthorised use.

(a) Deliberate or accidental damage, and loss
 (i) *Physical security* is the prevention of access and use to unauthorised personnel, by means of:
   - restricted access: locking rooms when not in use, or installing electronic badge-card operated locks for continuous use, or using security guards;
   - restricted use: use only by authorised names or under supervision for hardware, software and files;
   - precautions against burglary, etc., while unoccupied, with burglar alarms, security patrols, etc.
 (ii) *Natural hazards* such as fire should be anticipated by installing sprinkler systems or inert gas emitters. In certain situations, precautions should also be taken against flooding, subsidence or earthquake, and power surges due to lightning.
(iii) Precautions against *accidental loss* or *deliberate destruction* of *software* can be taken by using ROM, and involving operating system facilities, where available, to make software inaccessible (by password), read only or execute only. Security copies of all key files and software should be kept, and stored away from the computer room in fireproof safes, and log or journal records should be taken whenever a permanent change is made to a master file record, so that the current state of a master file can be speedily restored from the previous full copy.

(b) Unauthorised use of information and programs
There are three identifiable risks:
- access to files containing either company-confidential (for example,

production costs) or personal-confidential (for example, employee details) information;
- use of, or tampering with, programs for fraudulent purposes ('computer fraud');
- stealing or unauthorised copying of programs or files that have a commercial or competitive value.

The first risk includes the risk to privacy, and is discussed more fully from all angles in the next chapter. These risks can all be minimised by the stringent application of physical security in the computer department, and controls over input in the user department, and there is no evidence at all to suggest that data is not more secure stored in computer-readable form than in human-readable form. Nevertheless, computer crime exercises an unwarranted fascination because, by its nature, it is 'insider' crime perpetrated by qualified technical people who, like sophisticated bank robbers, may even attract sympathy for 'beating the system'.

However, an extra dimension to the problem arises from the availability of terminal access to a computer via public telecommunication lines, both of which are not controllable in the same way as internal computer equipment. There is no support for claims that any computer system can be accessed from any telephone (except in the sense of being able to dial any modem's number), nor that data transmission can be tapped with an acoustic 'black box'. Countermeasures against normal but unauthorised access can be made:
- by data encryption (the 'scrambling' of data by applying a mathematical operation with values known only to those authorised to read the data);
- with extensions of passwords;
- by further controls on terminal usage, including restricting users by badge-readers, voice-prints or signature printers to establish identity, and by in-built terminal address codes to stop 'strange' devices from logging in;
- with tamper-proof cabling in optical fibre.

Even supposing these measures failed, it is still necessary to decode the bit signals into data or instructions, and get through the layers of software protection to execute programs. In real life the undramatic truth is that confidentiality, integrity and security of software and files are most at risk from bored, unscrupulous or disgruntled employees, ex-employees and contractors, using regular but unauthorised means of access allied to their insiders' knowledge of how the software and programs work. Perhaps the most reliable precaution against such abuse is proper personnel management, and a totally 'professional' computer industry.

CHAPTER 10

COMPUTERS AND PEOPLE

It is only to be expected that the rise to prominence of the computer over the last four decades has had some effect on the lives of people in our society. That effect has, in the experience of the majority, been most evident in changed patterns of employment; many people, I think, would at the moment be hard pressed to name one other significant effect. This is partly because the breakout of computers from their business use is only just under way, so that the full effects, potentially, of computers as domestic machines like a television or the car are not yet realised. In the next chapter we look forward to these developments; in this chapter we examine the current situation in respect of:
- employment;
- education;
- civil rights and civil liberties;
- leisure.

10.1 COMPUTERS AND EMPLOYMENT

(a) The positive position

Fig. 9.1 showed the range of occupations created, or re-defined, by the use of computers within our large organisations, at clerical, technician, professional and managerial levels. Numerically this is the largest 'plus' effect of computers on employment. An informed estimate is that the computer accounts now for about 1.5 per cent of the total employment in Western societies — about 400 000 in the United Kingdom and about 2 million in the United State — and that about 90 per cent of those computer jobs are in the *computer or data processing departments* of other organisations. Other directly computer-related jobs are in the *computer manufacturing* sector (which is itself part of the wider electronics industry) and the *computer services* sector (software and systems houses, computer bureaux and consultants).

Other estimates indicate that there is now, and will continue to be, a shortfall of supply over demand, and also that there will continue to be an increase in total employment numbers. In an era in which full employment in general, and in particular industries, seems to have disappeared, employment in computing appears buoyant and stable. To that extent, then, computing has already arrived as a significant factor in our economy, and has thereby created a substructure in those aspects of our society that relate to employment and preparation for employment, particularly in education (see next section).

That positive and healthy picture conceals some contrary factors.

(b) Computers and unemployment

The majority of those in senior positions in the computer industry, by which is meant those who design, manufacture and sell computers as well as those who use them, did not start their careers in computing but have moved sideways, or sideways and upwards, from other careers. Nowadays there is an ever-growing intake of specially trained personnel into the industry and a fairly well-defined career pattern is emerging. The industry can absorb, certainly for the foreseeable future, all the products of computer science/studies and electronic/computer engineering courses that become available. This situation, however, is not likely to continue indefinitely. More new applications and users will rely on packages rather than on bespoke programming, and the next generation of computers are likely to be self-programmable, so that the job opportunities are likely to be for a smaller number of more highly trained systems and software designers. Apart from the computer professionals the industry has caused some other patterns of employment to change. For example, the pen-pushing clerk of the past has been replaced by data preparation and data control personnel. This change has, of course, been taking place over the last century but the recent past has seen its rapid acceleration. The trend is now towards capital-intensive, knowledge-based manufacturing and service occupations and away from labour-intensive, semi-skilled work. Much component assembly and many office procedures (see Chapter 11) have been replaced by advancing technology, and jobs have been lost.

It is difficult to give a true balance between the positive and negative effects of computers, partly because in most cases the negative effects are disguised as, for example, hidden job losses when people who leave are not replaced. Technological unemployment tends also in the short term to be swamped by trade recessions and other factors which affect the supply of jobs.

However, we do know of heavy job losses over the last ten years due to new microelectronic technology, ironically in the electronics and telecommunications industries. Even in computer manufacturing itself fewer people are needed to make more computers. Given the pressures on productivity in international markets and on public service organisations alike, then it is virtually impossible for them to avoid the opportunity of reducing their costs and increasing their effectiveness with more computers and fewer employees.

It is not necessary to believe some of the more dramatic claims made in the media about the potential effects of the microprocessor and all its associated products; it is sufficient merely to recognise that the introduction of computers is part of an overall trend, and the best that can be made of that trend is for the maximum exploitation of the employment opportunities which it offers in the supply, servicing and operation of the new technology.

(c) Computers and trade

In this respect the present situation also presents an unsatisfactory picture for the UK and for many other countries. The computer manufacturing industry itself is dominated world-wide by American companies, except perhaps in the protected markets of Japan and Eastern Europe, by a margin that must be unparallelled in any other sector of industry or commerce. US companies manufacture multinationally in Western Europe and elsewhere, and particularly exploit British software expertise and tax benefits in Eire. Even considering re-exports there remains a large and unhealthy balance of payments deficit in Western Europe on hardware and systems, and it is almost impossible to export to the highly protected US market to reduce the trade gap.

In fact, producing national profit-and-loss accounts is particularly difficult because (a) most computer manufacturers buy in components and even unit products like printers and discs from other companies; and (b) chips and other electronic components are made world-wide, with labour-intensive work (like mounting wafers) performed mostly in the Third World.

The situation is further complicated by the Japanese threat. Given their current dominance of the world consumer electronics market, it would be surprising if the Japanese manufacturers were not able to extend into computing, with their unique blend of manufacturing skills, subservient labour market, enterprise and Government aid. Japanese-made chips are already inside many otherwise impeccably western products, and Japanese processors, particularly plug-compatible models of IBM mainframes, are already on sale, though not always under manufacturers' names. Industry leaders are resigned to expecting Japanese dominance to extend to processors and peripherals by the end of the decade.

Given these competitive factors, what can be done to maintain a major share of the market for domestic products? The lesson is clear from those countries which are in that position, that is, the United States and Japan. The lesson is to establish a protected market by import controls or other means, and support the domestic suppliers with financial aid under a comprehensive plan. The home market will then establish a strong base and economies of scale from which some larger exports can be launched. This is precisely how it has been done in the United States and Japan; to do otherwise is a dereliction of duty by other governments to their native computer enterprises. Ironically, the United Kingdom has the strongest domestic supplier in the western world in ICL; had it received the support that American and Japanese companies enjoy, it could now be a world leader.

10.2 COMPUTERS IN EDUCATION

Since the computer industry, and the use of its products, are now important factors in employment, it would be expected that computers and computing would find a place in education and training, which have as one of their objectives, preparation for adulthood and employment. Computing courses are now available at all levels, and computing has taken its rightful place among other subjects, even though the demands that it places on teachers and resources are very great. Fig. 10.1 summarises some of these course provisions with the qualifications attached, which may be traced as the appropriate entry point to different career paths in computing on Fig. 9.1. What is equally important, and may be overlooked in our enthusiasm to teach computer programming, is that computers have a role to play in the education process.

Computer assisted learning (CAL) in its broadest sense relies on the computer as a model of the process of learning, the 'input, process and store then output' cycle of the computer matching the learning cycle of the provision of information, its retention in memory and its retrieval when required (see Fig. 10.2). It is of course not the only model of this process used in education, but it appears to be of particular value, firstly as a means of providing information in a graphic and appealing way (often by offering a simulation of a lesson that is more revealing than a verbal description), and secondly as a means of giving individual attention to pupils at their own pace. It is thought to be most rewarding as an aid to the teaching of backward children in remedial classes, and in cases of mentally handicapped children.

Computer-managed learning (CML) goes beyond the learning process into the management of the learning situation, by storing scores and assess-

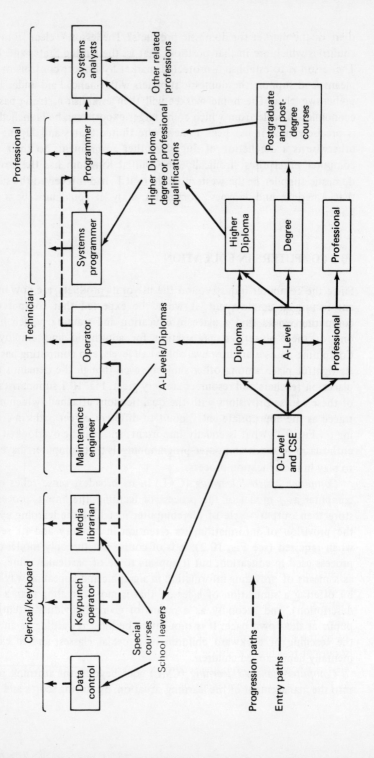

Fig 10.1 *qualifications, courses and career entry points in computing*

Fig 10.2 *the learning process and computer-assisted learning*

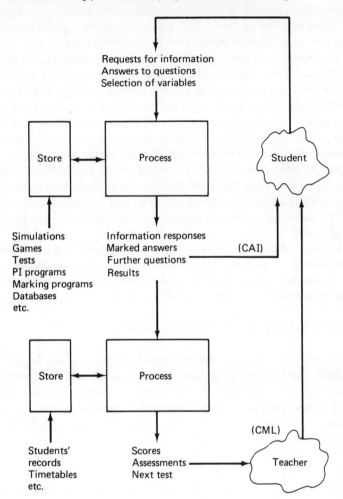

ments and then, among other outputs, determining which tests are to be taken next. Primarily, however, CML is data processing applied to the running of an educational establishment, built, like business data processing, around a set of master files of which the student records file is likely to be the most significant. The importance of CML also lies in the implicit model of real life which the school represents to the pupil. It is important that the computer should be seen to be playing the same role in the school as it does outside; lessons learnt at this stage about 'living with the computer' are likely to be more rewarding than difficult adjustments learnt afterwards, in the same way that changes like metrication are more difficult for those who have grown up with Imperial measures than for our children who have been taught in metric units from the beginning.

The relevance of the computer and similar new subjects such as micro-electronics, is symptomatic of the move away from a labour-intensive and labour-based economy towards an energy- and knowledge-based economy, in which lack of formal education and established mental skills will restrict youngsters to an uncertain employment future. The difficulty of finding employment for unskilled school-leavers is one of the most distressing features of 'structural unemployment', and it calls for an expansion of higher vocational education – an extension of the Robbins' principle that higher education should be available for all those who qualify for it. It is nonsensical that youngsters should be paid for being unemployed but not supported on courses to prepare them for purposeful and permanent employment.

In time, of course, our society's preoccupation with the need and the right to work – the 'work ethic' as it is known – may relax, in which case the computer's contribution to people's leisure time and leisure activities may become more important (see Section 10.4).

10.3 CIVIL RIGHTS AND CIVIL LIBERTIES

One immediate effect of the widespread adoption of the computer by business and government is one that every household must experience regularly – the appearance in mail boxes of computer-printed bills and invoices, and computer-printed forms and documents of many types. This indicates, as mentioned in Chapter 2, that the organisations that issue those letters, bills and documents have records on their files relating to the addressee (normally the head of the household). When you add to that total other organisations which keep computer files on individuals, but for different purposes, you arrive at a conclusion that a very large amount of information is held about individual persons – one estimate is about 50 K characters on average on every person – on computer files. This total is much greater than it could have been previously, simply because of the limitations of bulk imposed by pen-and-paper records.

There are three factors about the situation which cause concern: firstly because much of this information is confidential, for example, financial, medical, criminal data; secondly because it is now possible, through data transmission, for this information to be transferred between two computers with relative ease: and thirdly because this information may not be based on fact but on hearsay, rumours or allegation. This concern, along with proposals for safeguards, have been expressed inside and outside the computer industry for the last fifteen years, by private individuals and organisations dedicated to civil rights, and by computer professionals themselves. The concern has become known as the *privacy issue*, and has concentrated, but not exclusively, upon information held by government departments and other official organisations which, if put together (see Fig. 10.3) would create a comprehensive dossier about any citizen, information which would enable a government to exert a power over us incompatible with our current view of democratic rights.

Subsequent or current precedents have proved that there are grounds for these fears: both the US Government and its agencies during the Vietnam War, and the British Government in Northern Ireland have compiled such dossiers, and telephone-tapping and information-gathering, both internally and internationally, use all the latest semiconductor technology.

The first official investigation on the privacy issue concluded with the Younger Report in 1970, which enunciated ten principles that have become known as the Younger Committee Principles:

(i) Information should be regarded as held for a specific purpose and not be used, without appropriate authorisation, for other purposes.

(ii) Access to information should be confined to those authorised to have it for the purpose for which it was supplied.

(iii) The amount of information collected and held should be the minimum necessary for the achievement of a specified purpose.

(iv) In computerised systems handling information for statistical purposes, adequate provision should be made in their design and programs for separating identities from the rest of the data.

(v) There should be arrangements whereby the subject could be told about the information held concerning him.

(vi) The level of security to be achieved by a system should be specified in advance by the user and should include precautions against the deliberate abuse or misuse of information.

(vii) A monitoring system should be provided to facilitate the detection of any violation of the security system.

(viii) In the design of information systems, periods should be specified beyond which the information should not be retained.

(ix) Data held should be accurate. There should be machinery for the correction of inaccuracy and the updating of information.

(x) Care should be taken in coding value judgements.

These principles have become enshrined in privacy legislation which has been enacted in most Western countries, and adopted by the EEC. The essential features of these new laws are:

(i) an individual's right of privacy, that is, control over the disposal of confidential information about himself, is given some legal standing;

(ii) computer files containing such information are to be registered with

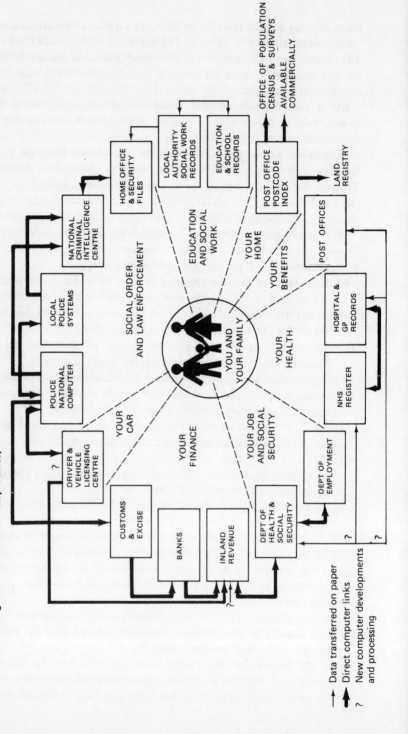

Fig 10.3 governmental and other official holdings of information about individuals in the United Kingdom (based on a diagram from the Sunday Times)

Data transferred on paper
Direct computer links
? New computer developments and processing

YOU AND YOUR FAMILY

SOCIAL ORDER AND LAW ENFORCEMENT
EDUCATION AND SOCIAL WORK
YOUR HOME
YOUR BENEFITS
YOUR HEALTH
YOUR CAR
YOUR FINANCE
YOUR JOB AND SOCIAL SECURITY

NATIONAL CRIMINAL INTELLIGENCE CENTRE
LOCAL POLICE SYSTEMS
POLICE NATIONAL COMPUTER
DRIVER & VEHICLE LICENSING CENTRE
HOME OFFICE & SECURITY FILES
LOCAL AUTHORITY SOCIAL WORK RECORDS
EDUCATION & SCHOOL RECORDS
OFFICE OF POPULATION CENSUS & SURVEYS AVAILABLE COMMERCIALLY
POST OFFICE POSTCODE INDEX
LAND REGISTRY
POST OFFICES
HOSPITAL & GP RECORDS
NHS REGISTER
DEPT OF EMPLOYMENT
DEPT OF HEALTH & SOCIAL SECURITY
INLAND REVENUE
BANKS
CUSTOMS & EXCISE

some central agency with constitutional powers, and are open to inspection by it;

(iii) misuse of such information is a statutory criminal and/or civil offence;

(iv) individuals may demand to have a full print-out of their computer records.

The shortcoming in the provisions in some countries (including the UK) is exemption for police, security and other governmental data files, which does appear to completely negate the purpose of the exercise for private citizens. In the face of somewhat cynical Government whitewashing, compounded by growing police powers of seizure of files, some security for the citizen is provided by the determination of some professional bodies to retain their traditional exercise of confidentiality in dealings with their clients and patients. Meanwhile the main abuse of confidential data held on files by commercial companies is likely to be no more serious than the selling of name-and-address files by a company which has the right to hold them (for example, for magazine subscriptions) to other organisations for use in personalised direct mail advertisements.

10.4 COMPUTERS AND LEISURE

One of the great and pleasant surprises of the last few years has been the breakout of computers from their purposeful and gainful use into both juvenile and adult leisure activities. The reduction in scale and cost of microprocessors has brought microprocessor-powered games and micro-computers within reach of both the important-event toy and DIY enthusiast market, and microprocessors are about to appear inside our important consumer durables: cars, washing machines, cookers and the like. There is no doubt that all of these products are at the top end of their respective markets, and create new sectors in the consumer electronics and publishing industries. There is some concern about the obsessive effects of home computers and video games (just as there was originally about the growth of TV as isolating the individual home). Equally their popularity may be seen as part of the growing trend towards choice in leisure activities, away from the rigid 'programming' of public broadcasting and other public services (we are all watching less TV than we did last year). Similarly, computer-based services can be seen to be providing alternative and less partial sources of information to those available in the newspapers, which are themselves suffering a slow and continuous decline in their sales.

What will undoubtedly be more important to all people is the inclusion of intelligence in the near-universal domestic devices of TV and telephone — TV in particular in the form of Prestel. Although this is promoted primarily as a leisure magazine, it has considerable potentialities as an educational aid for both vocational and leisure pursuits, as a home programmed-learning terminal and as a vehicle for electronic mail. Along with the intelligent telephone which can make telephone conversations more enjoyable, intelligent devices can be broadening influences in the home, even as a contrary influence to TV which has tended to isolate the unitary home.

Their ultimate contribution may be seen as a corrective to the main trend of the computer in its business use, which in general has produced a machine-driven discipline in many business activities. The mainframe computer is a symbol of the power of the large bureaucratic organisations over our lives. Microcomputers, on the other hand, are essentially personal, popular and democratic, and will help people to master and control that part of their lives over which they retain some self-determination.

SPECIMEN QUESTIONS

1. Answer **either** (a) A large amount of personal information can now be stored in data banks at locations anywhere in Great Britain.
   (i) Describe the data that are likely to be stored.
   (ii) Explain why this is a cause of concern to many people.
   (iii) Describe a realistic method by which individuals could have access to these data banks.
   or (b) Describe the effect on the general public of the increasing use of microcomputers and the rapid developments in microelectronics. Include in your answer references to employment, efficiency, new career opportunities and leisure activities. *

2. In the past ten years the use of computers has become widespread. The ordinary person is likely to become aware of the use of a computer in many different fields. Give one example, taken from each of three distinct fields, of such a use of a computer. Describe clearly the role of the computer in each case. Indicate the probable effects on employment of the increasing use of the microcomputer. The effects on employment in both the developed and underdeveloped countries should be considered. *

3. Microcomputers and microprocessors are having an increasing effect on the private and working lives of the majority of people in this country. **Either** (a) Describe the possible growth in the use of microcomputers and microprocessors in commerce.
   Or (b) Describe the possible growth in the use of microcomputers and microprocessors in industry.
   Include in your answers references to:
   (i) current and future developments;
   (ii) the effect on the people employed by various organisations using microprocessor based equipment;
   (iii) the advantages/disadvantages for the user/customer of such organisations. *

CHAPTER 11

COMPUTERS AND THE FUTURE

The years to the end of the 1980s will be years of relentless change, to which computers and energy will be the main contributors: computers because they will continue to expand, energy for the opposite reason. We cannot stop this change; in an increasingly world-wide competitive economy, the pace is being set elsewhere, and it is both inconceivable and virtually impossible to drop out of the race. In computing, the pattern of that change is already set:

- existing machines and products will reach an ever-wider market as they continue to drop in price;
- new products are already in the wings, based on the heavy R and D effort of the last five years;
- the pace of microelectronic development will be continuing to deliver more powerful microprocessors and denser storage chips, up to the point at which they defeat the skills of designers to incorporate them into systems. Before that point arrives, we (or the Japanese) will be able to construct computers from them that will afford a higher level of intelligence than our present machines provide (the so-called Fifth Generation Computers).

Equally, there is no doubt that the new products of which we are aware, and the longer-term innovations about which we can speculate, will find a ready market: in consumer products they will continue to offer flexibility and choice and an expanding framework for leisure activities, and in industrial products they will continue to help organisations to reduce costs and thereby remain competitive (in the commercial market) or meet reducing budgets (in the public sector).

As a result we shall see more computers and microcomputers in every aspect of our lives; at home in our electronic goods, at work in our business procedures, in shops, post offices, health centres and so forth. In particular they will advance further into some specific areas in which significant progress has already been made in the movement towards the Information Society:

- the electronic office;
- the home computer centre;
- the cashless society;
- the automatic factory.

11.1 MICROPROCESSORS WITH EVERYTHING

The application of microprocessors has only just begun, and it is clear that given the willingness and ability of designers to treat them as an engineering component, even the current units have an enormously wide potential for exploitation. When you add to that potential the low costs likely in volume production, and the further benefits of the more powerful microprocessor and denser storage units now about to be launched, then the speculation about the future seems justified. It can be stated without fear of contradiction that the take-up of microprocessors will continue with increasing momentum, in a number of different ways:
- in existing consumer products;
- in computing equipment;
- in new products related to the new markets identified above.

Their cheapness and cost effectiveness will create a number of different consequences according to their application:

(i) replacement of existing products, and potential loss of industry and jobs, such as that which occurred in the Swiss watch industry;

(ii) expansion of current markets because of increasing cheapness, especially computer systems themselves;

(iii) there will be completely new markets, like that which grew up for electronic calculators, some of which, but not all, will cause further displacement of manual labour by machines because of the changed break-even point in high-labour-cost economies in competition with the lower labour costs of the Third World.

There are two schools of thought: one that the replacements of labour will be permanent, leading to very much larger levels of structural unemployment unless some 'compulsory' form of work-sharing is introduced, and the second that new jobs, particularly in the electronic and computer industries, will grow up to replace those that are lost, and therefore no action is called for beyond the intermediate transitional stage. Those who take the first view often argue that the present situation is the start of a new Post-Industrial Society, in which perhaps all our material needs can be produced by only 10 per cent of the population, leaving enormous human resources and energy to be devoted to the service and welfare sectors. The technological revolution of microelectronics which has led to this scenario would call for a corresponding revolution in our cultural and political beliefs to accommodate such a situation. Those who hold the second, less dramatic opinion point to similar cycles of recession caused by technological innovation and subsequent revival (known as Kondratiev Cycles after the economist who first detected them). Unfortunately, these cycles have been of approximately fifty years duration, and this school of thought also generally holds *laissez-faire* and non-interventionist views about the expansion of higher education, government support of new industries and easing the distress of the (temporarily) unemployed which would make the intervening period shorter and less painful.

A moderate compromise view might therefore be that there is a potential gap between the national rates of job losses and job creation, which determined efforts by the government and the industry might close. The additional unknown factor in the equation is the rate of adoption of the new technology in the new concept areas, depending upon the acceptance of changed procedures and work/leisure patterns by those concerned. The resistance to those changes, as has occurred already in the newspaper industry, could, ironically, lose more jobs than the refusal to move will artificially preserve.

11.2 THE ELECTRONIC OFFICE

The conventional office is widely thought to be a large potential market for computer application, principally because it is labour-intensive and relatively untouched by capital-intensive machines or systems. The spearhead of this invasion is the *word processor*, a device based on either stand-alone microcomputers or special terminals attached to larger computers, whose function is to assist its operator in the preparation and production of typed letters and other documents with text-processing software.

One focus of attention in the word processor is its user terminal which is rapidly evolving into a multi-functional office workstation. This will consist, as now, of a high-quality display, keyboard and printer, plus other integrated features such as a voice message input/output and communication facilities. The displays themselves will have a multiple window feature so that different and concurrent office activities can be shown together, and thus perhaps to be made to look like a conventional desk top with separate areas for memos, in/out/pending trays, etc. Fig. 11.1 shows a typical structure for a multi-functional work-station, and below another impression of what such a machine may look like.

Such multi-function, multi-purpose workstations, will form the nucleus of the automated office, linked internally and externally by appropriate forms of data communications — Fig. 11.2 shows a typical layout. The transmission of documents externally between communications-based office systems will constitute one form of Electronic Mail, which will

Fig 11.1 *one forecast of the structure of the integrated work station . . .
and another (courtesy of* Computing*)*

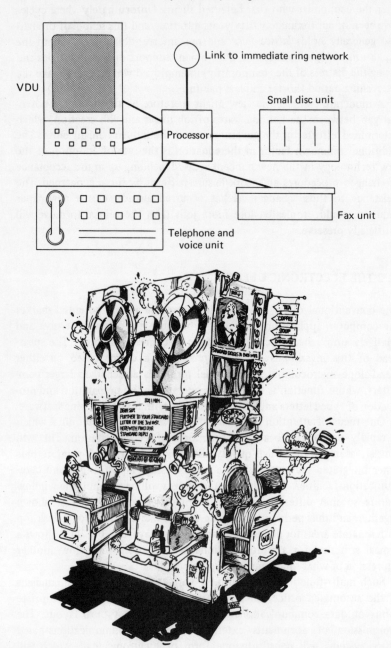

Fig 11.2 *how the electronic office might be structured*

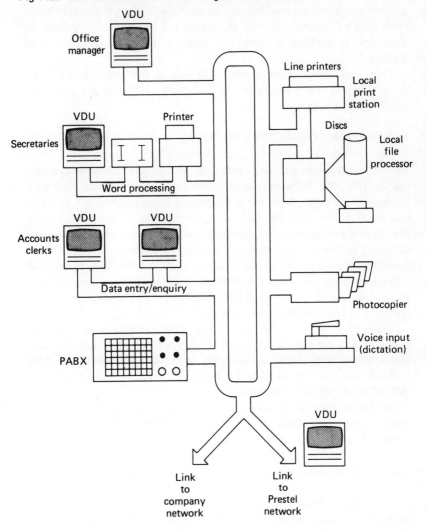

change the basis of formal communications between companies. The arrival of an electronic document from outside into an automated office system will trigger off processing activities as a consequence of its entry into an 'active' data-base of company documents. It is likely that such documents will identify themselves by a form of the Article Numbering System Code shown in Fig. 4.12, where the first five significant digits uniquely identify the company, and with the postcode used as the address;

in a similar way, employees will be referred to by their National Insurance number which will in effect become an all-purpose Identity Code. It is also likely that a Universal Standard Document will be required to permit the automatic recognition of company name, address and other items of identity.

These electronic office systems will change the conventional office more than any other innovation in its history, and with it the working life of millions of office workers.

11.3 THE HOME COMPUTER CENTRE

By contrast with the electronic office, in which there is frenetic commercial activity, the *home computer centre* remains very much more of a longer-term concept. As its name suggests, the concept refers to the eventual development of a domestic computer centre or electronic system that will be intelligent and computer-based. One reason why it is less well advanced is that its provision will be largely a public service, and its development may be left to the initiative of PTTs rather than to commercial undertakings. By general agreement, however, the centrepiece of the concept is a service already well-established in the United Kingdom and on the point of launch elsewhere – videotex.

Videotex is an internationally agreed generic name for all electronic systems that use a modified TV set to display computer-based information. Interactive systems, using a telephone line and a keyboard, are called viewdata (at least in the United Kingdom); broadcast services (like the BBC's Ceefax) are called *teletext*.

At the moment all videotex systems are used primarily as information display media – in effect, as Electronic Bookstalls – but in principle are fully interactive computer systems, using a general-purpose terminal comprising the TV set and adapter. Systems such as Prestel can also be used as private computer systems in which access is restricted, via passwords, to members of a Closed User Group. The TV adapter can also be used to connect directly to the serial bus of a home computer. The importance of this arrangement is not limited to public services operated by a PTT – private viewdata systems and software are also available on many computers, using the standards of the public service as a common protocol, including links, or 'Gateways' into normal private computer networks and to international networks.

Your TV set, therefore, with minor modifications, can become an all-purpose domestic computer terminal for private or public uses which have enormous possibilities and few restrictions. For private use, some companies are already using it to transmit instructions to and receive information from employees who are essentially home- rather than office-based, principally salesmen. The other main theme of the 1980s and the 1990s, the declining stocks of non-replaceable energy, has led to speculation that perhaps many more employees could in fact work from home — those who do not require constant face-to-face contact with other employees. All the necessary information and computing facilities can be provided by the home computer centre, with programs run for you either at the remote computer or on your own home computer; and the occasional meetings can be set up by an arrangement known as 'tele-conferencing' — essentially at the moment a telephone-switching arrangement in which a number of terminals are each in continuous contact with each other, but one which will ultimately require voice input/output at each terminal plus possibly a camera for image transmission — the video telephone as we used to call the notion — to carry both the voice and face of the participants to each other.

Working from home could save a large amount of energy (no petrol for travelling to work; no office central heating) at little marginal cost, since some people's homes will be heated anyway through the day and the telephone and TV set use only small amounts of electricity, which will largely be provided by nuclear energy or self-regenerating fuel. Declining stocks of petrol and other natural fuels may well force such action, with the aid of high scarcity prices, or perhaps a modified form of work location, a sort of cottage industry, which equally avoids large travelling bills. Incidentally, computer programming is one such activity that ideally lends itself to work at home, and some professional organisations have been using it for a number of years, primarily to allow mothers with young children to carry on their professional work.

The domestic possibilities are perhaps more difficult to pin down. School children might be provided with schoolwork at home, either in CAL or conventional exercise form; cooks could call for menus; services and goods could be requested (as is already available in Prestel) from local or central shops or mail order companies; and your mail could come in electronic form. As in some terminal-based computer systems, you might receive a message on your screen: Mail Waiting For You. You could then, by keying in a command, either see the mail displayed on the screen or call for it to be printed out on your printer, or both. If you have a Fax terminal you will of course receive a full facsimile. Also it has been predicted that the quarterly visits of meter readers could be replaced by invitations to input meter readings on your Prestel keypad.

The development of the domestic use of a home computer centre depends upon three unknown factors:

- wider social acceptance and larger sales, which would reduce hardware costs to an acceptable level;
- some governmental enterprise of the type displayed in France where every household in one region is to be equipped with a small videotex

screen to replace telephone directories for telephone enquiries;

- some financial pressures — perhaps a worldwide shortage of paper, or further increases in postal charges — to stimulate a transfer from physical to electronic communications.

Given progress along these lines, videotex systems could develop as shown in Fig. 11.3.

Ironically, the main restriction on the development of videotex as the hub of the Electronic Cottage is the existing communications channels — TV transmissions because they do not permit interaction, telephone because of low line speed. This could change for most subscribers as plans for domestic broadband cable connections mature. Originally conceived as a way of channelling TV programmes into the home from local centres fed by DBS (Direct Broadcasting by Satellite) receivers, with a capacity for up to 30 channels simultaneously, it is now planned to reserve at least one channel for data traffic from various sources, with full interactive capacity equal to many telephone lines. This data channel could be used both to feed the home computer/videotex terminal, and also to link other devices in the home directly to external computers. Trials are already under way in which specially adapted gas and electricity meters are to be remotely monitored in the interests of local load control; such an arrangement would also ultimately permit the automatic periodic calculation of units used and payments due. Another trial involves the adaptive monitoring of central heating controls from a central temperature recorder, in order to reduce energy consumption (the second main concern of the 1990s).

11.4 THE CASHLESS SOCIETY

One of the consequences of using a home computer terminal to request goods and services will certainly be to accelerate a trend that has steadily grown for several years — the payment for goods and services by cheques or credit cards without 'real' money. Financial settlement and account systems are already almost totally computerised, as Fig. 11. 4 shows, but using paper documents as vehicles.

(i) Credit card transaction slips and cheques are used as OCR/MICR or keypunched input to the store's computer system, which prints out periodic monthly account statements for credit, and taken to the bank's or finance house's computer system which maintains customer accounts.

(ii) Settlement of that credit debt may be by regular standing orders, or by the normal transfer of credit from a payer's to a payee's bank account in response to a cheque for the monthly total.

(iii) That debit is normally covered by the customer's regular salary, which may be either input by a cheque or credit transfer note printed-out by

Fig 11.3 *the present and potential capabilities of videotex as the basis of a home computer system (present facilities underlined)*

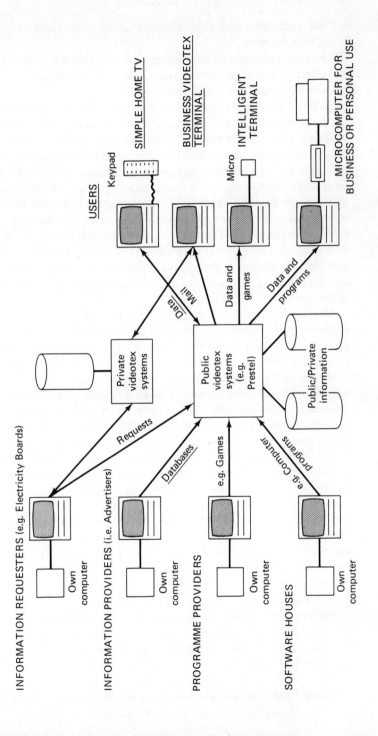

the computer-based payroll system of the customer's employer in reward for work.

(iv) Regular payments to supplier and other agencies may also be made directly from an employee's salary, and from a customer's account, by standing orders and direct deductions.

In this way a large proportion of many people's earnings and payments are made by paper and/or electronic means, without any real money passing hands at all. So the cashless society has been on the move very largely on the back of the computer. However, although the purchase of goods and services leaves the purchaser with the benefit 'in real-time', in most cases settlements of the credit occurs monthly when the batch processing of customer account transactions takes place. This is good for the customer, who may receive up to a month's free credit, but not very good for the supplier (who doesn't receive immediate payment) nor for the economy (it is of course very good for the banks). There is also the same, but shorter, gap between cashing a cheque and its processing which customers may also exploit along with other procedural causes of delay ('there's a cheque in the post').

Meanwhile, however, there has been a steady growth of paperless *electronic fund transfer systems* (EFTS), with all the clearing banks and their branches 'on the computer', with a computerised clearing bank system, and a world-wide financial transfer network, SWIFT. What is now proposed, and under trials, are fully integrated and on-line systems which will eliminate the delay between a financial transaction and the computer deduction of the payment from a bank account. Point of sale terminals (see Section 4.3) and credit card terminals will be on-line, either to the store's computer or a local credit card agency computer in the first place. It will be necessary to verify ownership of a presented credit or account probably by the electronic encoding of a signature at the point of sale and its checking against a stored signature held with the customer's record. Those computers will then use the coded address of the credit card holder's bank to access directly that bank's computer system and initiate an immediate debit from the payer's account and effect a credit transfer to the payee's account or to the credit card agency's account — no month's free credit, no three days' grace on a cheque either, if on-line cheque clearing terminals are introduced. Fig. 11.5 shows the revised version of Fig. 11.4 under these changed circumstances.

Further advances towards the disappearance of cash may come from the wider use of portable terminals in such mobile uses such as buses, or by your milkman, except that interaction with the bus or dairy company's computer will come at the end of a shift or a day rather than continuously.

There will of course be major problems as the cashless society advances. The most fundamental is that those 30 per cent of adults without a bank

Fig 11.4 *how the money goes (mostly without cash)*

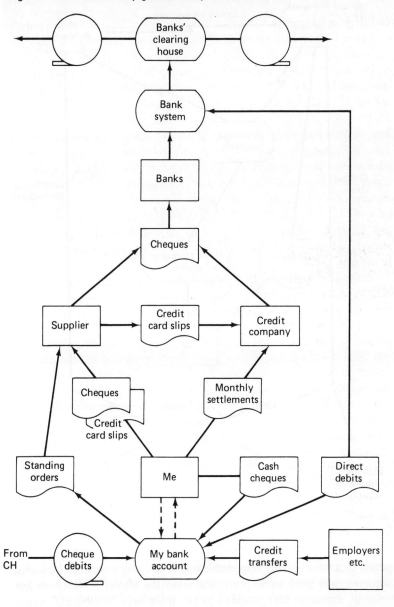

account will have to be persuaded to open one, to avoid the risk of further discrimination against them in financial matters. Perhaps an account will in future be opened automatically for everyone at the age of 18 as a part of the Social Security system, but with a national bank that will

Fig 11.5 *how the money will go (electronically)*

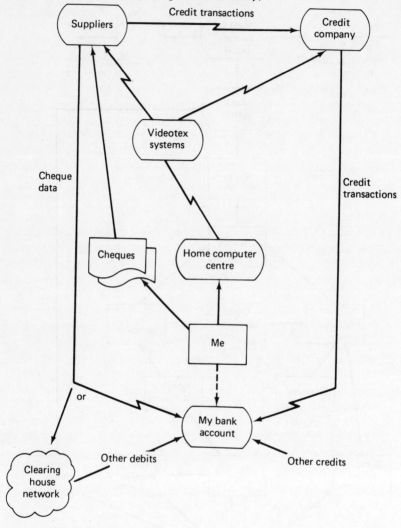

operate in a more socially responsible way than today's commercial banks. Customers will need some protection from the effects of hasty on-line decisions, similar to that provided by the three days' 'cooling-off' period in which an HP transaction can be cancelled. Cash will not, of course, ever disappear, but an end to the large holdings of cash by banks and stores, and movement of it, will only be regretted by bank and payroll robbers, who will anyway find richer pickings from computer fraud.

11.5 THE AUTOMATIC FACTORY

Large-scale process and machine automation, of the type described in Chapter 2, has already been widely achieved, with some of the most impressive successes implemented by computer manufacturers in printed circuit board and chip production. However, manufacturing processes that call for manual assembly and manipulation (including such operations as packaging) have resisted automation largely because of the need to see and handle the materials and items with tools. Much of the work itself is completely repetitive and predetermined, requiring little initiative or discretion. Now the advent of low-cost intelligence, and a lot of patient, detailed research, has made it possible and increasingly economic to automate such work of the type seen in the fully automated car assembly operations. The controlling devices are known as 'robots' (although they do not correspond in appearance to the popular meaning of that term).

A *robot* is a program-controlled device which can receive quasi-sensory inputs, from electronic 'eyes' and 'feelers', and perform tasks with arm-like jibs holding tools – tasks like painting, spraying, welding, lifting, handling and depositing, mostly in direct simulation of the movements and actions of a human operator. They are at the moment inelegant contraptions, functionally rather than aesthetically designed and numbered in hundreds, but they are already economic propositions in these applications because of better quality, no loss of service due to operators' strikes, and no risk to health in dirty jobs. The important breakthroughs have already been made, and they are capable of immediate exploitation in many similar tasks throughout industry.

There are also pre-production or development prototypes in operation for more demanding work, such as mobile searching, sorting and classification of objects, and for applying parts to fixtures. Given further refinement and long production runs to cover the high development costs, fully automatic versions of general-purpose engineering assembly lines, and of product handling and packaging lines, are a real possibility in the next ten years. The complete automatic factory is both an unachievable ideal (like the 'cashless society'), and meaningless in that the maintenance force will have to be much higher in numbers and skills than now, and the supplying companies will need hybrid engineers/cyberneticians. In most cases there will continue to be sections of the work that currently call for irreplaceable human activity, some of which, like final product testing, it may be possible to do to a higher level of customer satisfaction than at the moment.

One of the major problems, however, that this type of development, and incidentally, expansion of word processing in the electronic office, will bring is that the jobs replaced are largely performed (for 'cultural' rather than physical reasons) by women, while the jobs that they create are currently mostly performed by men – a reversal of recent trends which have been replacing 'men's jobs' in heavy industries with 'women's jobs' in light industries. The education system, and the parents of today's schoolchildren, must give their daughters the same encouragement and opportunities as their sons to enter the highly skilled, knowledge-based professions which will continue to be relevant. Computing is incidentally one occupation that has already started, and ironically even reverses the trends – keyboard skills, once the preserve of women, are now considered essential for all computer users.

Postscript

As computers continue to advance on so many fronts, it will be ever more necessary to ensure their humane use and human control. To this end, it is a salutary exercise to remind ourselves that today's computers, and computers in the future, are machines. Science fiction speculations of computers that can exhibit human intelligence and creativity, or indeed any function not specifically programmed into them by their human creators and operators, can be entirely discounted, and as machines, computers will continue to be the creations of men. True engineers have no respect for man-made objects, because anything made by one human hand can be made better by another, and engineers will continue to demonstrate this by making better and better computers. The true problem of machines like computers continues to be that they are means to an end, while society determines those ends, either deliberately or by default. If you do not like what computers are being used to do today, or you fear what computers may be used to do in the future, then the remedy is in your own hands. Equally, if you do not use computers to help control human progress in what will be an increasingly competitive and unfriendly world at the end of this century, then again the fault is yours, and mine. Mastering computers, and other machines, is ultimately an act of political and moral will, of which only people are capable.

SUGGESTIONS FOR FURTHER READING

Chapter 2
Digital Equipment Corporation (1980), *New Directions in Computing*
Race, J. (1977). *Computer-Based Systems* (Teach Yourself Books)
Bradbeer, R. (1982), *The Personal Computer Book*, 2nd edn (Gower Press)
Sommerville, I. (1982), *Information Unlimited* (Addison-Wesley)
Zorkoczy, P. (1982), *Information Technology* (Pitman)
Flewitt, P. (1980), *Word Processing − An Introduction* (Macmillan)

Chapter 3
Cripps, M. (1977), *An Introduction to Computer Hardware*
Gosling, P. and Laarhoven, Q. (1980), *Codes for Computers and Micro-computers* (Macmillan)
Halsall, F. and Lister, P. (1980), *Microprocessor Fundamentals* (Pitman)
Willis, N. and Kerridge, J. (1983), *Introduction to Computer Architecture* (Pitman)

Chapter 4
National Computer Centre (1982), *Handbook of Data Communications*, 2nd edn
Wilkinson, B. and Horrocks, P. (1980), *Computer Peripherals* (Hodder and Stoughton)
Wickham, P. (1983), *Keyboarding For All* (Pitman)

Chapter 5
Bingham, J. (1983), *Mastering Data Processing* (Macmillan)
Kilgannon, P. (1980), *Business Data Processing and Systems Analysis* (Arnold)
Edwards, C. (1982), *Developing Microcomputer-Based Business Systems* (Prentice-Hall)
Daniels, A. and Yeates, D. (1982), *Basic Systems Analysis* (Pitman)
Clifton, H. (1983), *Business Data Systems*, 2nd edn (Prentice-Hall)

Chapter 6
Gosling, P. (1982), *Mastering Computer Programming* (Macmillan)
Hutty, R. (1983), *Mastering COBOL* (Macmillan)
Huggins, E. (1983), *Mastering Pascal Programming* (Macmillan)

Chapter 7
Lister, A. (1979), *Fundamentals of Operating Systems* (Macmillan)
Brown, P. (1983), *Starting with UNIX* (Addison-Wesley)

Chapters 8 and 9
Yearsley, R. and Graham, R. (1974), *Handbook of Computer Management* (Gower)

Chapter 10
Careers Research and Advisory Centre (published annually), *Hobson's Computing Casebook* (CRAC, Cambridge)
National Computing Centre (1982), *Working With Computers*
Laver, M. (1980), *Computers and Social Change* (Cambridge University Press)
Coburn, P. *et al.* (1982), *A Practical Guide to Computers in Education* (Addison-Wesley)

Chapter 11
Forrester, T. (1980), *The Microelectronics Revolution* (Blackwell)

Specimen questions

Monson, C. C. and Bacon, S. J. (1980), *Revision Questions for Computer Studies* (ICL/CES).

GLOSSARY OF SIGNIFICANT TERMS IN COMPUTING

This glossary is intended for quick reference. If greater detail is required, check with the Index, where each principal entry (marked in bold type) refers the readers to the initial explanation of the term. See also *A Glossary of Computer Terms*, published by the British Computer Society.

Address   the unique value used to identify a location in internal storage, or an area of backing storage on a device which permits direct access (that is, direct access storage or DASD).

ALU (arithmetic and logic unit)   that part of a processor which performs arithmetic and logical operations on data fed to it.

Backing storage   devices which store data permanently and externally to the processor.

Batch processing   the processing in one machine run of an accumulated batch of input data.

Bit   a binary digit.

Byte   a set of 8 bits, treated as one unit for storage of data.

Character   one of a set of elementary symbols acceptable to a computer.

Compile   translate a source program into machine code.

CPU (central processing unit)   the central part of a computer containing the control unit, the ALU, and sometimes the internal storage unit.

Database   an independently organised set of files covering all the data needed in an installation.

Data transmission   the communication of data over distance by an appropriate medium.

Data preparation   the preparation of raw data for processing by converting it from its original medium to a computer-readable medium.

Direct access   permitting access to records on a file without a search from the beginning of the file; directly to an addressable location of storage.

File   an organised collection of records relating to the same set of items.

File organisation   the way that records are placed on a file with a view to their subsequent retrieval.

Graphics   relating to the display and output of data in graphical form, that is, as pictures, etc., rather than as characters.

HLL (high-level language)   a programming language in which programs may be written in a way that reflects the problem and the user's own language rather than the demands of the computer.

Indexed files files for which an index has been created which allows direct access to the lowest addressable unit of storage.

Information processing data processing which mainly or solely consists of the processing of non-numerical data.

Instruction set that set of elementary operations which a computer is built to perform.

Intelligent terminals terminals which have been provided, by the installation of MPUs, with the ability to perform some processing.

Interaction two-way communication between a machine and its operator.

Keyboards units permitting the input of data, and sometimes the output of that data on a computer-readable medium, by the depression of keys for the acceptable set of characters.

LLL (low-level language) a programming language which directly reflects the machine code of a computer.

LSI (large-scale integration) pertaining to processor and storage units which have been miniaturised and constructed on a silicon or other type of chip.

Machine code instructions from a machine's instruction set, which are either directly executable or executed via microprograms composed of micro-instructions.

Macro (-instruction) an instruction in a programming language which the compiler replaces with a pre-stored sequence of instructions in the same language.

Magnetic core internal storage consisting of arrays of small ferrite rings.

Magnetic discs backing storage units in which the data is stored on circular discs coated with a magnetic substance.

Magnetic tape backing storage in which data is stored on a recording tape.

Mainframes computers made by the original computer manufacturers and mainly designed as medium- or large-scale single-processor systems.

Memory An alternative term for 'storage'.

Micro-instruction an executable instruction below the level of a machine code instruction and corresponding to one small step in it.

Microcomputers small computers (in size but not necessarily in performance) built around microprocessor and storage components.

Microprocessor a processor or part of a processor built on a silicon chip (also known as an MPU − *micro*processor *u*nit).

Minicomputers medium- to small-scale computers designed for reliability and primarily to provide terminal and other device attachment.

Modem (modulator–demodulator) a small unit which converts digital data to analog form and vice versa for data transmission.

Multi-access referring to hardware and software which have been designed to allow a large number of terminal users to enjoy apparently simultaneous use of the computer by giving each terminal a small allocation of computer time in turn ('time-slice').

OCR (optical character recognition) the input of data by means of pre-printed characters in special fonts which can be recognised by optical scanners.

OMR (optical mark recognition) the input of data by means of pre-printed or hand-generated marks to represent digital values, which can be recognised by optical scanners.

Operating system that part of systems software which controls the running of programs on a computer.

Package standard off-the-shelf software.

Paper tape perforated tape used as computer input or output media.

Peripherals input/output and backing storage devices connected on-line to a computer.

Personal computers very small and cheap microcomputers designed for use in non-professional circumstances.

Plotters output devices that are able to plot continuous lines.

Printers output devices that print characters.

Processor see CPU.

Programming language a defined set of symbols and meanings in which programs may be written.

Punched cards cards used as input and output media.

Read-only storage internal storage which cannot normally be overwritten by a program.

Real-time referring to the processing of input within the time-scale of the wider machine system in which a computer is working (or 'embedded').

Registers special storage areas in the processor which are used to hold data and instructions immediately prior to and subsequent to processing and to hold results temporarily.

Semiconductor storage internal storage composed of solid state electronic units.

Sequential access permitting access to records on a file only by a search from the beginning of the file and thence in logical sequence.

Serial access permitting access to records on a file only by a search from the beginning of the file and thence in physical sequence.

Software computer programs.

Subroutine a sequence of instructions that is executed from another program, or by another instruction elsewhere in the program.

Systems analysis the task of analysing requirements and designing a computer-based system to meet those requirements.

Systems software software supplied along with a computer to enable it to perform its basic function of running programs.

Systems programming the task of generating and maintaining systems software and similar supplied packages.

Teletype a slow printer/keyboard terminal.

Terminal an input and output device, usually remote from the computer.

Transaction processing the processing of transactions as they arrive at the computer from terminals.

VDT (visual display terminal) and VDU (visual display unit) a screen/keyboard terminal.

Word the set of bits which constitutes one location of internal storage, usually a multiple of 8 bits.

Word processor a microcomputer with software to aid the secretarial task of producing typed letters and other text.

INDEX

A principal entry is set in bold type.